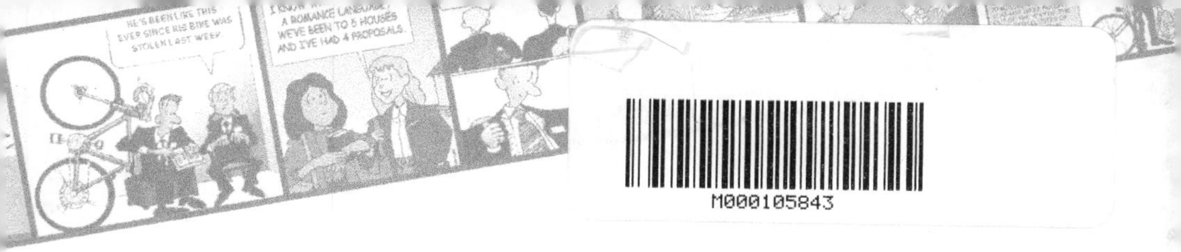
HE'S BEEN LIKE THIS EVER SINCE HIS BIKE WAS STOLEN LAST WEEK
A ROMANCE LANGUAGE? WE'VE BEEN TO 5 HOUSES AND I'VE HAD 4 PROPOSALS.

CALLED to LAUGH

The Lighter Side of Missionary Life

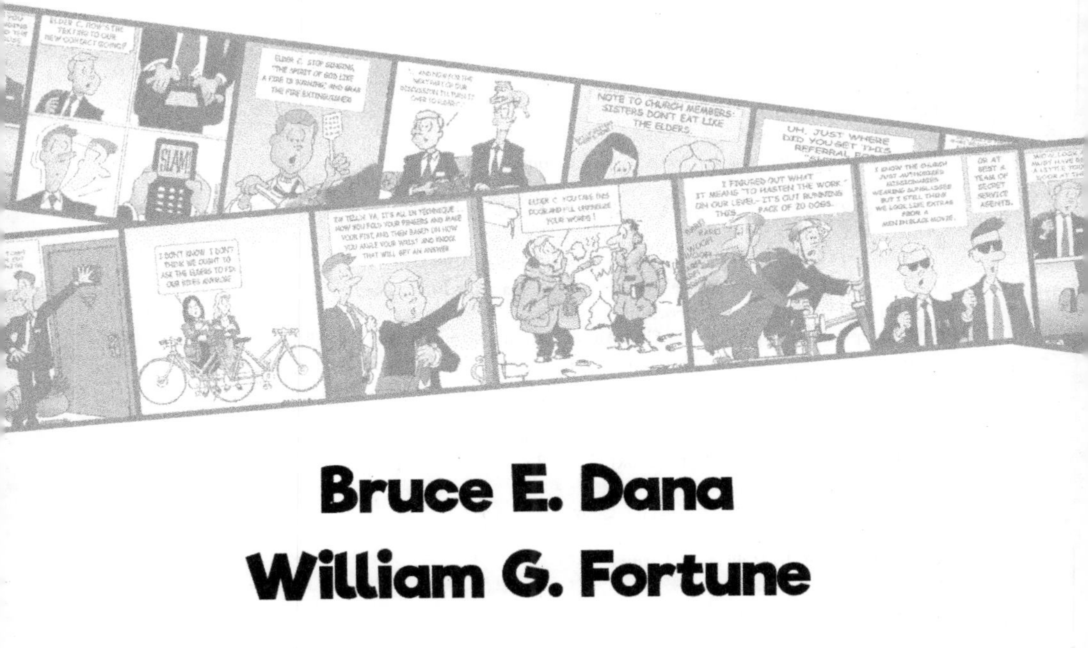
ELDER C. STOP SINGING "THE SPIRIT OF GOD LIKE A FIRE IS BURNING" AND GRAB THE FIRE EXTINGUISHER
SLAM!
NOTE TO CHURCH MEMBERS: SISTERS DON'T EAT LIKE THE ELDERS.
I FIGURED OUT WHAT IT MEANS "TO HASTEN THE WORK" ON OUR LEVEL— IT'S OUT RUNNING THIS PACK OF 20 DOGS.
I KNOW THE CHURCH JUST AUTHORIZED MISSIONARIES WEARING SUNGLASSES BUT I STILL THINK WE LOOK LIKE EXTRAS FROM A MEN IN BLACK MOVIE.
OR AT BEST A TEAM OF SECRET SERVICE AGENTS.
I DON'T KNOW. I DON'T THINK WE OUGHT TO ASK THE ELDERS TO FIX OUR BIKES ANYMORE
I'M TELLIN' YA, IT'S ALL IN TECHNIQUE... HOW YOU FOLD YOUR FINGERS AND MAKE YOUR FIST, AND THEN BASED ON HOW YOU ANGLE YOUR WRIST AND KNOCK THAT WILL GET AN ANSWER
ELDER C. YOU TAKE THIS DOOR AND I'LL UNFREEZE YOUR WORDS!

Bruce E. Dana

William G. Fortune

CFI

An imprint of Cedar Fort, Inc.

Springville, Utah

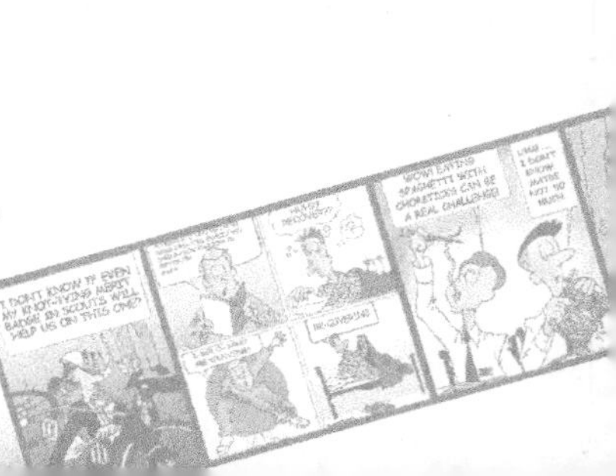
I DON'T KNOW IF EVEN MY KNOT-TYING MERIT BADGE IN SCOUTS WILL HELP US ON THIS ONE!
WOW! EATING SPAGHETTI WITH CHOPSTICKS CAN BE A REAL CHALLENGE!

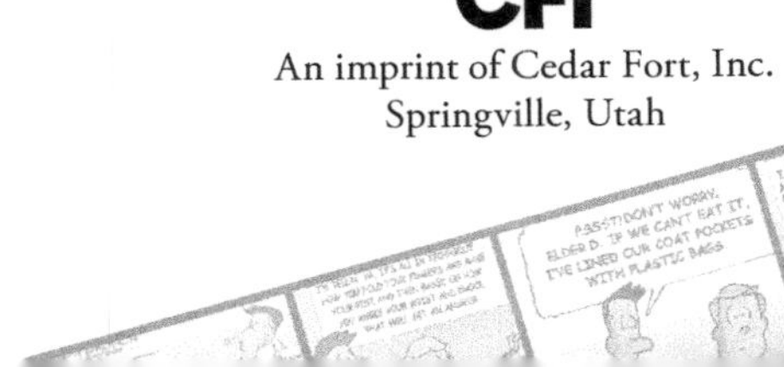
PSSST! DON'T WORRY, ELDER D. IF WE CAN'T EAT IT, I'VE LINED OUR COAT POCKETS WITH PLASTIC BAGS

ISBN 13: 978-1-4621-2265-3

Published by CFI, an imprint of Cedar Fort, Inc.
2373 W. 700 S., Springville, UT 84663
Distributed by Cedar Fort, Inc., www.cedarfort.com

LIBRARY OF CONGRESS CATALOGING-IN-PUBLICATION DATA

Names: Dana, Bruce E., compiler. | Fortune, William, 1941- compiler.
Title: Called to laugh : the lighter side of missionary life / Compiled by
    Bruce Dana and William Fortune.
Description: Springville, UT : CFI, An imprint of Cedar Fort, Inc., [2018]
Identifiers: LCCN 2018029013 (print) | LCCN 2018032523 (ebook) | ISBN
    9781462130054 (epub, pdf, mobi) | ISBN 9781462122653 (perfect bound : alk.
    paper)
Subjects: LCSH: Mormon missionaries--Humor. | LCGFT: Humor.
Classification: LCC BX8661 (ebook) | LCC BX8661 .C25 2018 (print) | DDC
    266/.93320207--dc23
LC record available at https://lccn.loc.gov/2018029013

Cover illustrations by William G. Fortune
Cover design by Jeff Harvey
Cover design © 2019 Cedar Fort, Inc.
Edited and typeset by Nicole Terry and Kaitlin Barwick

Printed in the United States of America

10 9 8 7 6 5 4 3 2 1

Printed on acid-free paper

I am forever indebted to my wife, Brenda, for allowing me valuable time to research and write. I am especially grateful for Bill's talented and humorous cartoons. And lastly, thankful for all who contributed to this enjoyable publication.

—Bruce

To my son Doug, who left us 20 years ago. You are the inspiration for Elder D. Your positive and happy outlook brought joy and happiness to all while you were with us and through the cartoons you will continue to do so.

—Bill

Also by

Bruce E. Dana

Mysteries of the Kingdom

Mary Mother of Jesus

Simon Peter

The Three Nephites and Other Translated Beings

Glad Tidings near Cumorah

The Eternal Father and His Son

The Apostleship

The Three Most Important Events

Prophetic Teachings on Death, Angels,
and Heavenly Manifestations

Stories & Jokes of Mormon Folks

CONTENTS

Introduction **1**
Missionary Glossary **2**

Prophets or Bullfrogs? **4**
The Right Mistake? **6**
A Foreign Mission—Don't Eat the Food or Drink the Water? . . . **7**
Carrots Help with Heavenly Visions? **9**
Priesthood or Monkeying Around? **10**
A Door Jam **13**
The Gospel Is True with or without Onions **15**
A Call to the Frozen **16**
Dueling Scriptures **18**
The Trouble with Speaking Softly **20**
Rubbing In the Gospel **23**
Weary of Being Leary **24**
A Test of Faith or Hearing? **26**
Good Thoughts or Bad Thoughts? **28**
Was That a Grapefruit or a Dove? **29**
Door-to-Door Panic **31**
Cheery or Cherry? **33**
Lost in Translation **34**
A Slight Doctrinal Misunderstanding **37**
Missionary Attraction **38**
No Alcohol, Tea, Coffee, or . . . Uh-Oh **39**
Mission Monkey Business **41**
Problems with a Romance Language **42**
Did They Teach the Tango at the MTC? **44**

How Does Your Garden Grow? Legally? **45**
What Do a Fire and Fistfight Have in Common? **47**
Just Testing the Waters of Baptism **48**
It's Baring Your Soul, Not the Body **49**
Door-to-Door Confusion **50**
The Axe of the Apostles **52**
Sick as a Horse **53**
Hair-Brained Ideas about the Church **54**
The True Origin of Saturn's Rings **55**
Flip? **56**
Stuffed Could Be a Delicate Condition **58**
Alien Elders All Over the Place **59**
Announcements Subject to Interpretation **61**
Who Let the Dogs Out? **62**
Homesickness or Farm Sickness? **65**
Keeping an FBI Out **66**
Herding Cats? **68**
The Right Timing Can Be Filling **71**
Look on the Bright Side **73**
Behold! A Voice of Thunder **74**
A Missionary Poem **76**
"Take No Thought . . . What Ye Shall Eat or Drink" **79**
Confusing Relationships **80**
Head over Heels on a Door Approach **82**
It's All Relative **83**
A Prayer without a Leg to Stand On **85**
No Good Deed Goes Unpunished **86**
Nobody but Us Chickens **89**
Two Wrong Turns Don't Make It Right **90**
Bridging Cultural Relations **92**
A Sobering Thought **95**
Not Crying over Spilled Milk, Just Mad **96**
A Humbling Stumble **97**

The Gift of Tongues 99
To Carry One Another's Burdens 100
A Case of Mistaken Identity 103
Nothing to Sneeze At 104
Social Media 106
How to Avoid a DUI: Join the Church 109
Mormons Have a Prophet Too? 111
Lack of Faith or Cell Phone? 112
Amend Your Ways 114
Trick-or-Tracting 116
For Crying Out Loud 117
Finding the Seat of the Problem 119
Lost Sleep in Translation 120
A Virtual Wreck 123
Give Me a Book Where the Buffalo Roam 124
Thought Peter Was a Fisherman? 126
Eating Your Own Words 129
Has the Devil Got a Hold on Me? 130
Primary Handful 132
Good Old Cookies 134
Many Are Chewin', but Some Are Full 135
Barking up the Wrong Sock 136
Expressions of Thanksgiving 138
A Focused Prayer 141
And on That Note, the Door Shut 142
Locked In and Locked Out 145
Feasting on the Gospel One Bowl at a Time 146
Which Day for Dessert? 147
Sacrament Bread and Butter 148

A Call for More Stories 149
About the Author 150
About the Illustrator 151

Introduction

Every member of the Church is a missionary and a teacher with the responsibility of teaching the gospel by word and deed to Heavenly Father's children. Elder Boyd K. Packer wrote the following enlightening words: "A sense of humor is a powerfully important attribute of a good teacher. The gospel is a happy and a pleasant gospel. There are times when we may be solemn almost to tears, but a good teacher will develop a sense of humor" (Boyd K. Packer, *Teach Ye Diligently*, [Salt Lake City: Deseret Book, 1975], 211; used by permission).

Mission presidents generally serve for three years, and full-time missionaries serve from eighteen months to two years, without financial help from the Church, devoting their time to proclaiming the message of the Restoration. During this time, there are naturally a few humorous moments that are unforgettable. The majority of the stories in this work have been collected by the authors from individuals who personally told their humorous experience while serving a mission, while other stories have been shared by relatives or friends who had been told the experience, and one story is from a printed work. It is further stated that some of the stories are direct quotes, while others are paraphrased.

Missionary Glossary

Mission: Various geographical areas designated by Church leadership for missionary work to be performed.

Missionary Training Center (also Language Training Center): A large structure to feed and house missionaries and to help prepare them to serve in their assigned missions.

Mission President: A leader called to oversee missionary activities in a mission. He is usually called to serve for three years.

Assistants to the President: Usually two elders are called to this position by a mission president to assist him with his responsibilities. This is the highest calling of a missionary in the mission field.

Zone Leader: A missionary who is responsible for overseeing the activities of two or more districts in a geographical area within a mission. A missionary called to be a zone leader has generally served first as a district leader.

District Leader: A missionary who is called to oversee four or more elders or sisters who are serving in a designated geographical area within a mission.

Elder: A male individual who has been called to serve in a mission, generally for two years.

Sister: A female individual who has been called to serve in a mission, generally for eighteen months.

Greenie: A designation for a new missionary.

Companionship: Generally two elders or two sisters; the smallest unit in a mission.

P Day: Preparation Day; a day of the week set aside for performing tasks such as laundry, letter writing, buying groceries, and some athletic activities.

Investigator: An individual being taught the gospel of Jesus Christ.

Golden Investigator: An individual who is not a member of the Church but who earnestly desires to join the Church.

Splits: When each missionary in a companionship goes with another missionary of another companionship, consisting usually of a district or zone leader or members of a local ward or stake, to do missionary work.

Tracting: This term has been used for years in various missions of the Church. This is where missionaries actively seek an investigator, whether it is going door-to-door, or visiting on the street, or using a variety of methods, to teach individuals the saving principles of the gospel of Jesus Christ.

District Meeting: A gathering in which the elders or sisters meet to discuss missionary activities in their assigned geographical area.

Zone Conference: A gathering in which several districts receive instructions and enlightenment from the zone leaders, mission president, or a visiting General Authority.

Prophets or Bullfrogs?

Background information:
The song "Joy to the World" was written by Hoyt Axton and made famous by the band Three Dog Night. The song is also popularly known by its opening lyric, "Jeremiah was a bullfrog."

"During the early 1970s, Elders in Atlanta, Georgia, worked hard with local Aaronic Priesthood leaders to prepare Young Men for missionary service by aggressively recruiting them for 'splits.' Elder Steven Nielsen recalls taking an almost inactive a seventeen-year-old out on a split. In what he thought would be a growing experience for the boy, [Elder Nielsen] asked him to bear his testimony of Joseph Smith to an investigator during the First Discussion. To his surprise, the young man bore a very solid witness of the Prophet Joseph's divine mission.

"'I know you believe Joseph Smith was a prophet,' said the investigator, 'but what about the ones in the Bible—do you believe, for example, that Abraham was a prophet?'

"'Of course,' answered the young man.

"'How about Isaiah?'

"Again, the answer was affirmative.

"'What about Jeremiah?' inquired the investigator. 'Was he a prophet?'

"The young man thought for a moment and said, 'No—Jeremiah was a bullfrog.'"

From Michael Bingham, *101 Missionary Stories You Won't Read in the Ensign* (Slickrock Books, 1998)

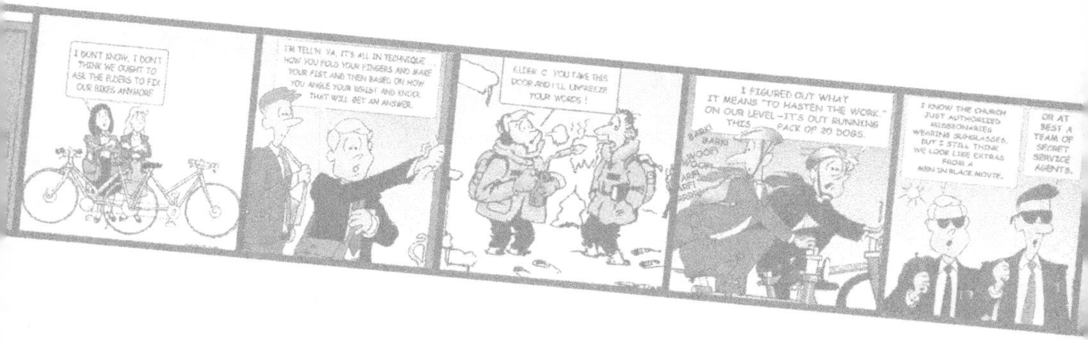
I DON'T KNOW, I DON'T THINK WE OUGHT TO ASK THE ELDERS TO FIX OUR BIKES ANYMORE
I'M TELL'N YA, IT'S ALL IN TECHNIQUE ... HOW YOU FOLD YOUR FINGERS AND MAKE YOUR FIST AND THEN BASED ON HOW YOU ANGLE YOUR WRIST AND KNOCK THAT WILL GET AN ANSWER.
ELDER C YOU TAKE THIS DOOR AND I'LL UNFREEZE YOUR WORDS!
I FIGURED OUT WHAT IT MEANS "TO HASTEN THE WORK." ON OUR LEVEL—IT'S OUT RUNNING THIS PACK OF 20 DOGS.
I KNOW THE CHURCH JUST AUTHORIZED MISSIONARIES WEARING SUNGLASSES, BUT I STILL THINK WE LOOK LIKE EXTRAS FROM A MEN IN BLACK MOVIE.
OR AT BEST A TEAM OF SECRET SERVICE AGENTS.

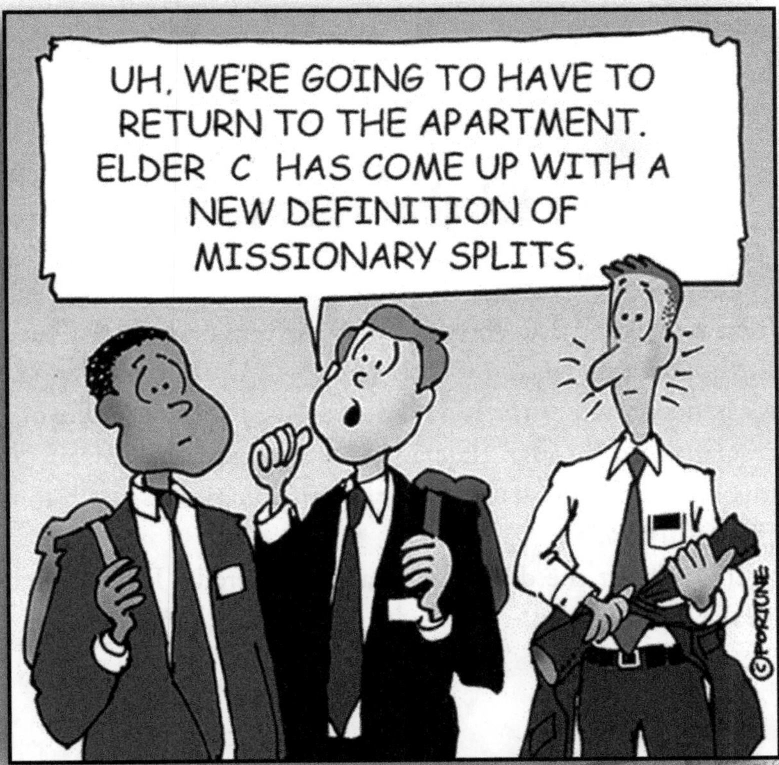
UH, WE'RE GOING TO HAVE TO RETURN TO THE APARTMENT. ELDER C HAS COME UP WITH A NEW DEFINITION OF MISSIONARY SPLITS.
©FORTUNE

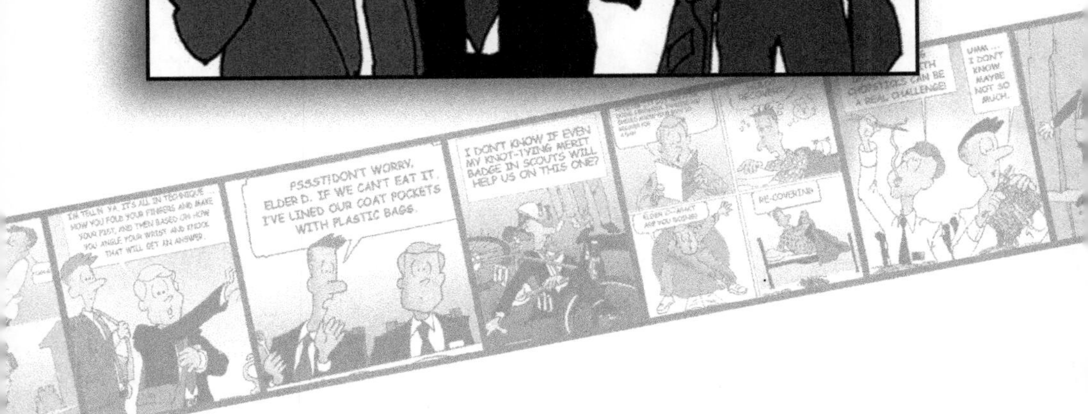
I'M TELL'N YA, IT'S ALL IN TECHNIQUE HOW YOU FOLD YOUR FINGERS AND MAKE YOUR FIST, AND THEN BASED ON HOW YOU ANGLE YOUR WRIST AND KNOCK THAT WILL GET AN ANSWER.
PSSST! DON'T WORRY, ELDER D. IF WE CAN'T EAT IT, I'VE LINED OUR COAT POCKETS WITH PLASTIC BAGS.
I DON'T KNOW IF EVEN MY KNOT-TYING MERIT BADGE IN SCOUTS WILL HELP US ON THIS ONE?
UMM... I DON'T KNOW MAYBE NOT SO MUCH.

The Right Mistake?

When a priest adviser took a group of young men for a visit to the Missionary Training Center in Provo, Utah, the elder at the desk handed each of the boys a descriptive pamphlet. One of the priests glanced through the pamphlet and gasped. "This must be a mistake," he said. "It says that the missionaries rise each morning at 6:00 a.m."

The elder at the desk smiled and answered, "It's definitely a mistake, but it's true!"

A Foreign Mission—Don't Eat the Food or Drink the Water?

Sister Ivins was called to serve in South America. When her parents dropped her off at the Missionary Training Center, her overly concerned mother put her arms around Sister Ivins and seriously said, "When in South America, don't eat the food or drink the water!"

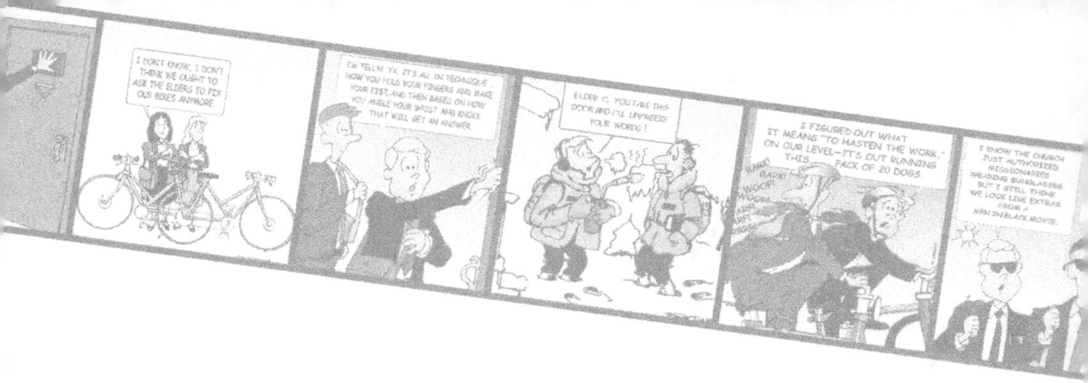
I DON'T KNOW, I DON'T THINK WE OUGHT TO ASK THE ELDERS TO FIX OUR BIKES ANYMORE.
I'M TELL'N YA, IT'S ALL IN TECHNIQUE... HOW YOU FOLD YOUR FINGERS AND MAKE YOUR FIST, AND THEN BASED ON HOW YOU ANGLE YOUR WRIST AND KNOCK THAT WILL GET AN ANSWER.
ELDER C, YOU TAKE THIS DOOR AND I'LL UNFREEZE YOUR WORDS!
I FIGURED OUT WHAT IT MEANS "TO HASTEN THE WORK" ON OUR LEVEL—IT'S OUT RUNNING THIS PACK OF 20 DOGS.
I KNOW THE CHURCH JUST AUTHORIZED MISSIONARIES WEARING SUNGLASSES. BUT I STILL THINK WE LOOK LIKE EXTRAS FROM A MEN IN BLACK MOVIE.

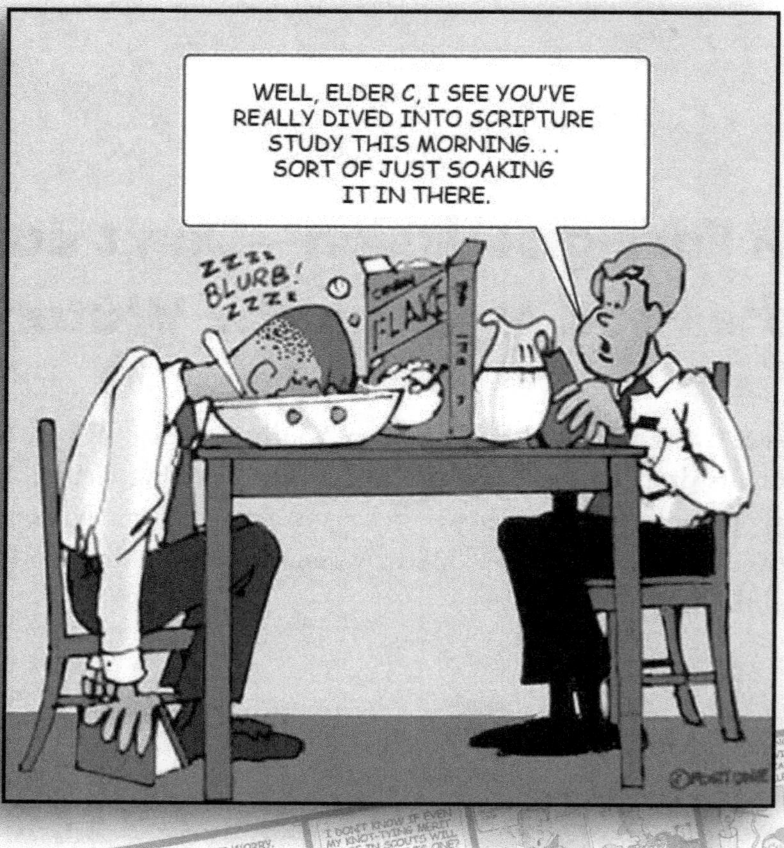
WELL, ELDER C, I SEE YOU'VE REALLY DIVED INTO SCRIPTURE STUDY THIS MORNING... SORT OF JUST SOAKING IT IN THERE.
ZZZZ
BLURB!
ZZZZ
FLAKES

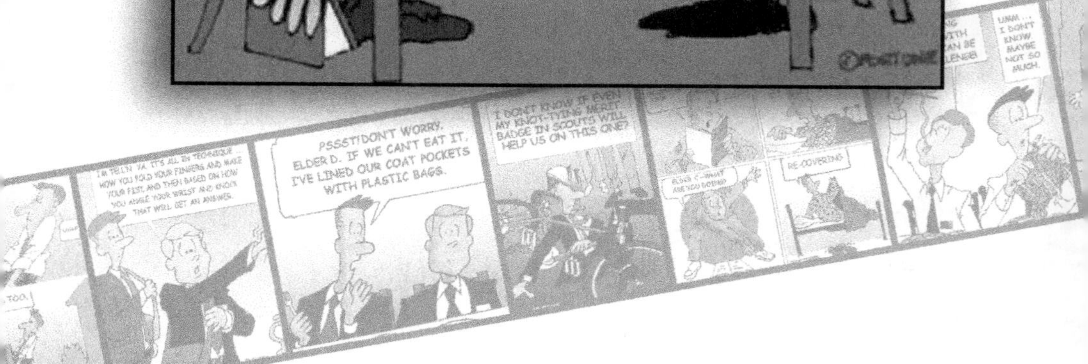
I'M TELL'N YA, IT'S ALL IN TECHNIQUE... HOW YOU FOLD YOUR FINGERS AND MAKE YOUR FIST, AND THEN BASED ON HOW YOU ANGLE YOUR WRIST AND KNOCK THAT WILL GET AN ANSWER.
PSSST! DON'T WORRY, ELDER D. IF WE CAN'T EAT IT, I'VE LINED OUR COAT POCKETS WITH PLASTIC BAGS.
I DON'T KNOW IF EVEN MY KNOT-TYING MERIT BADGE IN SCOUTS WILL HELP US ON THIS ONE?
RE-COVERING
UMM... I DON'T KNOW MAYBE NOT SO MUCH.

Carrots Help with Heavenly Visions?

While laboring in Nagoya, Japan, Elder Saxton, a zone leader, was doing a split with Elder Carson for the day. When they got to the next home, a lady answered the door. After the missionaries introduced themselves, Elder Carson excitedly told the lady about a young boy named Joseph Smith, who went to a grove of trees to pray and received a visitation from two heavenly beings. However, Elder Carson mispronounced a word in Japanese and said that Joseph Smith received a visit from two heavenly carrots.

Priesthood or
Monkeying Around?

In Rosario, Argentina, Elder Niles made Church history a little more interesting when he confused the word for "hands" (*manos*) with the word *monos*. In speaking of priesthood restoration, he declared to an investigator family that John the Baptist laid monkeys on the heads of Joseph Smith and Oliver Cowdery when ordaining them to the Aaronic Priesthood.

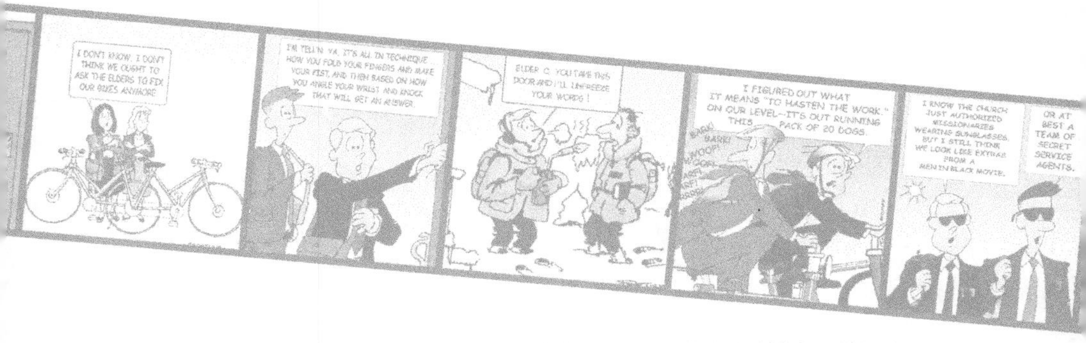
I FIGURED OUT WHAT IT MEANS "TO HASTEN THE WORK." ON OUR LEVEL--IT'S OUT RUNNING THIS PACK OF 20 DOGS.
OR AT BEST A TEAM OF SECRET SERVICE AGENTS.

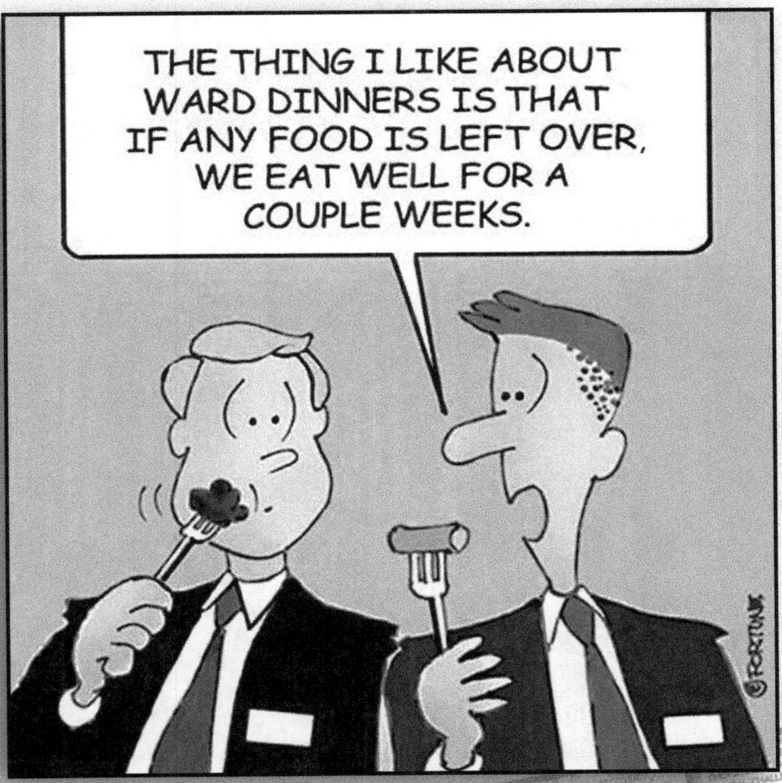
THE THING I LIKE ABOUT WARD DINNERS IS THAT IF ANY FOOD IS LEFT OVER, WE EAT WELL FOR A COUPLE WEEKS.
©FORTUNE

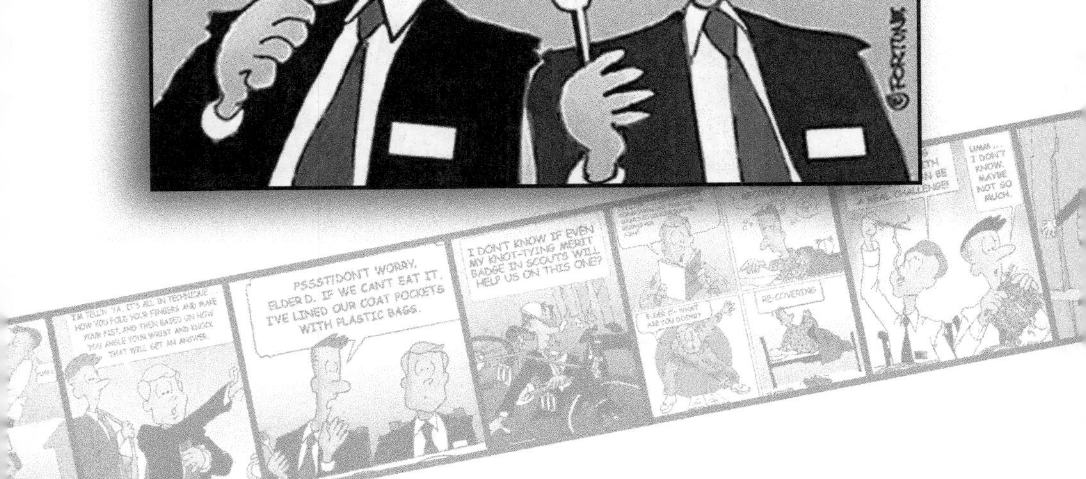
PSSST! DON'T WORRY, ELDER D. IF WE CAN'T EAT IT, I'VE LINED OUR COAT POCKETS WITH PLASTIC BAGS.
I DON'T KNOW IF EVEN MY KNOT-TYING MERIT BADGE IN SCOUTS WILL HELP US ON THIS ONE?
UMM... I DON'T KNOW. MAYBE NOT SO MUCH.

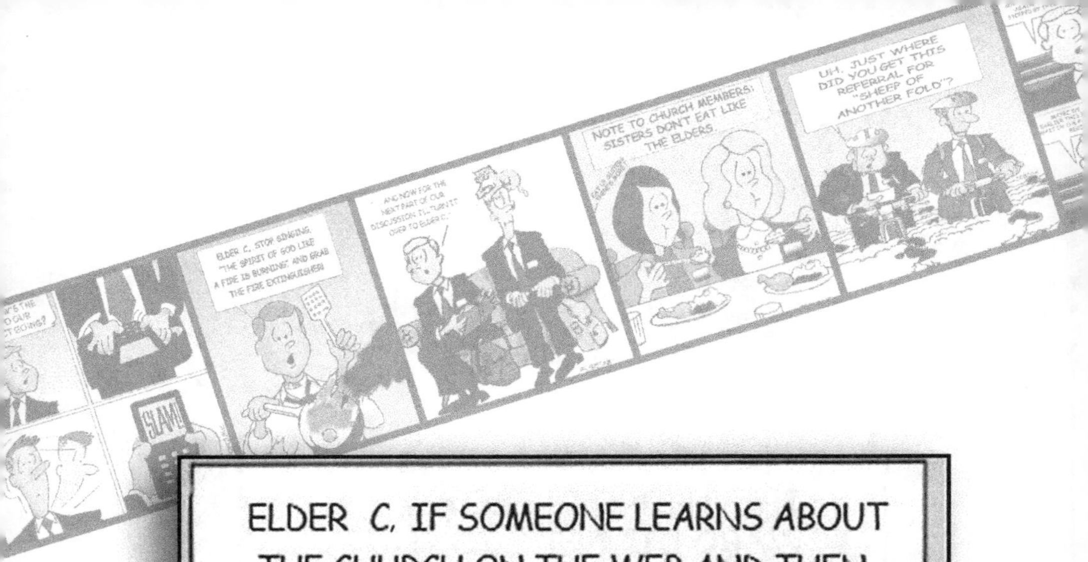
SLAM!
ELDER C, STOP SINGING "THE SPIRIT OF GOD LIKE A FIRE IS BURNING" AND GRAB THE FIRE EXTINGUISHER
AND NOW FOR THE NEXT PART OF OUR DISCUSSION I'LL TURN IT OVER TO ELDER C.
NOTE TO CHURCH MEMBERS: SISTERS DON'T EAT LIKE THE ELDERS.
UH, JUST WHERE DID YOU GET THIS REFERRAL FOR "SHEEP OF ANOTHER FOLD"?

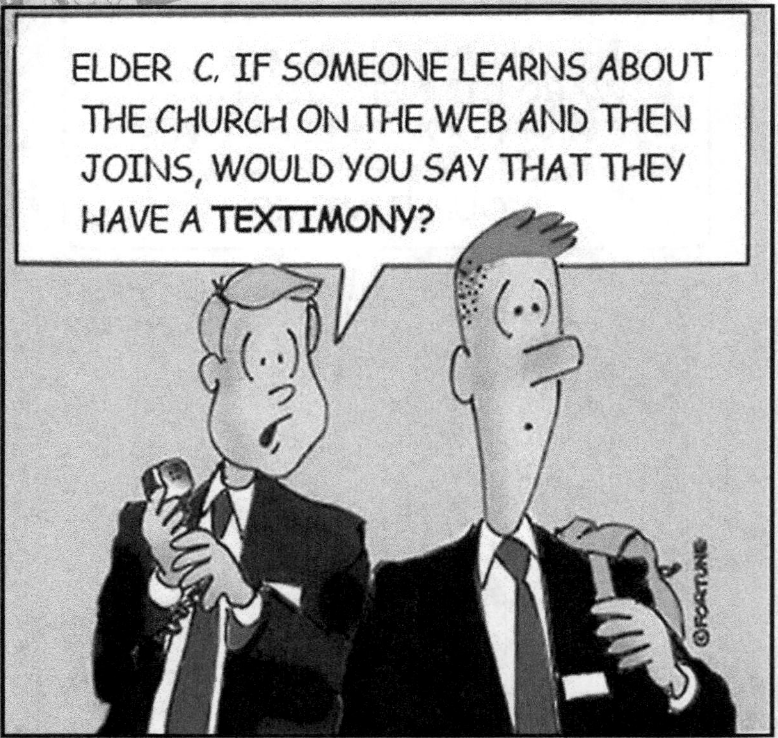
ELDER C, IF SOMEONE LEARNS ABOUT THE CHURCH ON THE WEB AND THEN JOINS, WOULD YOU SAY THAT THEY HAVE A TEXTIMONY?
©FORTUNE

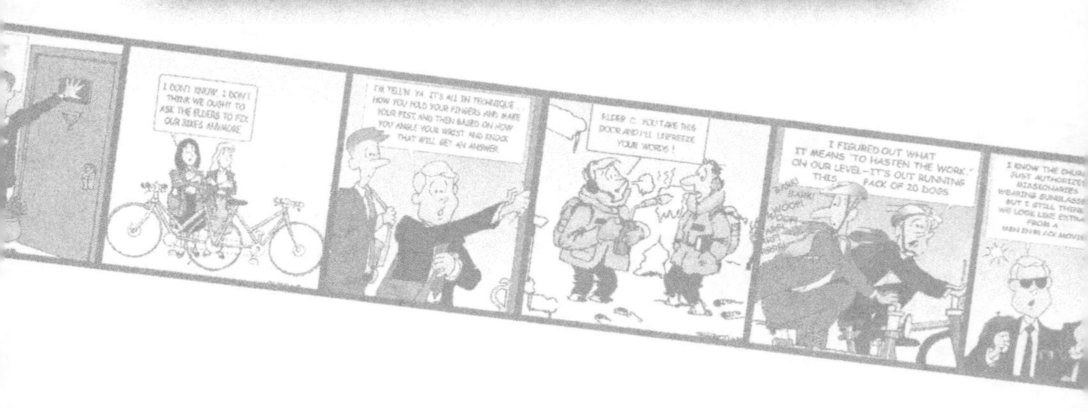
I DON'T KNOW, I DON'T THINK WE OUGHT TO ASK THE ELDERS TO FIX OUR BIKES ANYMORE
I'M TELL'N YA, IT'S ALL IN TECHNIQUE... HOW YOU HOLD YOUR FINGERS AND MAKE YOUR FIST AND THEN BASED ON HOW YOU ANGLE YOUR WRIST AND KNOCK THAT WILL GET AN ANSWER
ELDER C. YOU TAKE THIS DOOR AND I'LL UNFREEZE YOUR WORDS!
I FIGURED OUT WHAT IT MEANS "TO HASTEN THE WORK" ON OUR LEVEL—IT'S OUT RUNNING THIS PACK OF 20 DOGS

A Door Jam

In Las Vegas, Nevada, Elders Arnold and Lee were proselyting and knocked on the door of a woman who was not happy to see them. She said, in no uncertain terms, that she did not want to hear their message and slammed the door in their faces. To her surprise, however, the door did not close and, in fact, bounced back open. This time she really put her body into it and slammed the door again with the same result—the door bounced back open. Convinced that one of these young Mormons was sticking his foot in the door, she reared back to give it a slam that would teach them a lesson, when Elder Arnold exclaimed, "Ma'am, before you do that again, you need to move your cat."

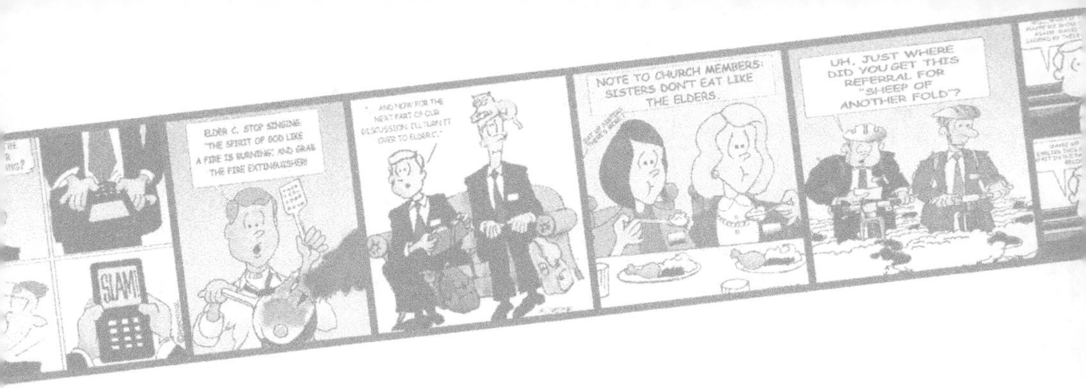
SLAM!
ELDER C. STOP SINGING "THE SPIRIT OF GOD LIKE A FIRE IS BURNING," AND GRAB THE FIRE EXTINGUISHER!
AND NOW FOR THE NEXT PART OF OUR DISCUSSION, I'LL TURN IT OVER TO ELDER C."
NOTE TO CHURCH MEMBERS: SISTERS DON'T EAT LIKE THE ELDERS.
UH, JUST WHERE DID YOU GET THIS REFERRAL FOR "SHEEP OF ANOTHER FOLD"?

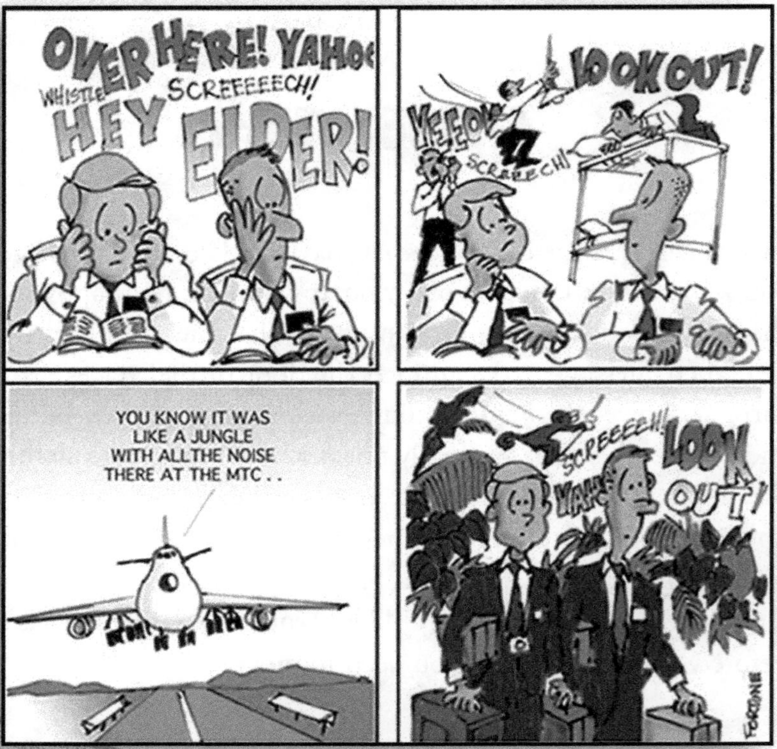
OVER HERE! YAHO
WHISTLE
SCREEEEECH!
HEY ELDER!
LOOK OUT!
SCREEECH!
YOU KNOW IT WAS LIKE A JUNGLE WITH ALL THE NOISE THERE AT THE MTC . .
SCREEEEH!
LOOK OUT!
FORTUNE

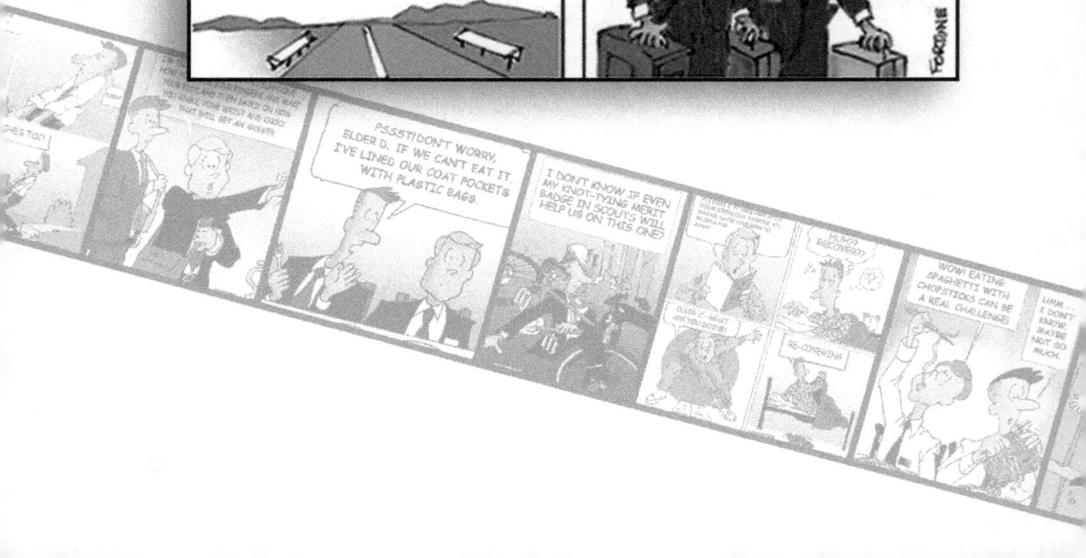
PSSST! DON'T WORRY, ELDER D. IF WE CAN'T EAT IT, I'VE LINED OUR COAT POCKETS WITH PLASTIC BAGS.
I DON'T KNOW IF EVEN MY KNOT-TYING MERIT BADGE IN SCOUTS WILL HELP US ON THIS ONE?
HUH?? RECOVER??
RE-COVERING
WOW! EATING SPAGHETTI WITH CHOPSTICKS CAN BE A REAL CHALLENGE!
UMM... I DON'T KNOW. MAYBE NOT SO MUCH.

The Gospel Is True with or without Onions

Background information:
In German, the word "doubt" is *Zweifel*.
The word "onion" is *Zwiebel*.

While serving as a greenie missionary in Berlin, Germany, Sister Bracken and her trainer, Sister Allen, were asked to speak in sacrament meeting. At the end of her talk, Sister Bracken unintentionally switched words and declared, "I know without a shadow of *onion* the gospel of Jesus Christ is true."

A Call to the Frozen

Prior to her call to serve in Anchorage, Alaska, Sister Ivy lived in Tampa, Florida. She struggled to keep warm during a very cold January in Alaska. At a zone conference, Sister Ivy spoke with the zone leader, Elder Mason, and sincerely said, "I don't know why I was called to Alaska, for I'm having a very difficult time with cold weather."

Mingling scripture with reality, Elder Mason smiled and said, "Remember, Sister, many are called, but few are frozen."

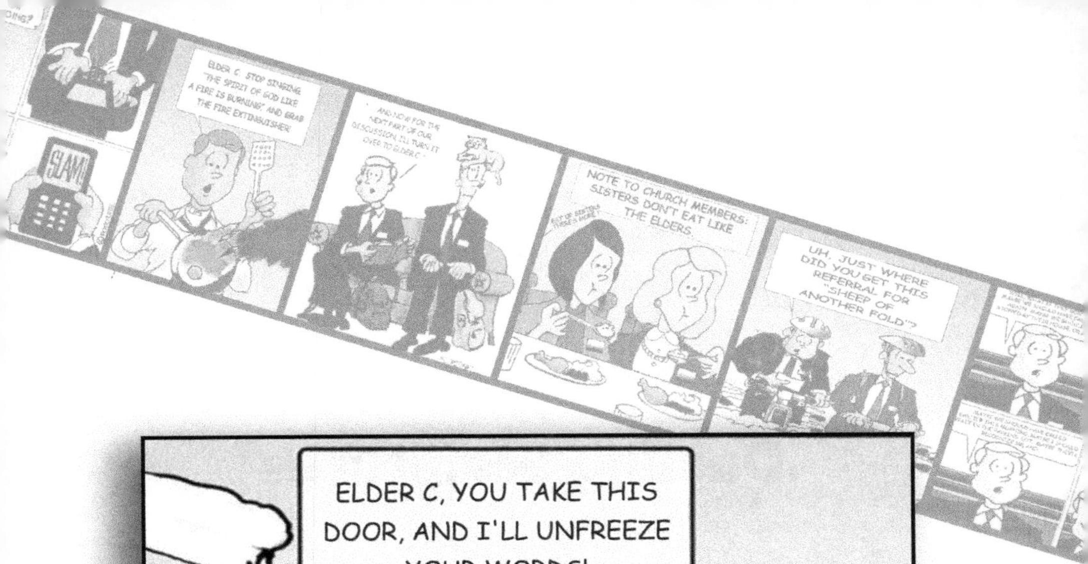
ELDER C, STOP SINGING "THE SPIRIT OF GOD LIKE A FIRE IS BURNING" AND GRAB THE FIRE EXTINGUISHER!
SLAM!
AND NOW FOR THE NEXT PART OF OUR DISCUSSION, I'LL TURN IT OVER TO ELDER C.
NOTE TO CHURCH MEMBERS: SISTERS DON'T EAT LIKE THE ELDERS.
UH, JUST WHERE DID YOU GET THIS REFERRAL FOR "SHEEP OF ANOTHER FOLD"?

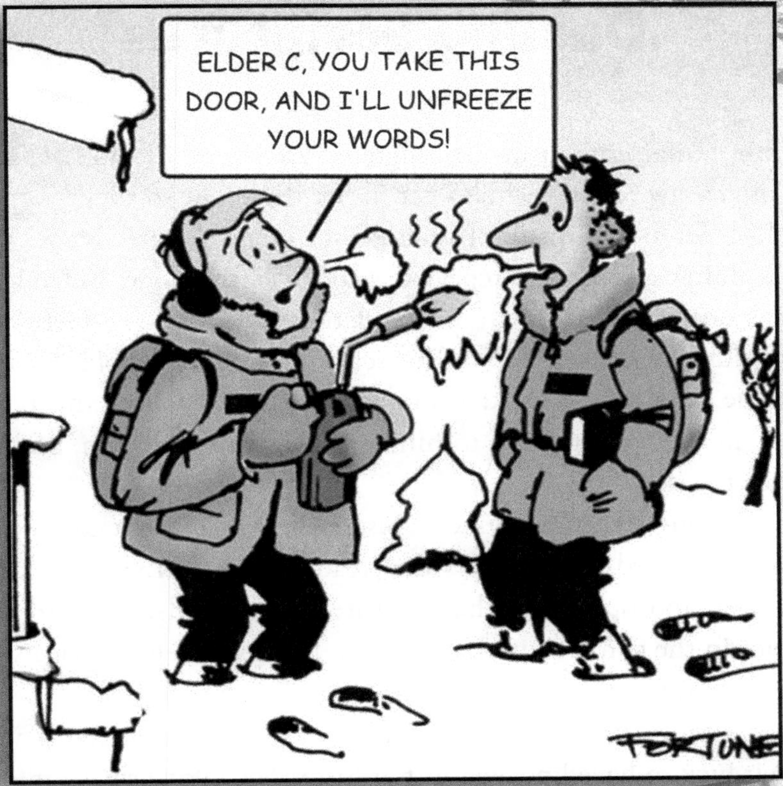
ELDER C, YOU TAKE THIS DOOR, AND I'LL UNFREEZE YOUR WORDS!
FORTUNE

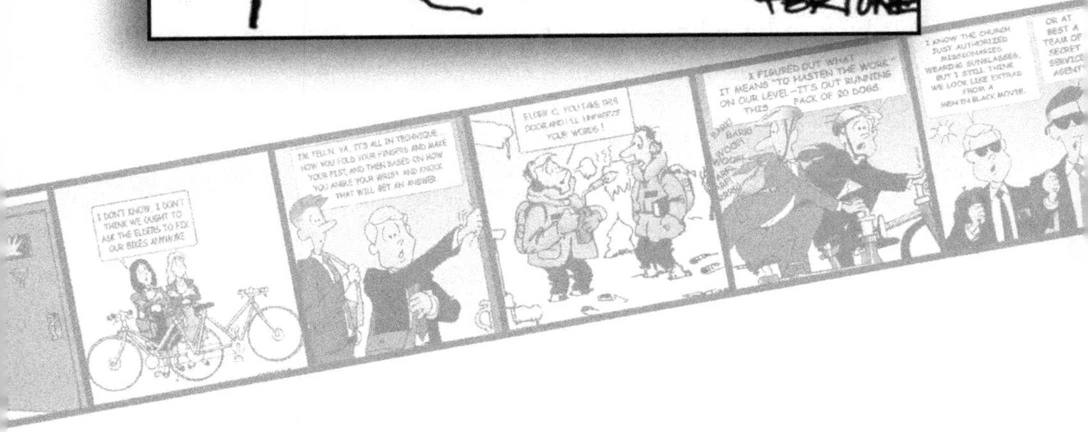
I DON'T KNOW. I DON'T THINK WE OUGHT TO ASK THE ELDERS TO FIX OUR BIKES ANYWAY.
ELDER C, YOU TAKE THIS DOOR AND I'LL UNFREEZE YOUR WORDS!
I FIGURED OUT WHAT IT MEANS "TO HASTEN THE WORK" ON OUR LEVEL—IT'S OUT RUNNING THIS PACK OF 20 DOGS.
I KNOW THE CHURCH JUST AUTHORIZED MISSIONARIES WEARING SUNGLASSES, BUT I STILL THINK WE LOOK LIKE EXTRAS FROM A MEN IN BLACK MOVIE.
OR AT BEST A TEAM OF SECRET SERVICE AGENTS

Dueling Scriptures

On a hot afternoon in Birmingham, Alabama, Elders Lyle and Conger saw Sister Nichols's car in her driveway, so they stopped to ask for a cold drink of water. They knew she was home, but she didn't answer the repeated knocks at the door. Elder Lyle took one of his cards, wrote "Revelation 3:20" on it, and left it in the side of the front door. (This scripture reads, "Behold, I stand at the door, and knock: if any man hear my voice, and open the door, I will come in to him, and will sup with him, and he with me.")

In church the next Sunday, Sister Nichols, without comment, handed a card to the elders that read, "Moses 4:16." The elders hurried and opened to the scripture, which reads, "I heard thy voice in the garden, and I was afraid, because I beheld that I was naked, and I hid myself."

Talking later to Sister Nichols, the elders discovered it was their luck to have knocked just as Sister Nichols was getting out of the shower.

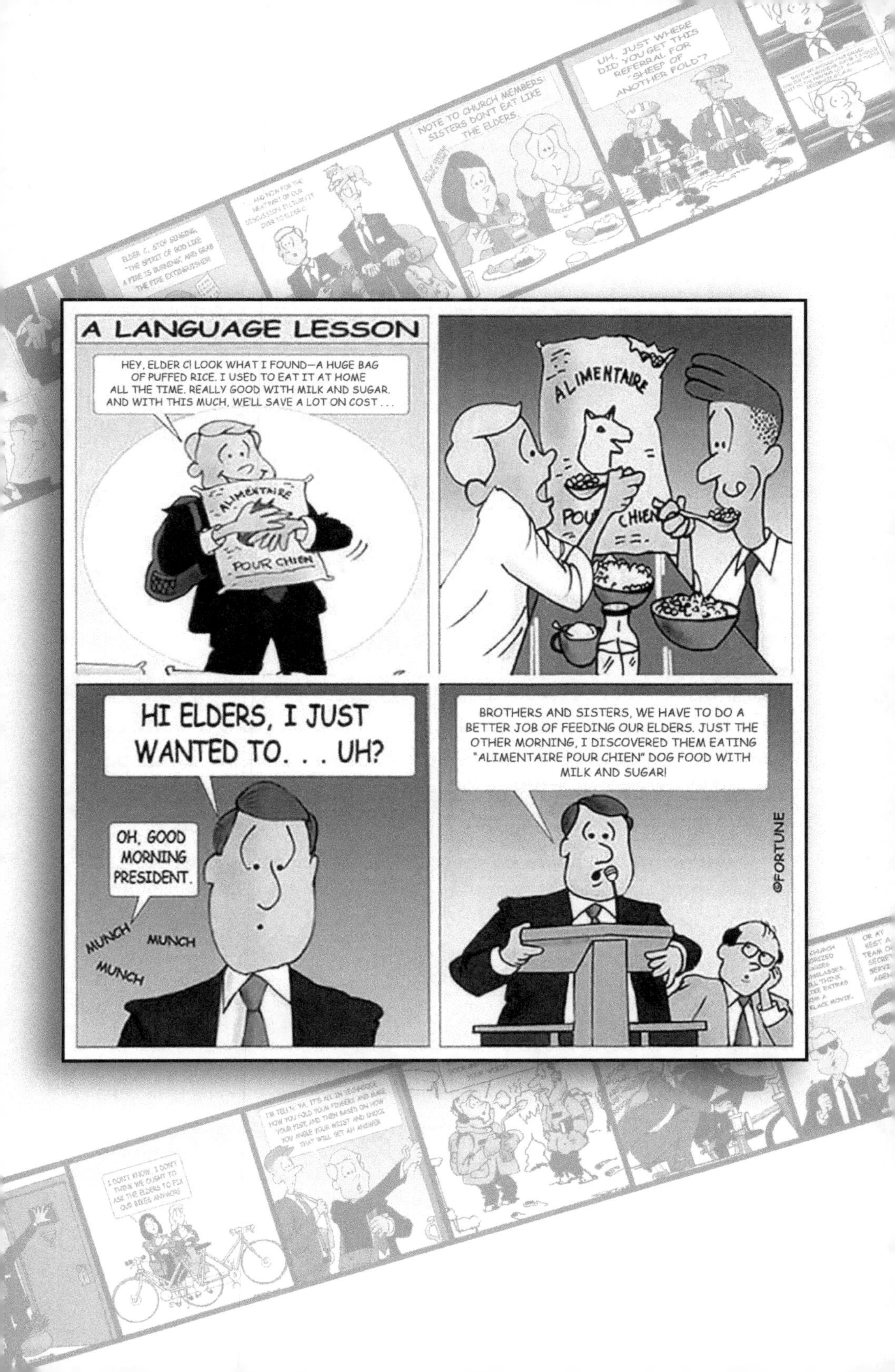
A LANGUAGE LESSON
HEY, ELDER C! LOOK WHAT I FOUND—A HUGE BAG OF PUFFED RICE. I USED TO EAT IT AT HOME ALL THE TIME. REALLY GOOD WITH MILK AND SUGAR. AND WITH THIS MUCH, WE'LL SAVE A LOT ON COST . . .
ALIMENTAIRE POUR CHIEN
ALIMENTAIRE POUR CHIEN
HI ELDERS, I JUST WANTED TO. . . UH?
OH, GOOD MORNING PRESIDENT.
MUNCH MUNCH MUNCH
BROTHERS AND SISTERS, WE HAVE TO DO A BETTER JOB OF FEEDING OUR ELDERS. JUST THE OTHER MORNING, I DISCOVERED THEM EATING "ALIMENTAIRE POUR CHIEN" DOG FOOD WITH MILK AND SUGAR!
©FORTUNE
NOTE TO CHURCH MEMBERS: SISTERS DON'T EAT LIKE THE ELDERS.
UH, JUST WHERE DID YOU GET THIS REFERRAL FOR "SHEEP OF ANOTHER FOLD"?

The Trouble with Speaking Softly

Elder Nelson and Elder Taylor were proselyting in Oakland, California. Elder Nelson was suffering with laryngitis but otherwise felt fine. He knocked on a front door, and a beautiful seventeen-year-old girl answered the door. At barely a whisper, Elder Nelson said, "We are representatives from The Church of Jesus Christ of Latter-day Saints. Are your parents home?"

Glancing quickly from side to side, she smiled and whispered back, "No, come on in."

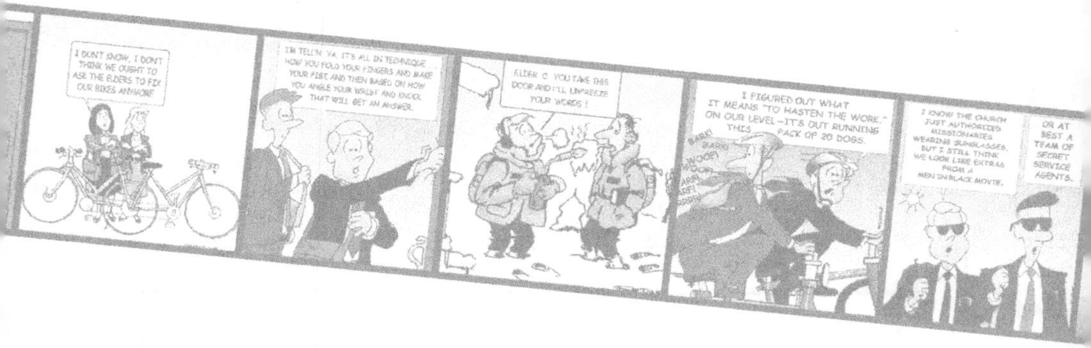
I DON'T KNOW, I DON'T THINK WE OUGHT TO ASK THE ELDERS TO FIX OUR BIKES ANYMORE
I'M TELL'N YA, IT'S ALL IN TECHNIQUE ... HOW YOU FOLD YOUR FINGERS AND MAKE YOUR FIST, AND THEN BASED ON HOW YOU ANGLE YOUR WRIST AND KNOCK THAT WILL GET AN ANSWER.
ELDER C. YOU TAKE THIS DOOR AND I'LL UNFREEZE YOUR WORDS!
I FIGURED OUT WHAT IT MEANS "TO HASTEN THE WORK." ON OUR LEVEL—IT'S OUT RUNNING THIS ... PACK OF 20 DOGS.
BARK!
WOOF!
I KNOW THE CHURCH JUST AUTHORIZED MISSIONARIES WEARING SUNGLASSES, BUT I STILL THINK WE LOOK LIKE EXTRAS FROM A MEN IN BLACK MOVIE.
OR AT BEST A TEAM OF SECRET SERVICE AGENTS.

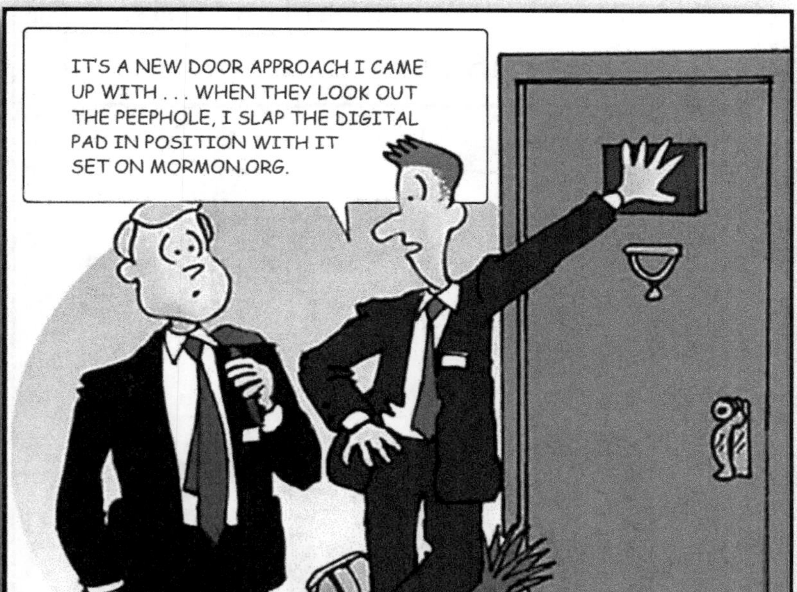
IT'S A NEW DOOR APPROACH I CAME UP WITH . . . WHEN THEY LOOK OUT THE PEEPHOLE, I SLAP THE DIGITAL PAD IN POSITION WITH IT SET ON MORMON.ORG.
FORTUNE

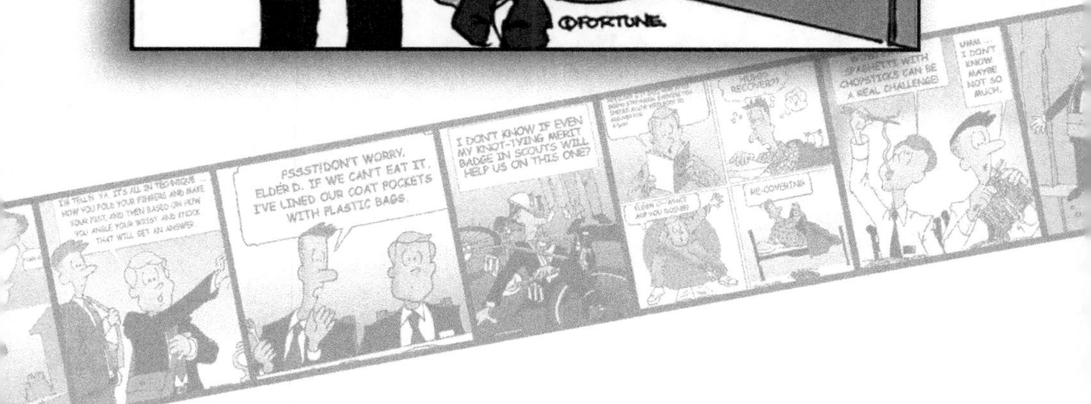
I'M TELL'N YA, IT'S ALL IN TECHNIQUE ... HOW YOU FOLD YOUR FINGERS AND MAKE YOUR FIST, AND THEN BASED ON HOW YOU ANGLE YOUR WRIST AND KNOCK THAT WILL GET AN ANSWER.
PSSST! DON'T WORRY, ELDER D. IF WE CAN'T EAT IT, I'VE LINED OUR COAT POCKETS WITH PLASTIC BAGS.
I DON'T KNOW IF EVEN MY KNOT-TYING MERIT BADGE IN SCOUTS WILL HELP US ON THIS ONE?
RECOVER??
RE-COVERING
SPAGHETTI WITH CHOPSTICKS CAN BE A REAL CHALLENGE!
UMM ... I DON'T KNOW MAYBE NOT SO MUCH.

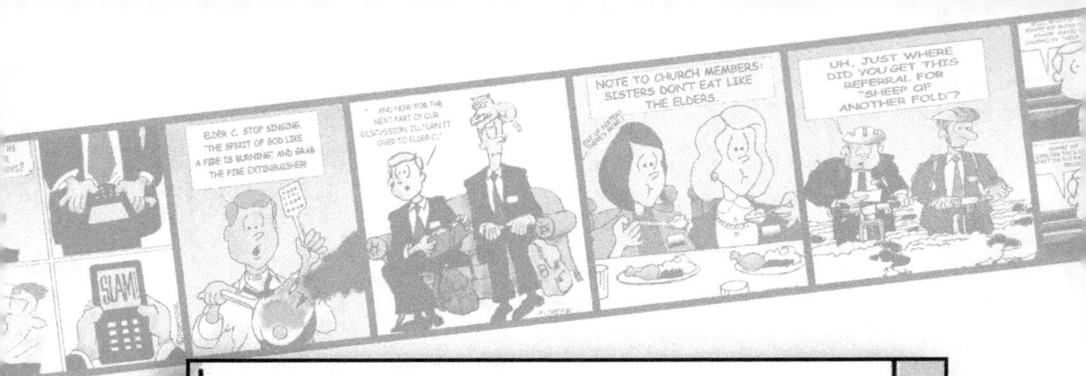
ELDER C. STOP SINGING "THE SPIRIT OF GOD LIKE A FIRE IS BURNING" AND GRAB THE FIRE EXTINGUISHER!
SLAM!
NOTE TO CHURCH MEMBERS: SISTERS DON'T EAT LIKE THE ELDERS.
UH, JUST WHERE DID YOU GET THIS REFERRAL FOR "SHEEP OF ANOTHER FOLD"?

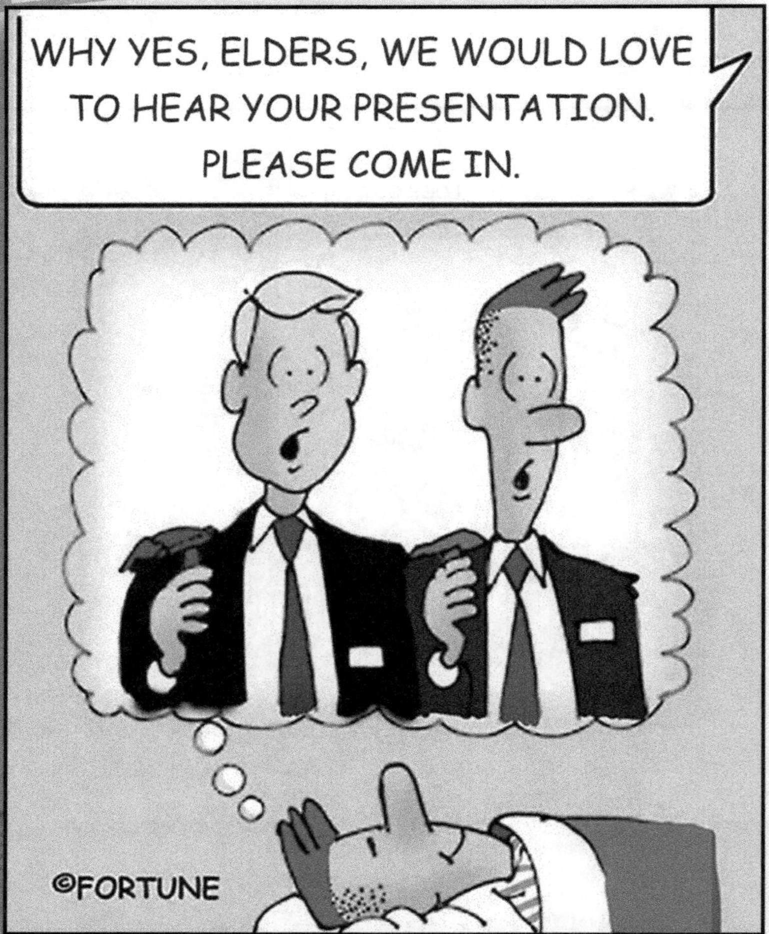
WHY YES, ELDERS, WE WOULD LOVE TO HEAR YOUR PRESENTATION. PLEASE COME IN.
©FORTUNE

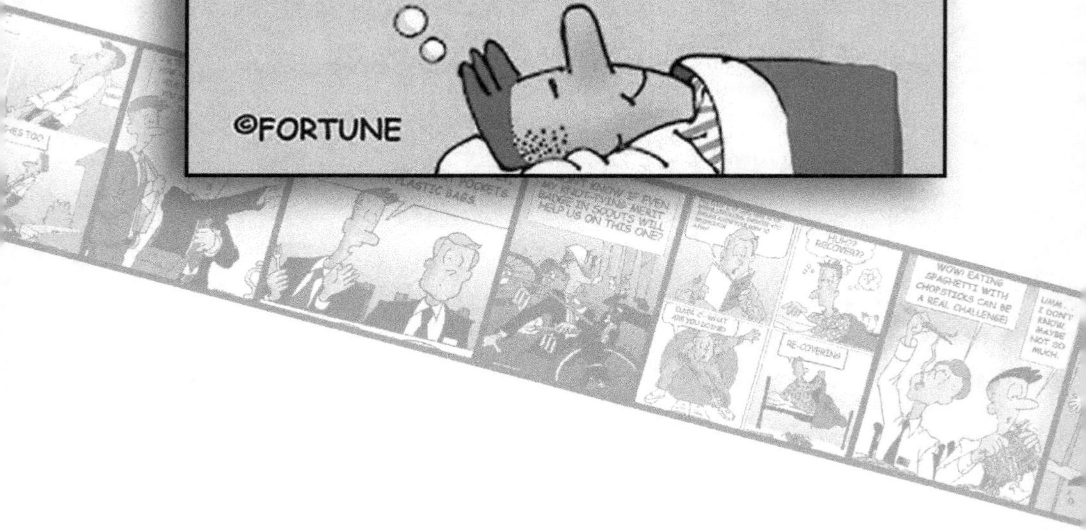
HUH?? RECOVER??
RE-COVERING
WOW! EATING SPAGHETTI WITH CHOPSTICKS CAN BE A REAL CHALLENGE!
UMM... I DON'T KNOW. MAYBE NOT SO MUCH.

Rubbing In the Gospel

Background information:
In Spanish, the word "message" is *mensaje.*
The word "massage" is *masaje.*

Elder Barnett was a greenie missionary assigned to train with Elder Sanchez. While serving for three weeks in Guadalajara, Mexico, Elder Barnett knocked on the front door of a home. An attractive woman opened the door, and Elder Barnett introduced himself and his companion and then surprised the woman by saying, "We are representatives from The Church of Jesus Christ of Latter-day Saints, and we have a great massage we want to give you."

Weary of Being Leary

"But ye, brethren, be not weary in well doing." (2 Thess. 3:13)

Coming home late one evening from missionary appointments, Elder Adams and Elder Leary were both tired. As they prepared to retire for the evening, Elder Adams went into the bathroom to brush his teeth. When he emerged from the room, he noticed Elder Leary was lying on his bed but not asleep. Looking up at Elder Adams, Elder Leary said, "Tonight I'm not Elder Leary—I'm Elder Weary. Let's have prayer."

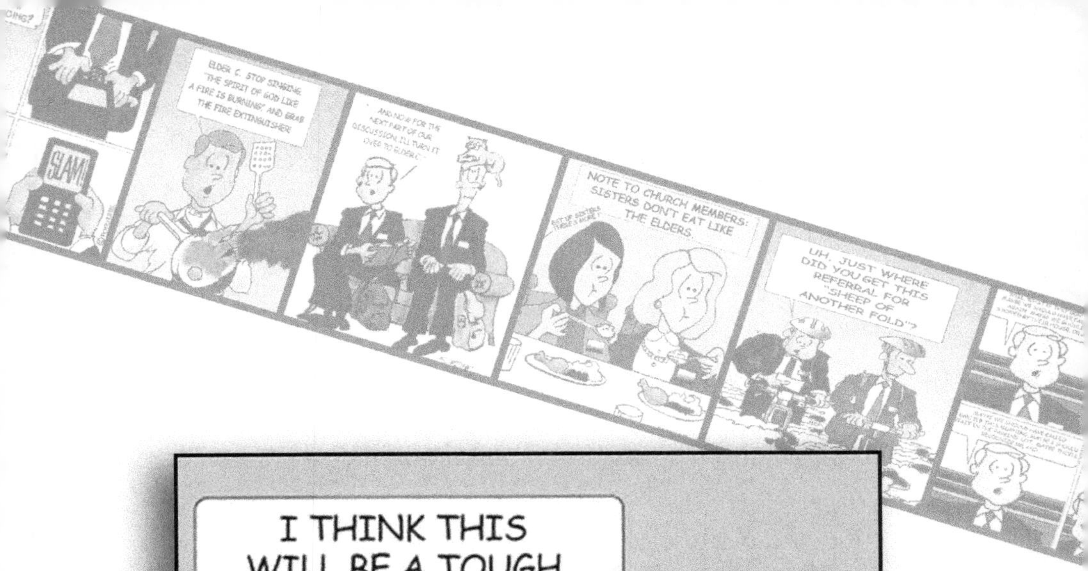
ELDER C. STOP SINGING "THE SPIRIT OF GOD LIKE A FIRE IS BURNING" AND GRAB THE FIRE EXTINGUISHER!
NOTE TO CHURCH MEMBERS: SISTERS DON'T EAT LIKE THE ELDERS.
UH, JUST WHERE DID YOU GET THIS REFERRAL FOR "SHEEP OF ANOTHER FOLD"?

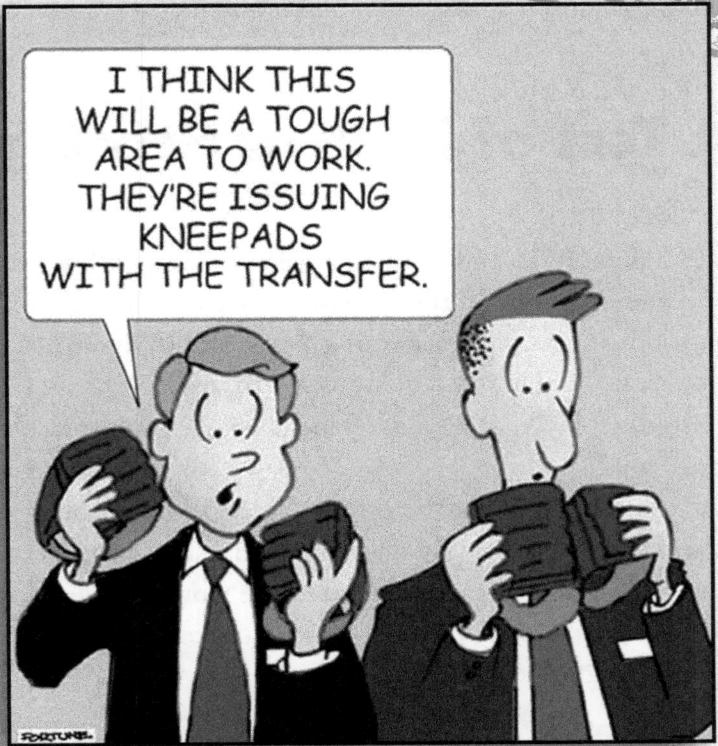
I THINK THIS WILL BE A TOUGH AREA TO WORK. THEY'RE ISSUING KNEEPADS WITH THE TRANSFER.

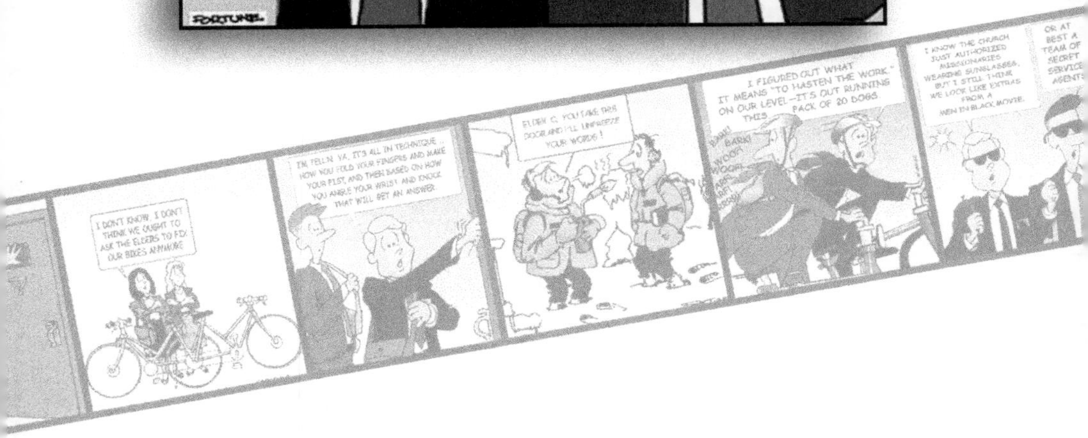
I DON'T KNOW. I DON'T THINK WE OUGHT TO ASK THE ELDERS TO FIX OUR BIKES ANYMORE.
I FIGURED OUT WHAT IT MEANS "TO HASTEN THE WORK" ON OUR LEVEL—IT'S OUT RUNNING THIS PACK OF 20 DOGS.

A Test of Faith or Hearing?

While Elders Todd and Williams were visiting with a member family one evening, Brother Treasure asked if the elders would like to join the family in evening prayer. Both agreed. One of the five-year-old daughters volunteered to say the prayer. During her lengthy prayer, she said, "Please help Mom and Dad to keep us safe."

At the conclusion of the prayer, Elder Todd curiously asked Brother Treasure what his daughter had asked in that part of her prayer. Brother Treasure repeated the words. Relieved, Elder Todd seriously said, "I thought your daughter said, 'Please help Mom and Dad to keep the faith.'"

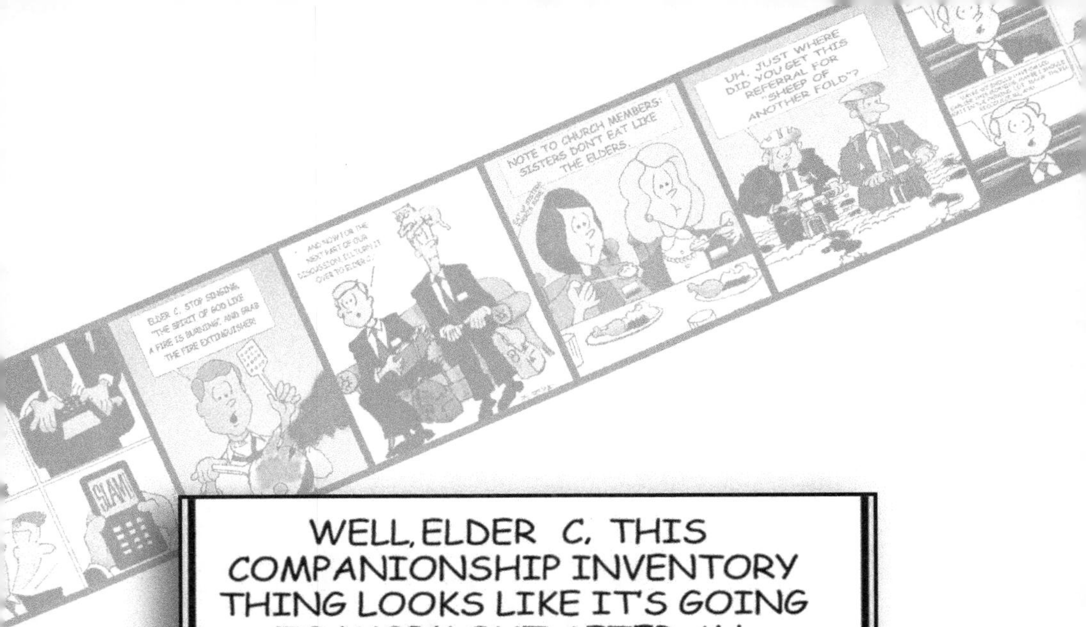
SLAM!
ELDER C. STOP SINGING "THE SPIRIT OF GOD LIKE A FIRE IS BURNING" AND GRAB THE FIRE EXTINGUISHER!
NOTE TO CHURCH MEMBERS: SISTERS DON'T EAT LIKE THE ELDERS.
UH, JUST WHERE DID YOU GET THIS REFERRAL FOR "SHEEP OF ANOTHER FOLD"?

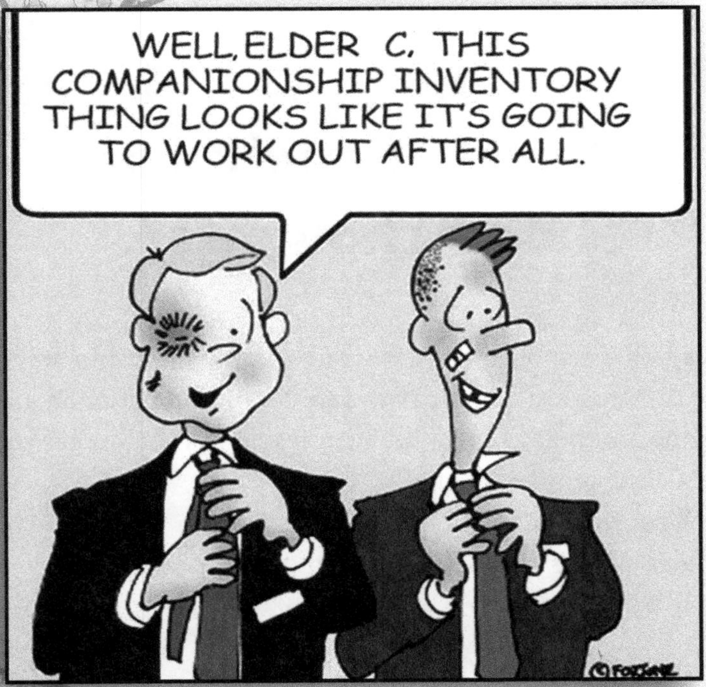
WELL, ELDER C. THIS COMPANIONSHIP INVENTORY THING LOOKS LIKE IT'S GOING TO WORK OUT AFTER ALL.

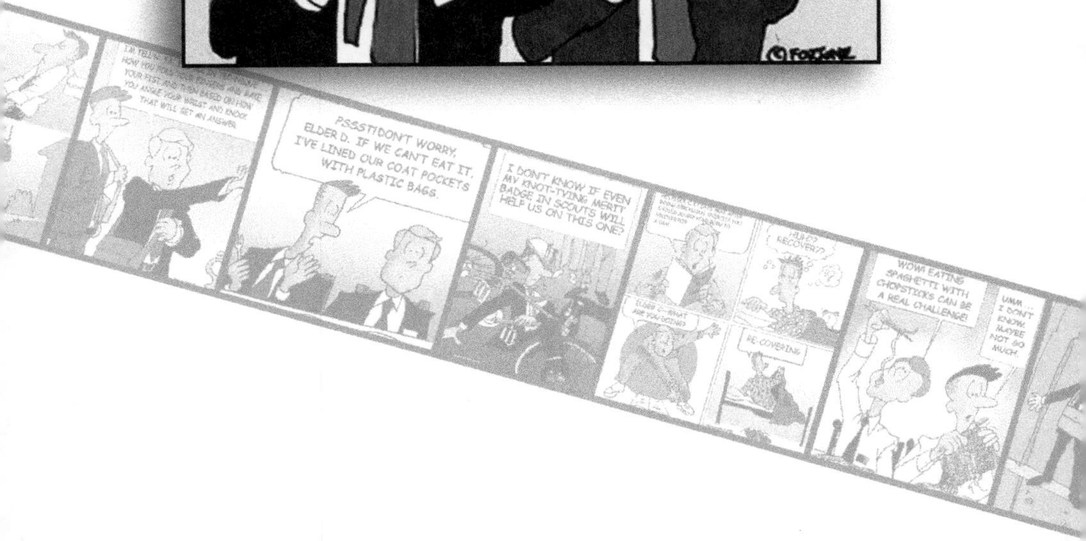
PSSST! DON'T WORRY, ELDER D. IF WE CAN'T EAT IT, I'VE LINED OUR COAT POCKETS WITH PLASTIC BAGS.
I DON'T KNOW IF EVEN MY KNOT-TYING MERIT BADGE IN SCOUTS WILL HELP US ON THIS ONE?
HUH? RECOVER?
RE-COVERING
WOW! EATING SPAGHETTI WITH CHOPSTICKS CAN BE A REAL CHALLENGE!
UMM... I DON'T KNOW. MAYBE NOT SO MUCH.

Good Thoughts or
Bad Thoughts?

Elders Wilkes and Smart were a new companionship serving in Omaha, Nebraska. As the two were becoming better acquainted with one another, Elder Wilkes confessed that before his mission he was quite temperamental.

"What do you mean?" asked Elder Smart.

Elder Wilkes replied, "More temper than mental."

Was That a Grapefruit
or a Dove?

Background information:
In Spanish, the word for "grapefruit" is *pomelo,*
and the word for "dove" is *paloma.*

As a greenie in Uruguay, Elder Cramer didn't speak the best Spanish, so any teaching situation with him was an adventure. Elder Cramer confused the words *pomelo* and *paloma*—and confused his investigators—when he explained the separate nature of the Godhead by stating that at the baptism of the Savior, the voice of God the Father came from heaven, and the Holy Ghost descended upon Jesus in the form of a grapefruit.

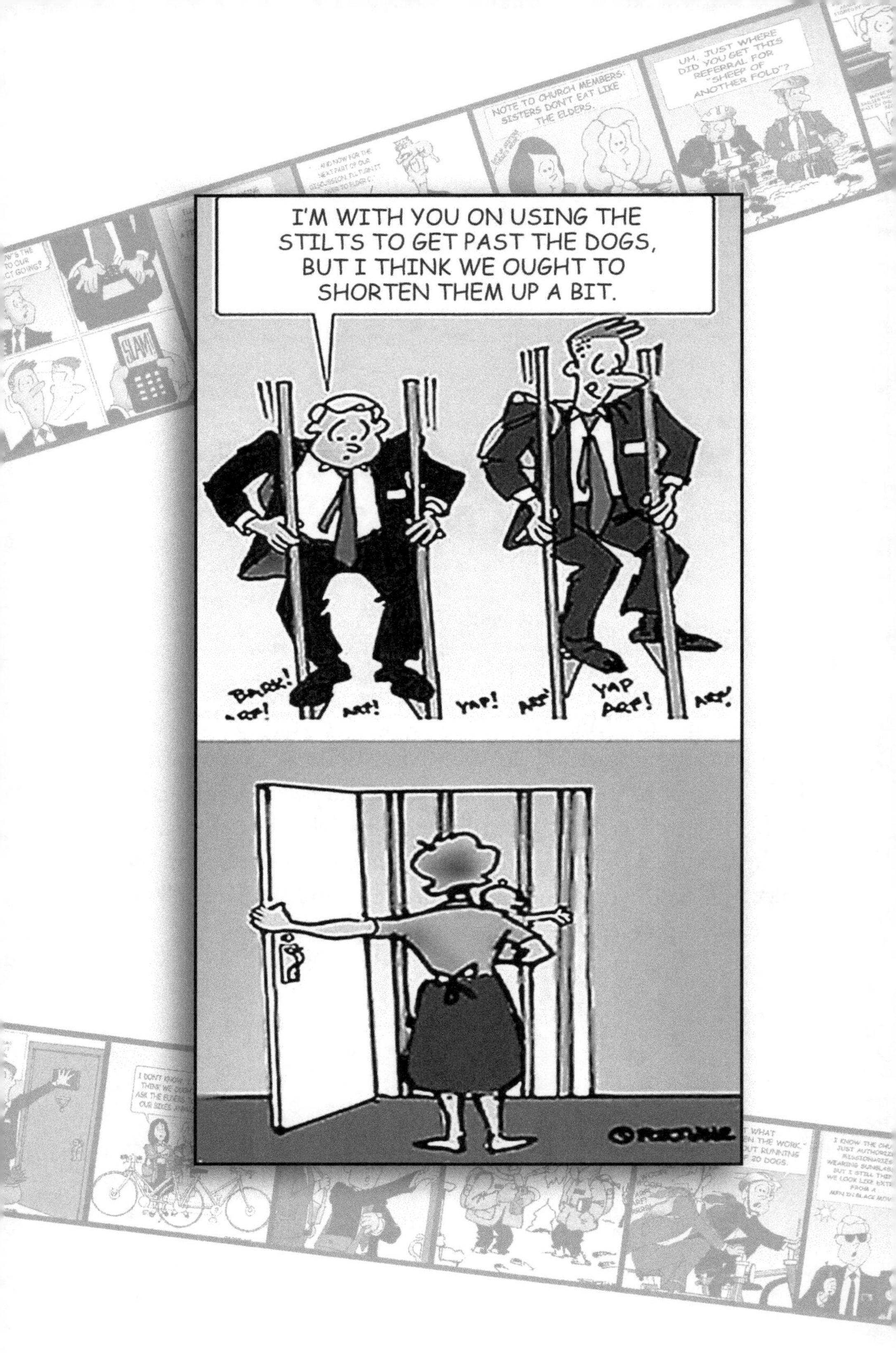

NOTE TO CHURCH MEMBERS: SISTERS DON'T EAT LIKE THE ELDERS.
UM, JUST WHERE DID YOU GET THIS REFERRAL FOR "SHEEP OF ANOTHER FOLD"?
I'M WITH YOU ON USING THE STILTS TO GET PAST THE DOGS, BUT I THINK WE OUGHT TO SHORTEN THEM UP A BIT.
BARK!
YAP!
YAP ARF!

Door-to-Door Panic

Elder Wells worked hard in the MTC to learn the Spanish language, but it was very difficult for him. Full of faith, but with limited words, he arrived in Mexico City and was assigned to a native companion, Elder Torres. Elder Wells was six feet, four inches tall and weighed 240 pounds. Elder Torres was five feet, one inch tall and weighed 135 pounds. They were quite a sight as they proselyted together.

Teaching Elder Wells, Elder Torres spoke at the first five doors they knocked on. When they got to the sixth door, it was the greenie's turn. Fearfully, he knocked, and a woman who didn't speak English came to the door.

Elder Wells's mind went blank, and he couldn't think of anything to say. Suddenly, he remembered a phrase of Spanish from the first discussion he learned in the Language Training Center. Turning to his right side, he quickly picked Elder Torres up, placed him in front of the lady, and said, *"This is My Beloved Son. Hear Him!"*

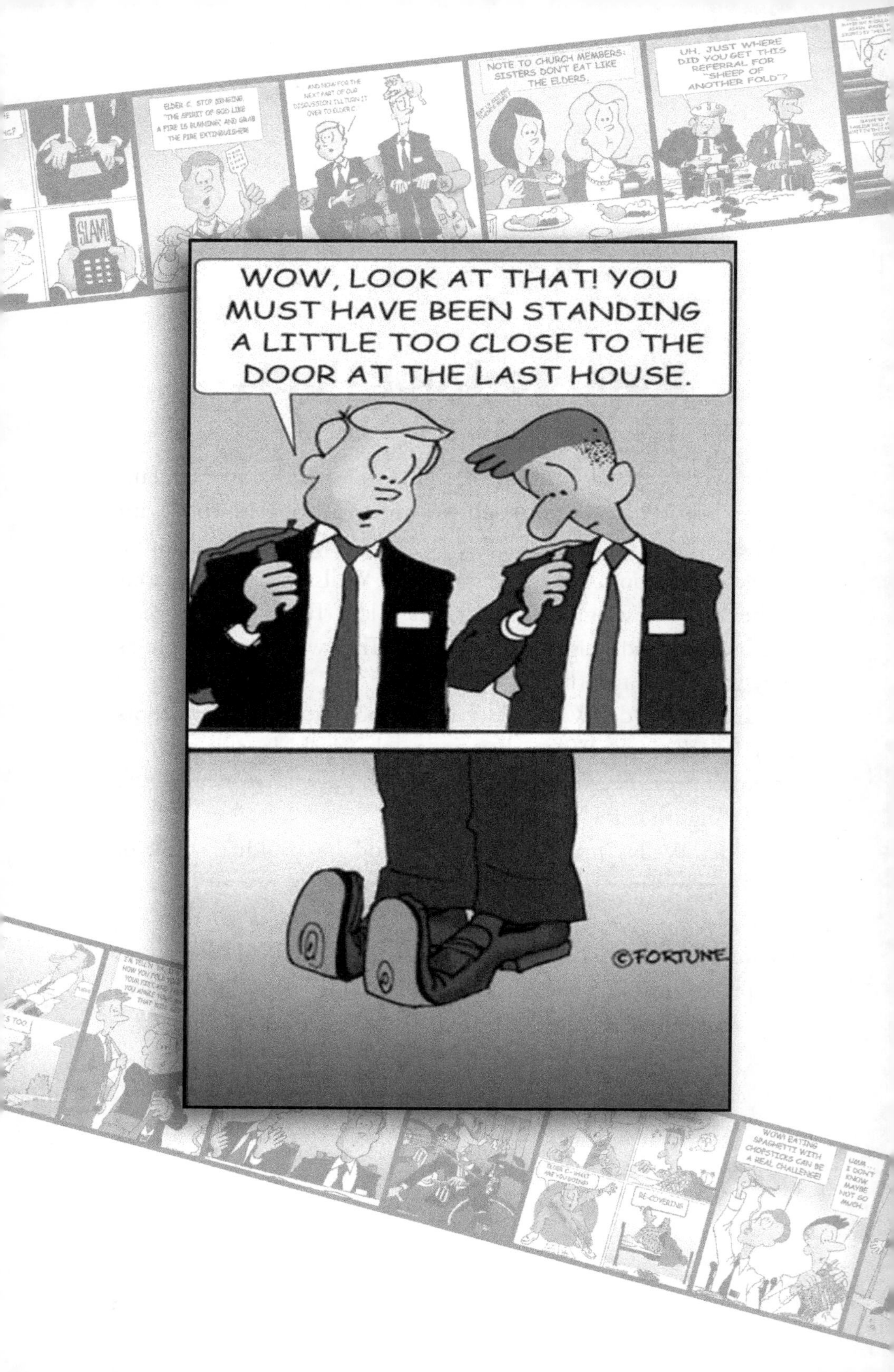
WOW, LOOK AT THAT! YOU MUST HAVE BEEN STANDING A LITTLE TOO CLOSE TO THE DOOR AT THE LAST HOUSE.
©FORTUNE
ELDER C. STOP SINGING, "THE SPIRIT OF GOD LIKE A FIRE IS BURNING," AND GRAB THE FIRE EXTINGUISHER!
SLAM!
NOTE TO CHURCH MEMBERS: SISTERS DON'T EAT LIKE THE ELDERS.
UH, JUST WHERE DID YOU GET THIS REFERRAL FOR "SHEEP OF ANOTHER FOLD"?
RE-COVERING
WOW! EATING SPAGHETTI WITH CHOPSTICKS CAN BE A REAL CHALLENGE!

Cheery or Cherry?

After reading from Joseph Smith—History, Elder Matthew looked at his companion and exclaimed that he wanted to be like the Prophet and have a "cheery temperament" (JS—H 1:28).

Not having told his companion that he had received a "Dear John" letter from his girlfriend the day before, Elder Stone somberly stated, "Today I have a cherry temperament."

"What do you mean?" asked Elder Matthew.

"It's the pits."

Lost in Translation

A new convert asked Elder Michaels what being translated meant. After he explained it, the elder said that he was told by an angel in a dream that he would be translated the next morning.

"Really?" asked the convert.

With a smile on his face, Elder Michaels teasingly answered, "I told the angel that I was not worthy!"

Then Elder Michaels continued, "The angel quickly responded, 'You'll have to stay on your mission for bearing false witness.'"

John Brockbank

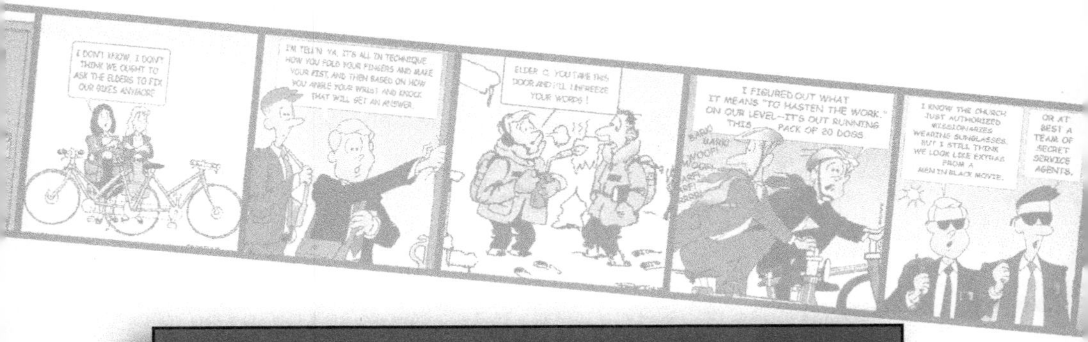
I DON'T KNOW. I DON'T THINK WE OUGHT TO ASK THE ELDERS TO FIX OUR BIKES ANYMORE
I'M TELL'N YA, IT'S ALL IN TECHNIQUE. HOW YOU FOLD YOUR FINGERS AND MAKE YOUR FIST, AND THEN BASED ON HOW YOU ANGLE YOUR WRIST AND KNOCK THAT WILL GET AN ANSWER.
ELDER C. YOU TAKE THIS DOOR AND I'LL UNFREEZE YOUR WORDS !
I FIGURED OUT WHAT IT MEANS "TO HASTEN THE WORK." ON OUR LEVEL--IT'S OUT RUNNING THIS PACK OF 20 DOGS.
I KNOW THE CHURCH JUST AUTHORIZED MISSIONARIES WEARING SUNGLASSES. BUT I STILL THINK WE LOOK LIKE EXTRAS FROM A MEN IN BLACK MOVIE.
OR AT BEST A TEAM OF SECRET SERVICE AGENTS.

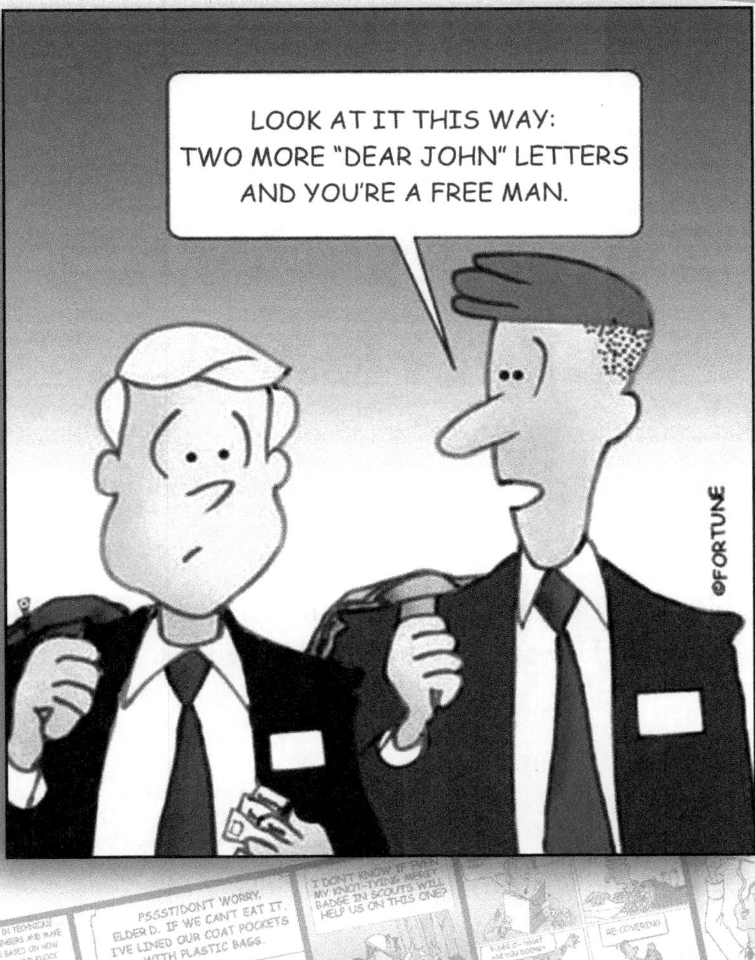
LOOK AT IT THIS WAY:
TWO MORE "DEAR JOHN" LETTERS
AND YOU'RE A FREE MAN.
©FORTUNE

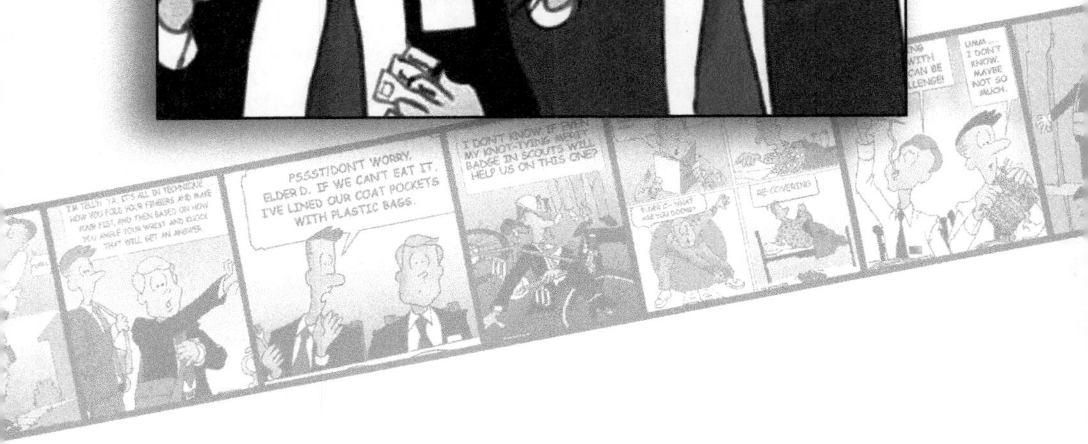
UMM... I DON'T KNOW. MAYBE NOT SO MUCH.
I'M TELL'N YA, IT'S ALL IN TECHNIQUE. HOW YOU FOLD YOUR FINGERS AND MAKE YOUR FIST, AND THEN BASED ON HOW YOU ANGLE YOUR WRIST AND KNOCK THAT WILL GET AN ANSWER.
PSSST! DON'T WORRY, ELDER D. IF WE CAN'T EAT IT, I'VE LINED OUR COAT POCKETS WITH PLASTIC BAGS.
I DON'T KNOW IF EVEN MY KNOT-TYING MERIT BADGE IN SCOUTS WILL HELP US ON THIS ONE?
ELDER C-- WHAT ARE YOU DOING?
RE-COVERING

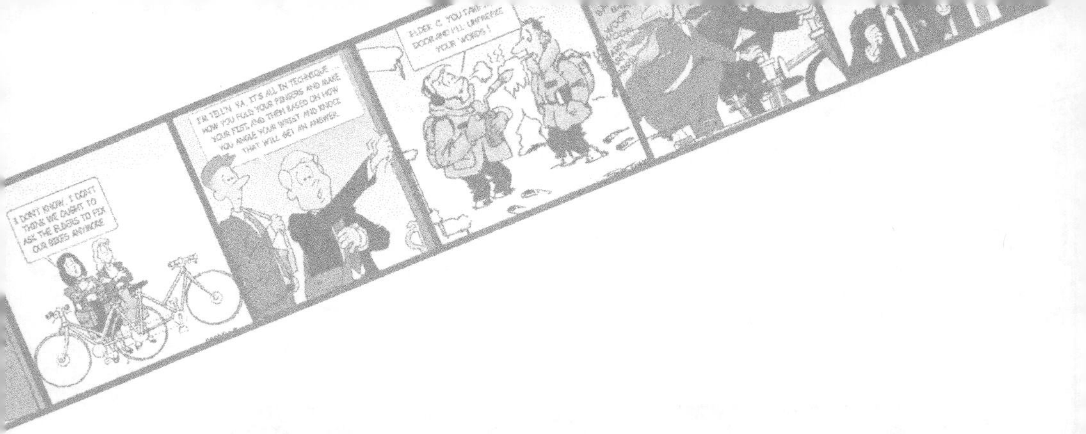
I DON'T KNOW. I DON'T THINK WE OUGHT TO ASK THE ELDERS TO FIX OUR BIKES ANYMORE
I'M TELLIN YA, IT'S ALL IN TECHNIQUE... HOW YOU FOLD YOUR FINGERS AND MAKE YOUR FIST, AND THEN BASED ON HOW YOU ANGLE YOUR WRIST AND KNOCK THAT WILL GET AN ANSWER.

Sister Missionary Experiences

The following are emails sent to Bill Fortune by sister missionaries.

NOTE: The following emails are real; none are fabricated. However, wording has been edited.

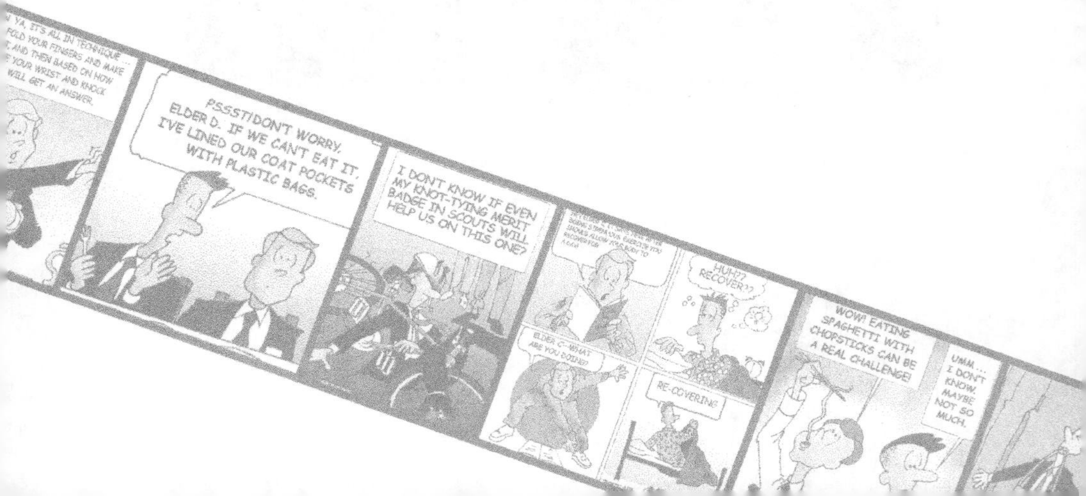
PSSST! DON'T WORRY, ELDER D. IF WE CAN'T EAT IT, I'VE LINED OUR COAT POCKETS WITH PLASTIC BAGS.
I DON'T KNOW IF EVEN MY KNOT-TYING MERIT BADGE IN SCOUTS WILL HELP US ON THIS ONE?
HUH?? RECOVER??
ELDER C--WHAT ARE YOU DOING?
RE-COVERING
WOW! EATING SPAGHETTI WITH CHOPSTICKS CAN BE A REAL CHALLENGE!
UMM... I DON'T KNOW. MAYBE NOT SO MUCH.

Subject: Missionary experiences in Switzerland

A Slight Doctrinal Misunderstanding

"[An individual] heard that we could help the dead go to heaven, and [we were] given an address to meet someone at ________. [My companion and I] arrived there, and [to our surprise] it was for a body to be baptized that was in a coffin."

Cori

Missionary Attraction

"An elderly lady approached [me] and said, 'You're not ugly enough to go on a mission.'

"So, being feisty, [I] answered, 'How else do you expect the Church to get more men in it?'

"[The lady] replied, 'Yep, this church has it right.'"

Cori

Subject: Missionary experiences in Brazil

No Alcohol, Tea, Coffee, or . . . Uh-Oh

"We were having a lesson on the Word of Wisdom, when an investigator told us that he would have no problem with alcohol, tea, or coffee issues, [but] nonchalantly added, 'Just cocaine.' Not what we were expecting."

Kristine

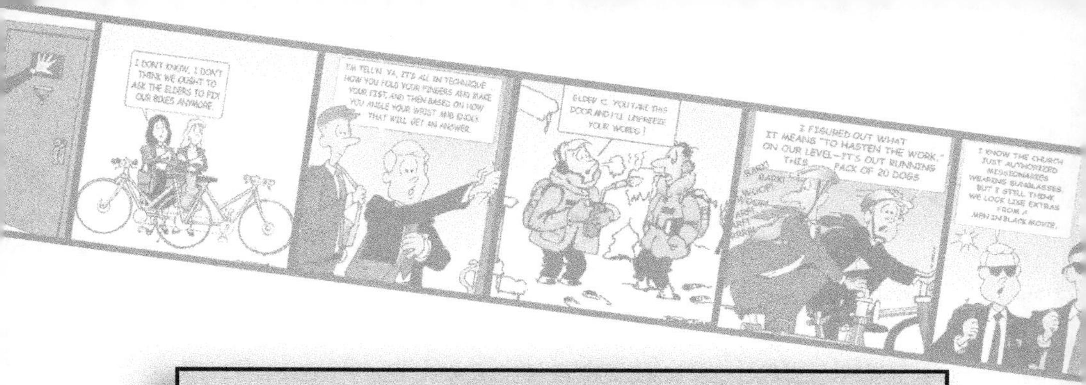
I DON'T KNOW, I DON'T THINK WE OUGHT TO ASK THE ELDERS TO FIX OUR BIKES ANYMORE.
I'M TELL'N YA, IT'S ALL IN TECHNIQUE. HOW YOU FOLD YOUR FINGERS AND MAKE YOUR FIST, AND THEN BASED ON HOW YOU ANGLE YOUR WRIST AND KNOCK THAT WILL GET AN ANSWER.
ELDER C. YOU TAKE THIS DOOR AND I'LL UNFREEZE YOUR WORDS!
I FIGURED OUT WHAT IT MEANS "TO HASTEN THE WORK." ON OUR LEVEL—IT'S OUT RUNNING THIS...... PACK OF 20 DOGS
I KNOW THE CHURCH JUST AUTHORIZED MISSIONARIES WEARING SUNGLASSES, BUT I STILL THINK WE LOOK LIKE EXTRAS FROM A MEN IN BLACK MOVIE.

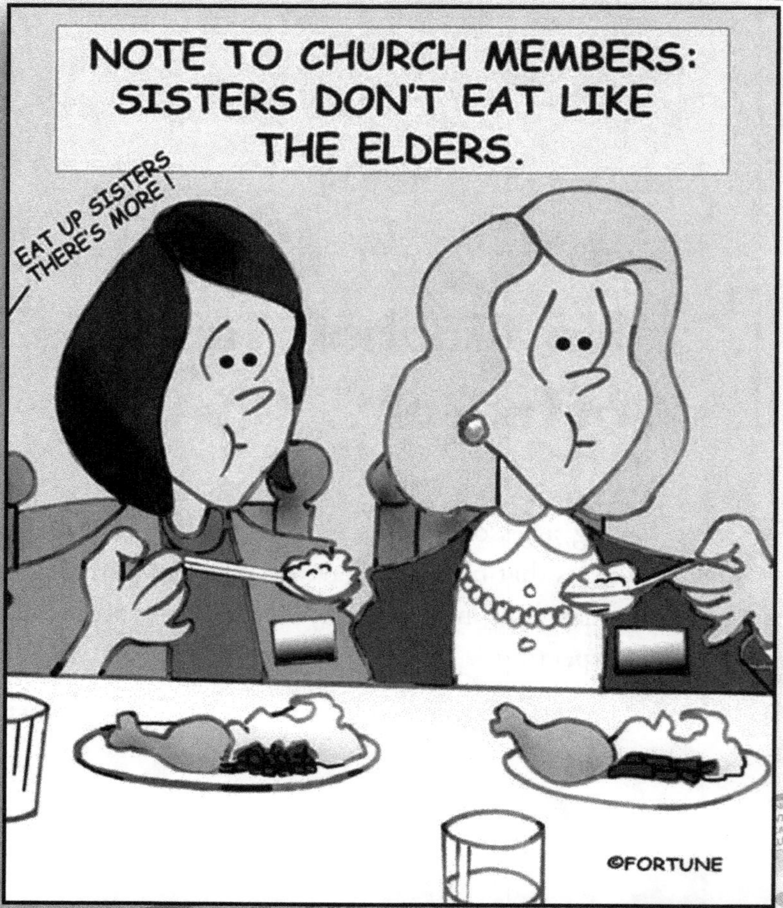
NOTE TO CHURCH MEMBERS: SISTERS DON'T EAT LIKE THE ELDERS.
EAT UP SISTERS THERE'S MORE!
©FORTUNE

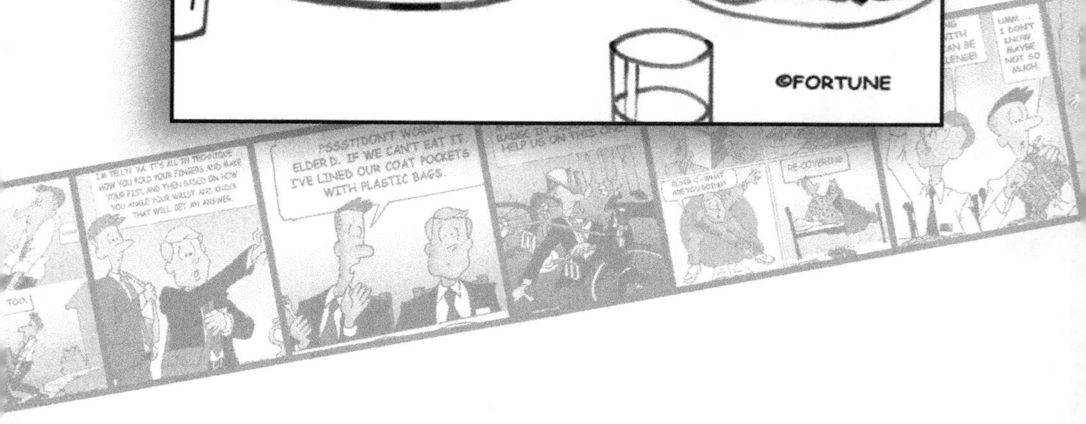
I'M TELL'N YA, IT'S ALL IN TECHNIQUE. HOW YOU FOLD YOUR FINGERS AND MAKE YOUR FIST, AND THEN BASED ON HOW YOU ANGLE YOUR WRIST AND KNOCK THAT WILL GET AN ANSWER.
ELDER D. IF WE CAN'T EAT IT, I'VE LINED OUR COAT POCKETS WITH PLASTIC BAGS.
RE-COVERING
UMM... I DON'T KNOW. MAYBE NOT SO MUCH.

Mission Monkey Business

"[While I was] sitting on the edge of a couch giving a lesson, a monkey crawled under my long skirt and jumped on my thigh and grabbed it. I shot up about four feet high and scared the poor thing."

Kristine

Subject: Missionary experiences in Montevideo, Uruguay

Problems with a Romance Language

"[My companion and I were] proposed to or offered 'benefit' relationships all the time. My blonde companions were the worst—poor things. A funny moment: My [greenie companion] didn't speak a lot of Spanish and didn't quite [understand] the 'opportunity' the guy was offering her. I had [to] deny on her behalf, and the [guy] seemed [really] disappointed."

Aubrey

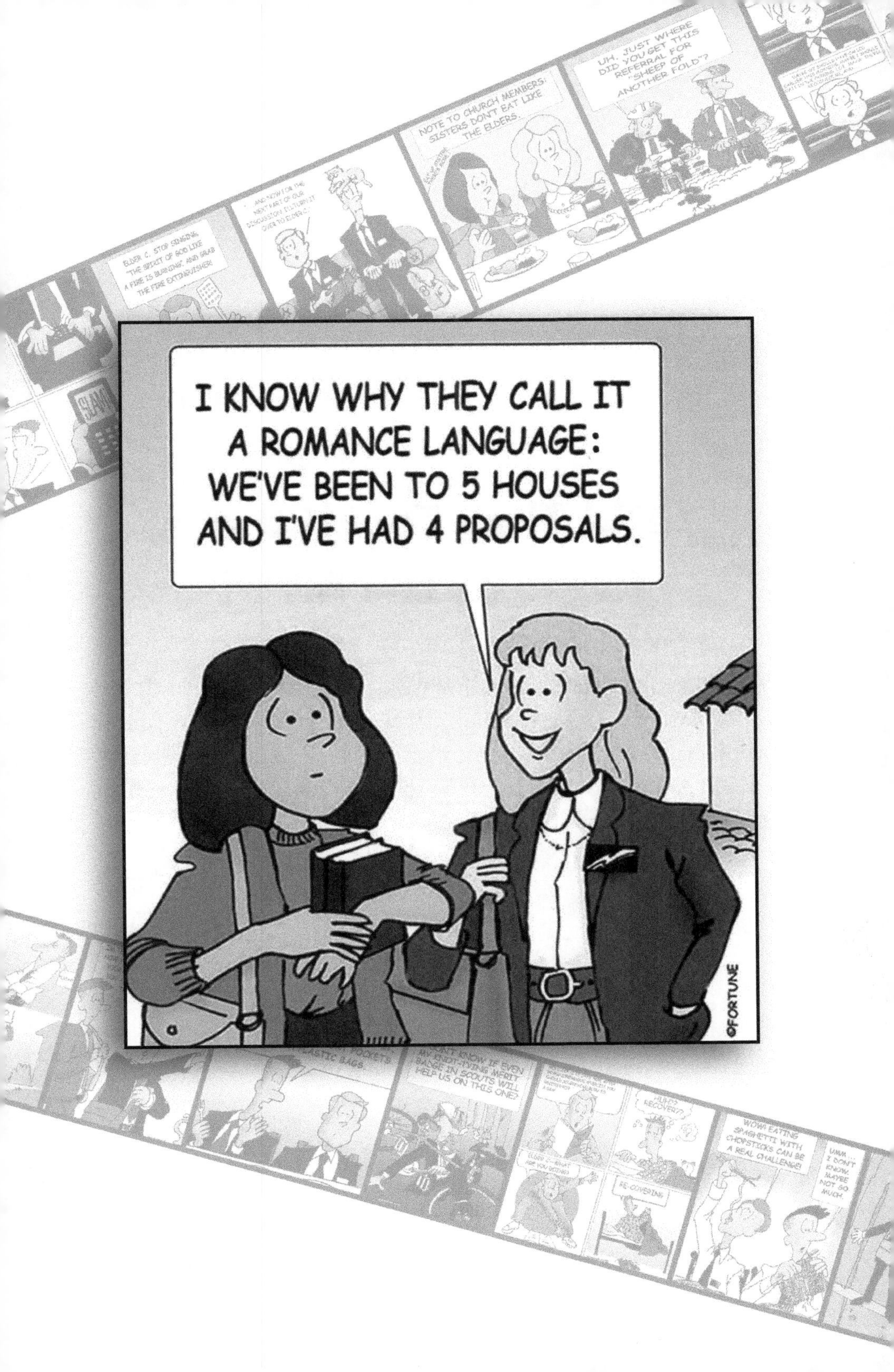
I KNOW WHY THEY CALL IT A ROMANCE LANGUAGE: WE'VE BEEN TO 5 HOUSES AND I'VE HAD 4 PROPOSALS.
©FORTUNE
ELDER C, STOP SINGING "THE SPIRIT OF GOD LIKE A FIRE IS BURNING" AND GRAB THE FIRE EXTINGUISHER!
NOTE TO CHURCH MEMBERS: SISTERS DON'T EAT LIKE THE ELDERS.
UH, JUST WHERE DID YOU GET THIS REFERRAL FOR "SHEEP OF ANOTHER FOLD"?
HUH? RECOVER??
RE-COVERING
WOW! EATING SPAGHETTI WITH CHOPSTICKS CAN BE A REAL CHALLENGE!
UMM... I DON'T KNOW. MAYBE NOT SO MUCH.

Did They Teach the Tango at the MTC?

"[With] another companion, [we were asked] to sing in Un Choro de los Ancients (Elderly Choir). It was us [and] a room full of people, [age] 60+. [I was in] my second area, [and] I was [really] sure 'El Amor Salvage,' the tango they had us singing, was not an [LDS] hymn. Good times, though."

Aubrey

How Does Your Garden Grow? Legally?

"[Doing a service project], we helped someone put in a greenhouse/garden patch. [Later], we found out [this man] was using it to grow marijuana. Oops!"

Aubrey

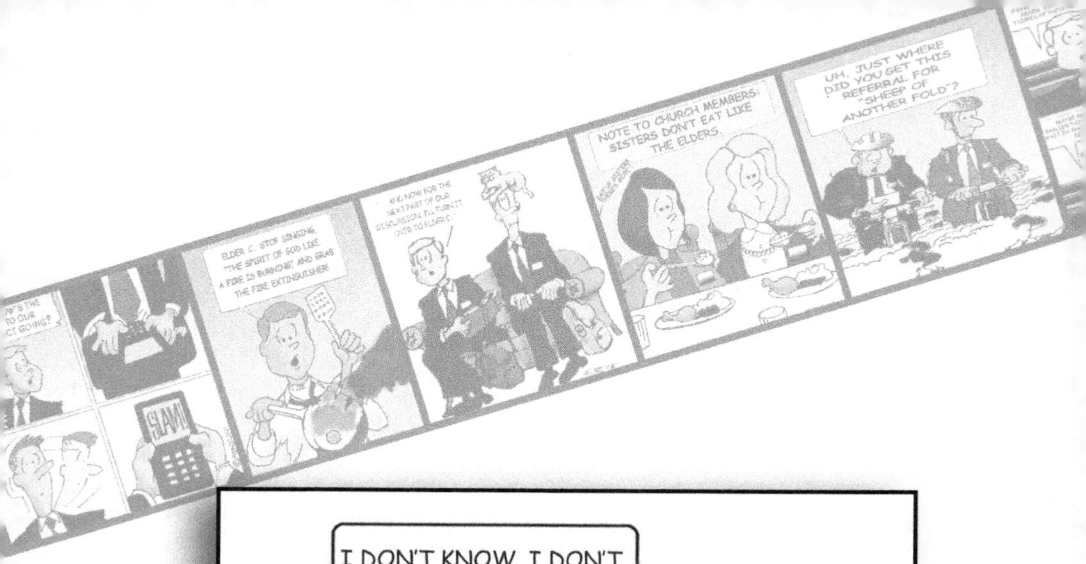
ELDER C. STOP SINGING "THE SPIRIT OF GOD LIKE A FIRE IS BURNING" AND GRAB THE FIRE EXTINGUISHER!
SLAM!
AND NOW FOR THE NEXT PART OF OUR DISCUSSION, I'LL TURN IT OVER TO ELDER C.
NOTE TO CHURCH MEMBERS: SISTERS DON'T EAT LIKE THE ELDERS.
UH, JUST WHERE DID YOU GET THIS REFERRAL FOR "SHEEP OF ANOTHER FOLD"?

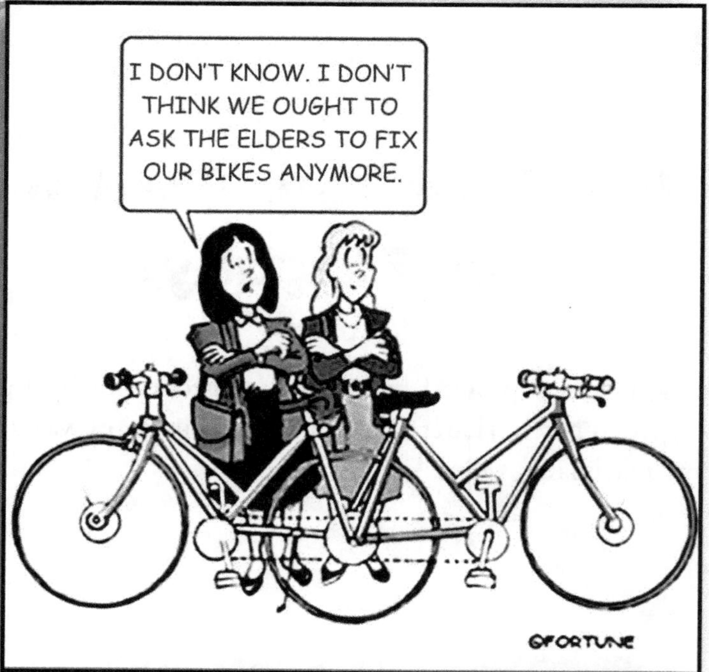
I DON'T KNOW. I DON'T THINK WE OUGHT TO ASK THE ELDERS TO FIX OUR BIKES ANYMORE.
©FORTUNE

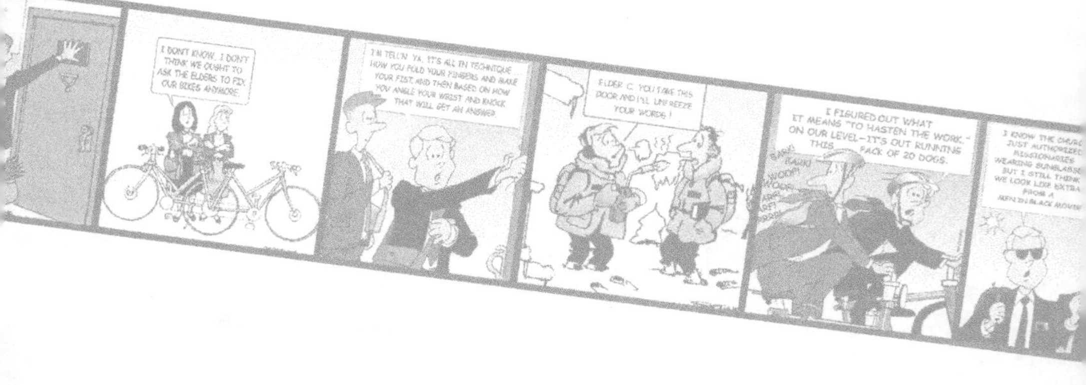
I DON'T KNOW. I DON'T THINK WE OUGHT TO ASK THE ELDERS TO FIX OUR BIKES ANYMORE.
ELDER C, YOU TAKE THIS DOOR AND I'LL UNFREEZE YOUR WORDS!
I FIGURED OUT WHAT IT MEANS "TO HASTEN THE WORK" ON OUR LEVEL—IT'S OUT RUNNING THIS PACK OF 20 DOGS.

What Do a Fire and Fistfight Have in Common?

A Baptism, of Course

"The church [house] caught fire during a baptism. I couldn't read technical Spanish, but fortunately one of our recent converts knew how to work the fire extinguisher. [The fire was] put out, but not before someone called the police, which caused a fist fight outside the church. Ah, baptism . . ."

Aubrey

Subject: Missionary experience in the Mexico Puebla North Mission

Just Testing the Waters of Baptism

"The sisters in our district had a baptism. When we arrived 30 minutes before the baptism, we realized that the font had not been filled, [so] we started filling it with buckets of water as fast as possible. At the very end, when [the font] was full, I bent down to feel how cold the water was—and I FELL IN. [All who] saw me soaking wet, they ALL about died laughing. Oh well. Life moves on."

Mother: Sandi
Missionary: Kalin

Subject: A friend's experience while serving in
Christchurch, New Zealand, 25 years ago

It's Baring Your Soul, Not the Body

"[While proselyting, I knocked on a door, and] a naked man answered. I'm pretty sure he was expecting someone else. I was a greenie (out 3 weeks) and offered him a Book of Mormon, while he [quickly] covered himself up with the area rug by the door. My companion told the elders that I had left him 'clothed in the glory of the spirit.' The elders kept the next appointment!"

From VJ
Missionary: Kay

Subject: Sister missionary story; mission not given

Door-to-Door Confusion

"My companion and I were serving in an area that had always been an elders' area. Because of this, most people thought we were Jehovah's Witnesses. One day we were out proselyting along an old country road and a car came toward us. The lady driving the car had her window rolled down, leaned out the window, and waved both hands at us yelling, 'Hi, girls! I am a Witness too!'

"[After the lady drove by us] I looked at my companion and sadly said, 'Great! Even the Jehovah's Witnesses think we are Jehovah's Witnesses.'"

Dawn

END OF EMAILS TO BILL

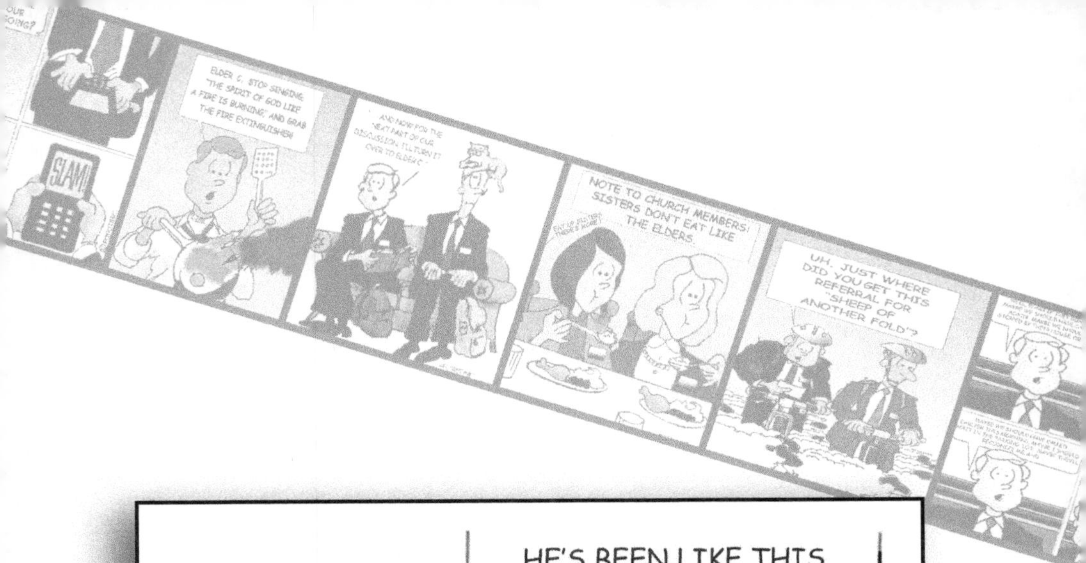
ELDER C, STOP SINGING "THE SPIRIT OF GOD LIKE A FIRE IS BURNING" AND GRAB THE FIRE EXTINGUISHER!
SLAM!
AND NOW FOR THE NEXT PART OF OUR DISCUSSION, I'LL TURN IT OVER TO ELDER C
NOTE TO CHURCH MEMBERS: SISTERS DON'T EAT LIKE THE ELDERS.
UH, JUST WHERE DID YOU GET THIS REFERRAL FOR "SHEEP OF ANOTHER FOLD"?

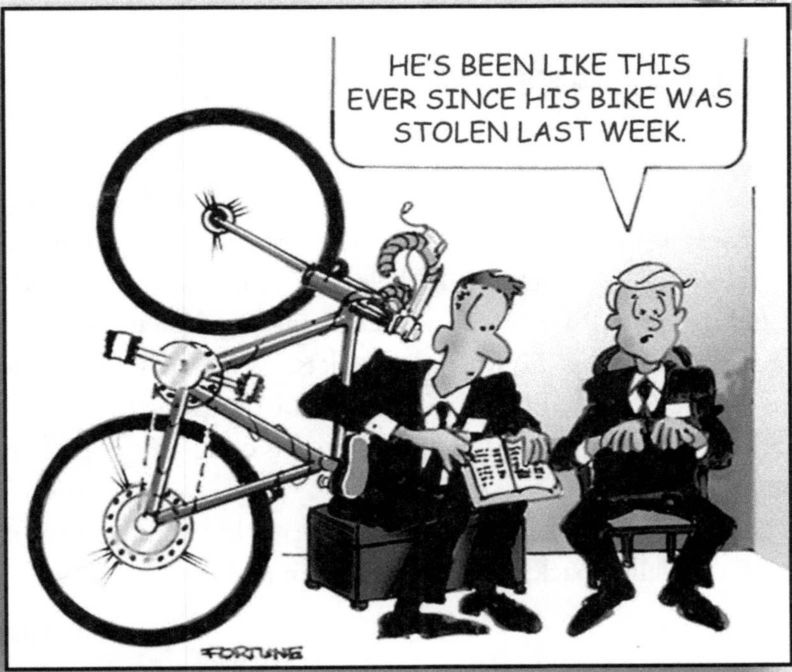
HE'S BEEN LIKE THIS EVER SINCE HIS BIKE WAS STOLEN LAST WEEK.
FORTUNE

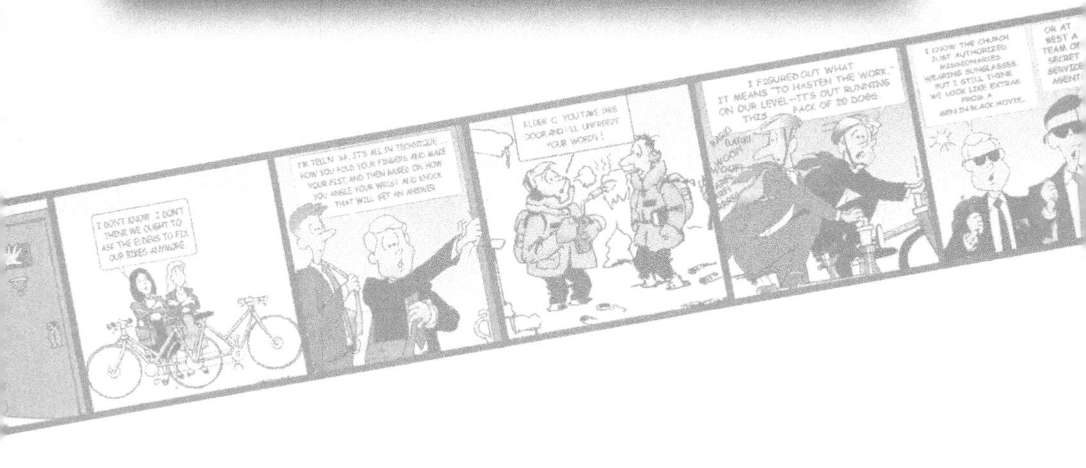
I DON'T KNOW. I DON'T THINK WE OUGHT TO ASK THE ELDERS TO FIX OUR BIKES ANYMORE.
ELDER C, YOU TAKE THIS DOOR AND I'LL UNFREEZE YOUR WORDS!
I FIGURED OUT WHAT IT MEANS "TO HASTEN THE WORK." ON OUR LEVEL--IT'S OUT RUNNING THIS PACK OF 20 DOGS.
I KNOW THE CHURCH JUST AUTHORIZED MISSIONARIES WEARING SUNGLASSES, BUT I STILL THINK WE LOOK LIKE EXTRAS FROM A MEN IN BLACK MOVIE.

The Axe of the Apostles

While serving in Melbourne, Australia, Elder Roberts and his companion lived in apartments (called flats) that had water heaters fueled by coal pellets. To help start the heaters, the elders would use a small axe to cut wood shavings, and then they would place the shavings in with the pellets. While his companion was in the shower, Elder Roberts was in the front room. Elder Roberts, wanting to cut wood, yelled to his companion, "Where's the axe?"

His companion could not hear correctly over the running water and yelled back, "It's between John and Romans!"

Darrell Robison

Sick as a Horse

Elder Tyler and Elder Simmons were visiting an investigator family. The family was halfway through the discussions when William, a ten-year-old, developed a bad head cold. Trying to cheer him up, Elder Simmons said, "My dad would often say to me when I had a cold, 'You have a COLT in your head, which makes you a little HORSE.'"

Hair-Brained Ideas about the Church

When Brother Skidmore's father was serving a mission in Canada many years ago, he and his companion knocked on a door, and a lady with puffy, bright-red hair answered. After the missionaries introduced themselves, this lady really railed on them and accused them of taking women back to Utah and putting them in Temple Square, by the Great Salt Lake, so they could not escape. His companion wryly stated, "You're right. And today we're looking for redheads."

The True Origin of Saturn's Rings

Elder Perkins had been transferred several times on his mission, and invariably his luggage would be misplaced. On one transfer, he met his companion, Elder Sterling, and they waited at the airport for the luggage to be unloaded. Well, to his dismay, Elder Perkins's luggage never arrived, and the airline could not locate it. Frustrated, Elder Perkins said to the baggage manager, "I'm sure if you were to look closely at the rings around Saturn, you'd discover they are lost airline luggage."

Flip?

Elder Tyson was an Idaho farm boy. He really struggled with controlling his "farm language." His words were made manifest in the presence of his mission president twice. President Fielding finally told Elder Tyson that if he didn't control his "farm language," President Fielding was going to put tape over the elder's mouth.

In the Pacific Northwest Mission, the popular word missionaries used as an expression of exasperation was "flip." On his way to a tri-zone conference, Elder Tyson was approaching the stake center when a seagull flew by and made a direct deposit on his dark brown hair. About one hundred yards away, President Fielding was outside the building greeting missionaries. With all the control he could muster, Elder Tyson yelled loudly, "FLIP!"

To Elder Tyson's great surprise, President Fielding went red in the face and yelled, "D**n you, Elder Tyson!"

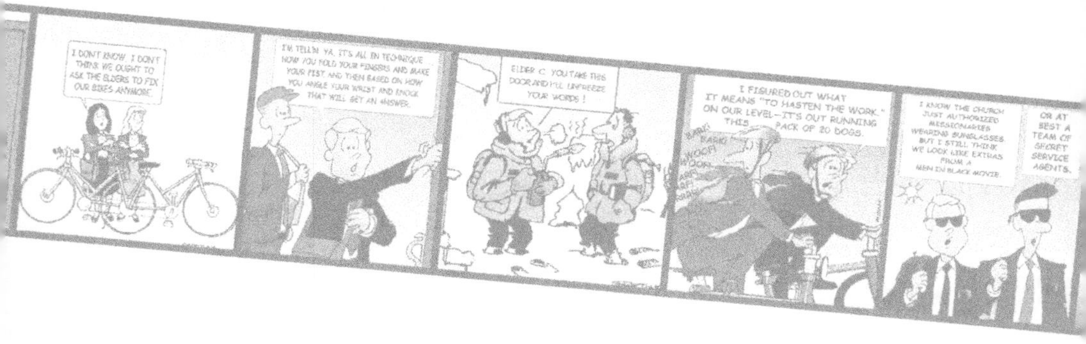
I DON'T KNOW. I DON'T THINK WE OUGHT TO ASK THE ELDERS TO FIX OUR BIKES ANYMORE.
ELDER C. YOU TAKE THIS DOOR AND I'LL UNFREEZE YOUR WORDS!
I FIGURED OUT WHAT IT MEANS "TO HASTEN THE WORK." ON OUR LEVEL—IT'S OUT RUNNING THIS PACK OF 20 DOGS.
I KNOW THE CHURCH JUST AUTHORIZED MISSIONARIES WEARING SUNGLASSES BUT I STILL THINK WE LOOK LIKE EXTRAS FROM A MEN IN BLACK MOVIE.
OR AT BEST A TEAM OF SECRET SERVICE AGENTS.

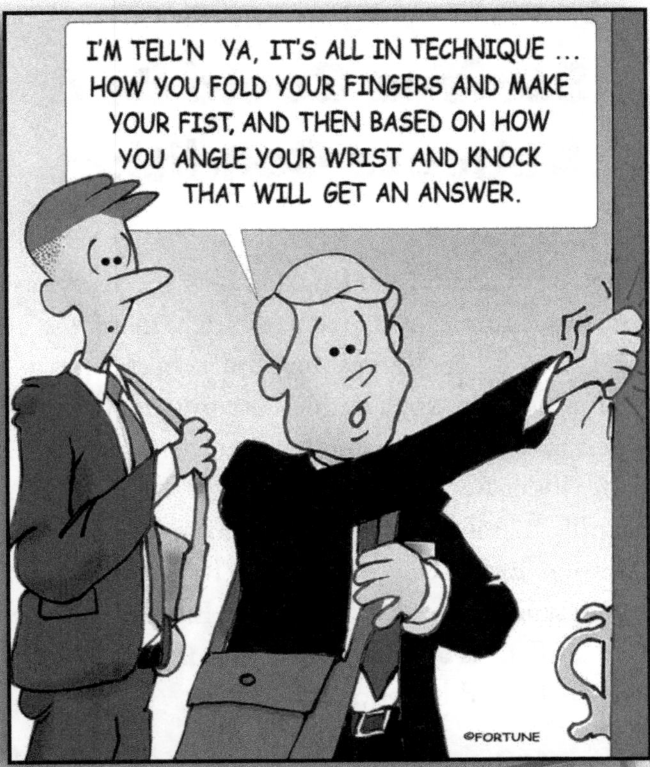
I'M TELL'N YA, IT'S ALL IN TECHNIQUE ... HOW YOU FOLD YOUR FINGERS AND MAKE YOUR FIST, AND THEN BASED ON HOW YOU ANGLE YOUR WRIST AND KNOCK THAT WILL GET AN ANSWER.
©FORTUNE

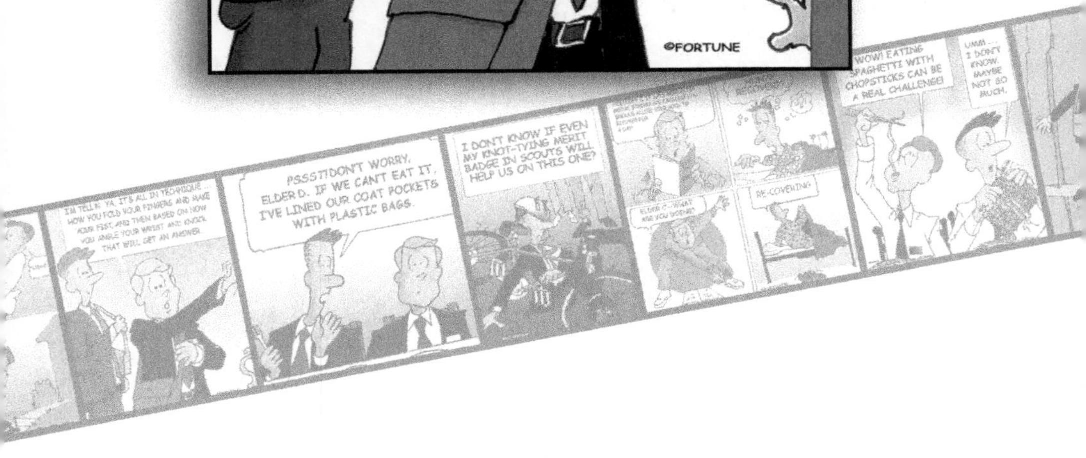
PSSST! DON'T WORRY, ELDER D. IF WE CAN'T EAT IT, I'VE LINED OUR COAT POCKETS WITH PLASTIC BAGS.
I DON'T KNOW IF EVEN MY KNOT-TYING MERIT BADGE IN SCOUTS WILL HELP US ON THIS ONE?
RE-COVERING
WOW! EATING SPAGHETTI WITH CHOPSTICKS CAN BE A REAL CHALLENGE!
UMM ... I DON'T KNOW. MAYBE NOT SO MUCH.

Stuffed Could Be a Delicate Condition

Many a greenie missionary in England over the years has enjoyed a generous and ample meal from Church members and non-members alike. Elder Reeves had only been in the United Kingdom for two days when he and his companion, Elder Wright, were invited to a member home for the evening meal. Finishing the last bite, Elder Reeves verbally declared, "I'm stuffed."

The family members, as well as his companion, gave a hearty laugh. Curious, Elder Reeves asked, "Why did you laugh?"

"So you will know in the future, Elder," answered Sister McElroy, "'stuffed' is a common slang word for being pregnant in most of the United Kingdom."

Lynn Arave

Alien Elders All Over the Place

Elders Stewart and King were in Cardiff, South Wales, serving in the England Bristol Mission in the early 1970s. They were residing in "digs" (apartments) where other residents were Cardiff University students. Together the residents ate a meal prepared by the landlady each evening. One night after putting the food out, the landlady turned on the "telly" (TV) to the British sci-fi series *Dr. Who*, about a man who travels in time and space around the galaxy. This was the first time the elders had ever seen or heard of this program. In this episode, the "Doctor" meets aliens and asks their identity.

"We're the Elders," the aliens responded.

The Cardiff students looked at the two missionaries, laughing, and proclaimed, "They're everywhere!"

Lynn Arave

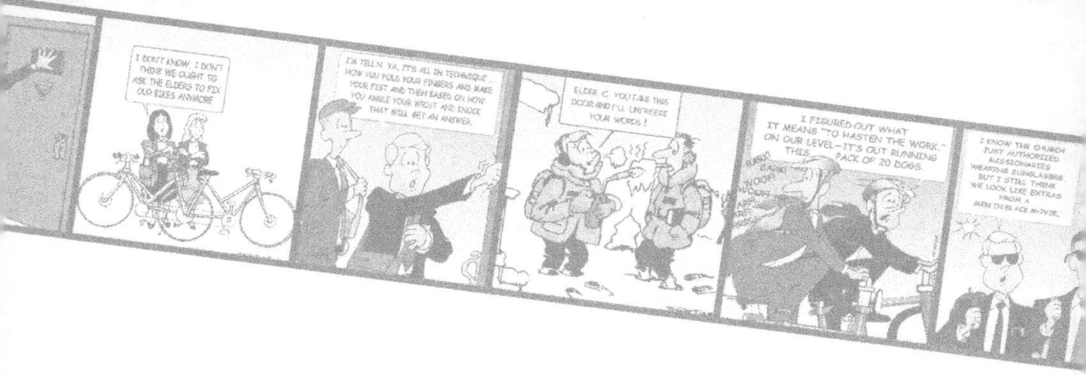
I DON'T KNOW. I DON'T THINK WE OUGHT TO ASK THE ELDERS TO FIX OUR BIKES ANYMORE
I'M TELLN' YA, IT'S ALL IN TECHNIQUE... HOW YOU FOLD YOUR FINGERS AND MAKE YOUR FIST AND THEN BASED ON HOW YOU ANGLE YOUR WRIST AND KNOCK THAT WILL GET AN ANSWER.
ELDER C, YOU TAKE THIS DOOR AND I'LL UNFREEZE YOUR WORDS!
I FIGURED OUT WHAT IT MEANS "TO HASTEN THE WORK." ON OUR LEVEL--IT'S OUT RUNNING THIS... PACK OF 20 DOGS.
I KNOW THE CHURCH JUST AUTHORIZED MISSIONARIES WEARING SUNGLASSES BUT I STILL THINK WE LOOK LIKE EXTRAS FROM A MEN IN BLACK MOVIE.

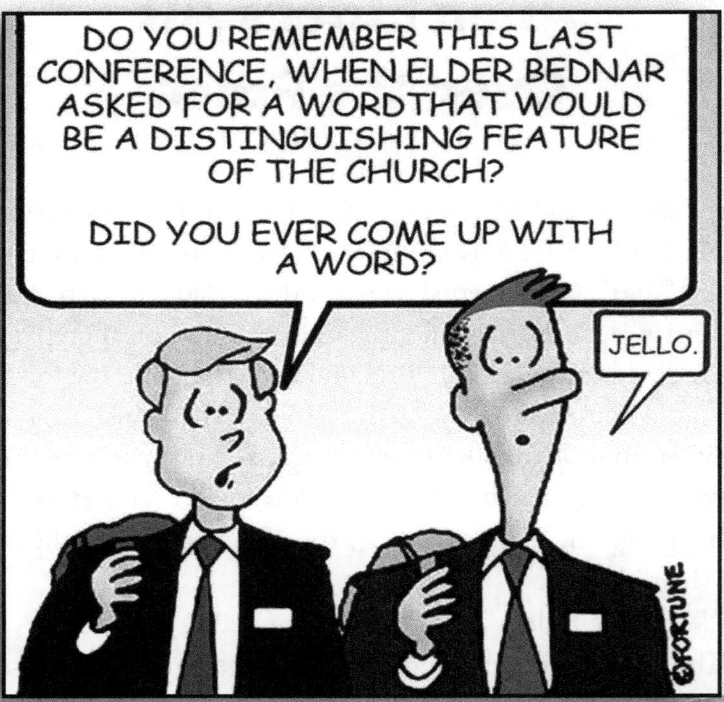
DO YOU REMEMBER THIS LAST CONFERENCE, WHEN ELDER BEDNAR ASKED FOR A WORDTHAT WOULD BE A DISTINGUISHING FEATURE OF THE CHURCH?
DID YOU EVER COME UP WITH A WORD?
JELLO.
©FORTUNE

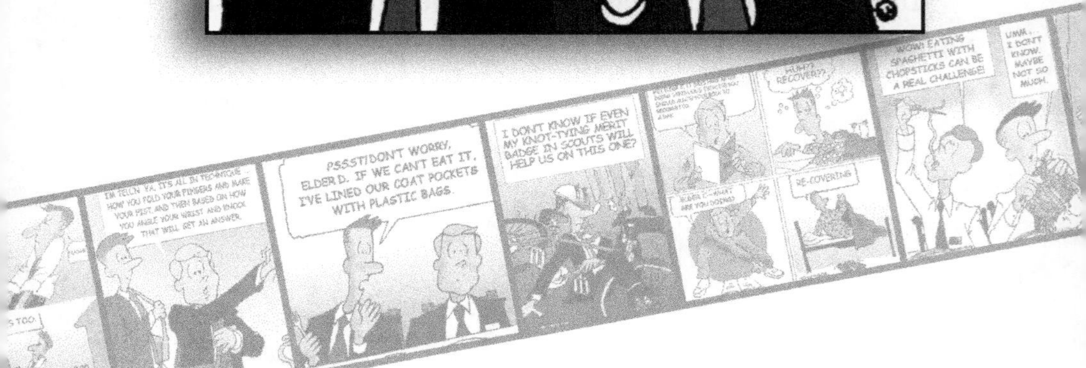
I'M TELLN' YA, IT'S ALL IN TECHNIQUE... HOW YOU FOLD YOUR FINGERS AND MAKE YOUR FIST AND THEN BASED ON HOW YOU ANGLE YOUR WRIST AND KNOCK THAT WILL GET AN ANSWER.
PSSST! DON'T WORRY, ELDER D. IF WE CAN'T EAT IT, I'VE LINED OUR COAT POCKETS WITH PLASTIC BAGS.
I DON'T KNOW IF EVEN MY KNOT-TYING MERIT BADGE IN SCOUTS WILL HELP US ON THIS ONE?
HUH? RECOVER??
ELDER C--WHAT ARE YOU DOING?
RE-COVERING
WOW! EATING SPAGHETTI WITH CHOPSTICKS CAN BE A REAL CHALLENGE!
UMM... I DON'T KNOW. MAYBE NOT SO MUCH.

Announcements Subject to Interpretation

Elders Rose and Simms were asked to speak in sacrament meeting. Brother Frost, the second counselor in the bishopric, conducted. He was a good man who was prone to change words unintentionally. After his welcoming remarks, Brother Frost announced who was leading the singing and that "Sister Playbody will pea the piano."

Quickly the bishop stood up and quietly corrected his counselor.

"Sorry," Brother Frost said. "Sister *Pea*body will *play* the piano."

Then he announced, "At Relief Society Wednesday evening, the sisters in the ward will learn crotching."

Again, the bishop stood up.

"Sorry, it is *crocheting*."

Mary Higgins

Who Let the Dogs Out?

A mission president was leading an orientation meeting for eight new missionaries. During President Allen's remarks, he quipped, "When a big, mean dog chases after you, remember that you don't have to run faster than the dog—you just have to outrun your companion."

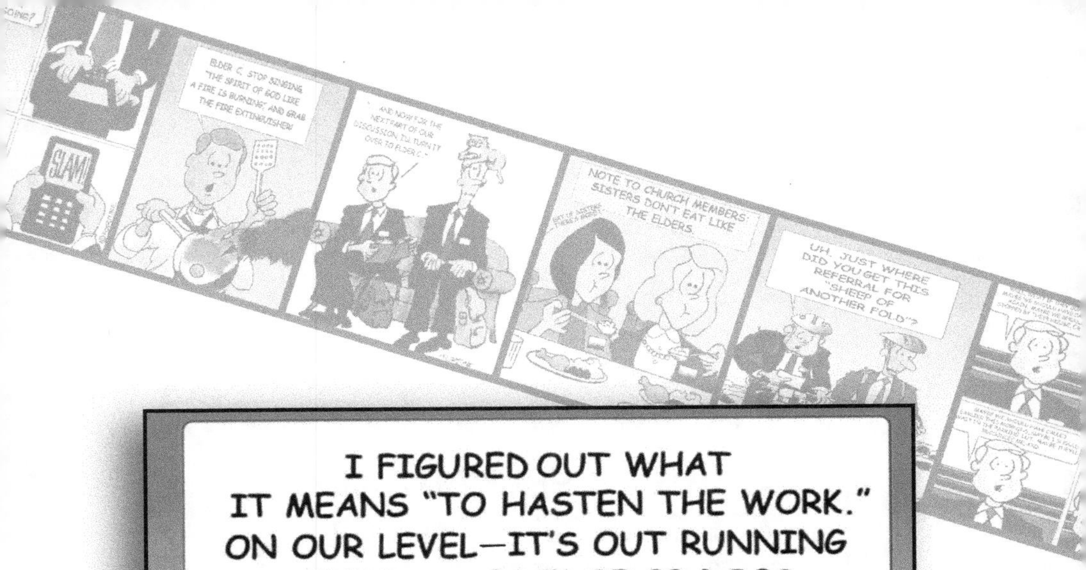
SLAM!
ELDER C, STOP SINGING "THE SPIRIT OF GOD LIKE A FIRE IS BURNING" AND GRAB THE FIRE EXTINGUISHER!
AND NOW FOR THE NEXT PART OF OUR DISCUSSION, I'LL TURN IT OVER TO ELDER C.
NOTE TO CHURCH MEMBERS: SISTERS DON'T EAT LIKE THE ELDERS.
UH, JUST WHERE DID YOU GET THIS REFERRAL FOR "SHEEP OF ANOTHER FOLD"?

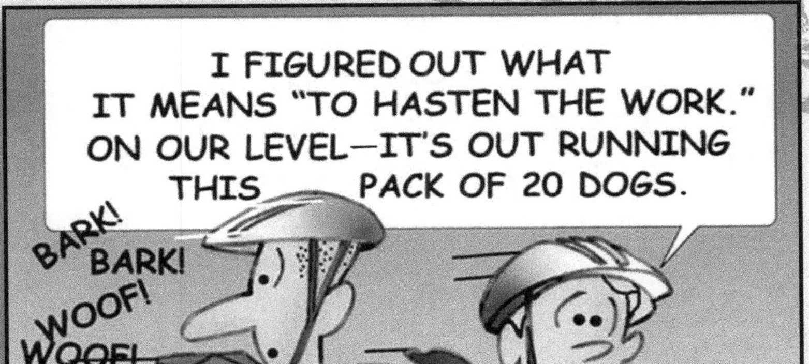
I FIGURED OUT WHAT IT MEANS "TO HASTEN THE WORK." ON OUR LEVEL—IT'S OUT RUNNING THIS PACK OF 20 DOGS.
BARK! BARK!
WOOF! WOOF!
ARF! ARF!
GRRRR!
©FORTUNE

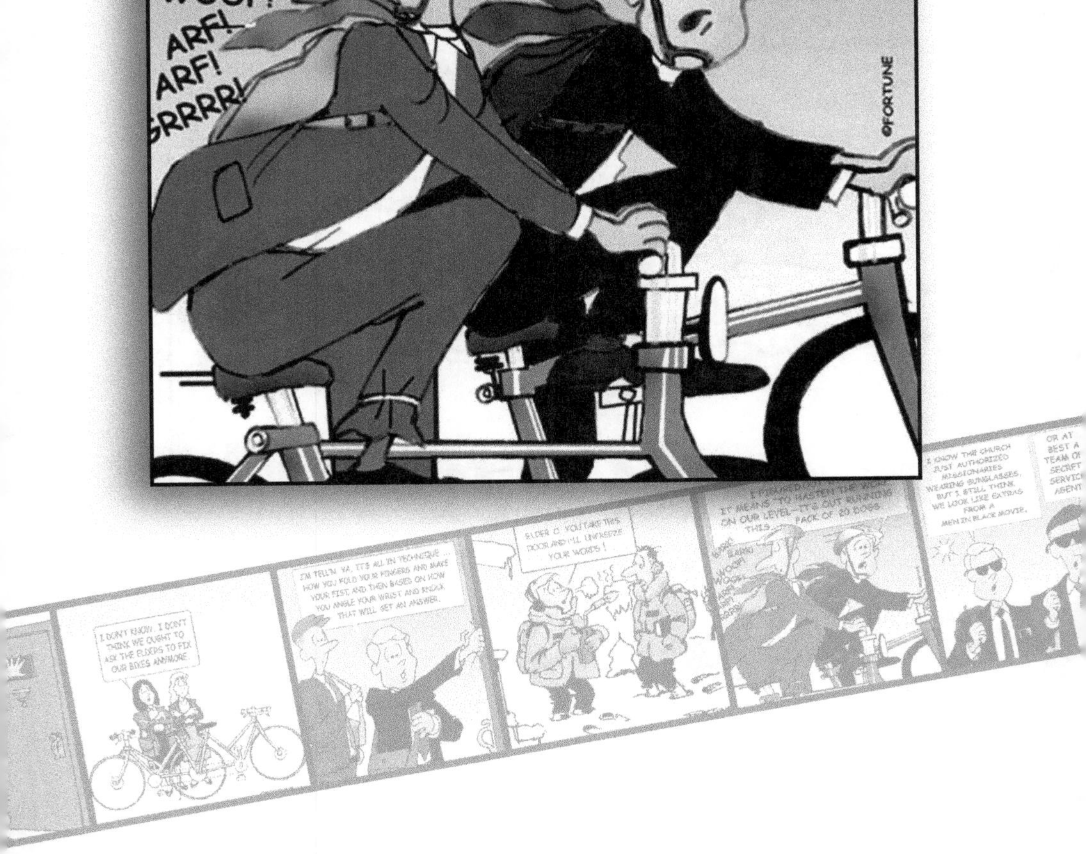
I DON'T KNOW, I DON'T THINK WE OUGHT TO ASK THE ELDERS TO FIX OUR BIKES ANYMORE.
I'M TELL'N YA, IT'S ALL IN TECHNIQUE... HOW YOU FOLD YOUR FINGERS AND MAKE YOUR FIST AND THEN BASED ON HOW YOU ANGLE YOUR WRIST AND KNOCK THAT WILL GET AN ANSWER.
ELDER C. YOU TAKE THIS DOOR AND I'LL UNFREEZE YOUR WORDS!
I FIGURED OUT WHAT IT MEANS "TO HASTEN THE WORK." ON OUR LEVEL—IT'S OUT RUNNING THIS PACK OF 20 DOGS
I KNOW THE CHURCH JUST AUTHORIZED MISSIONARIES WEARING SUNGLASSES, BUT I STILL THINK WE LOOK LIKE EXTRAS FROM A MEN IN BLACK MOVIE.

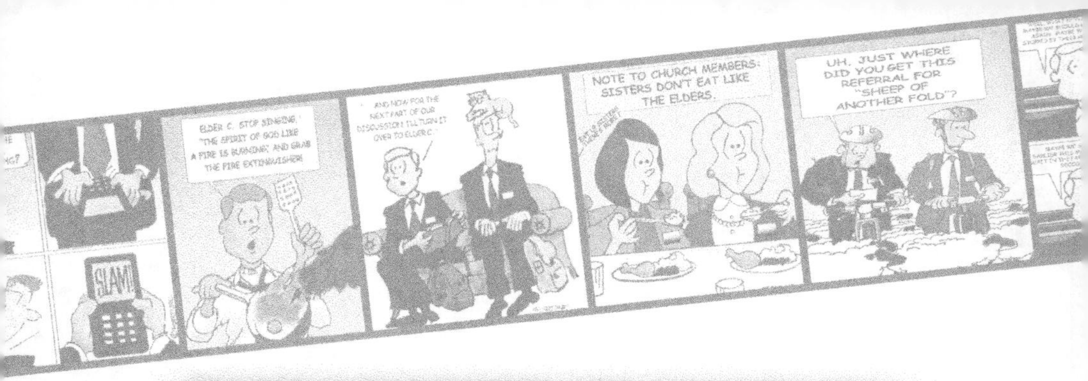
ELDER C. STOP SINGING, "THE SPIRIT OF GOD LIKE A FIRE IS BURNING," AND GRAB THE FIRE EXTINGUISHER!
SLAM!
AND NOW FOR THE NEXT PART OF OUR DISCUSSION! I'LL TURN IT OVER TO ELDER C.
NOTE TO CHURCH MEMBERS: SISTERS DON'T EAT LIKE THE ELDERS.
UH, JUST WHERE DID YOU GET THIS REFERRAL FOR "SHEEP OF ANOTHER FOLD"?

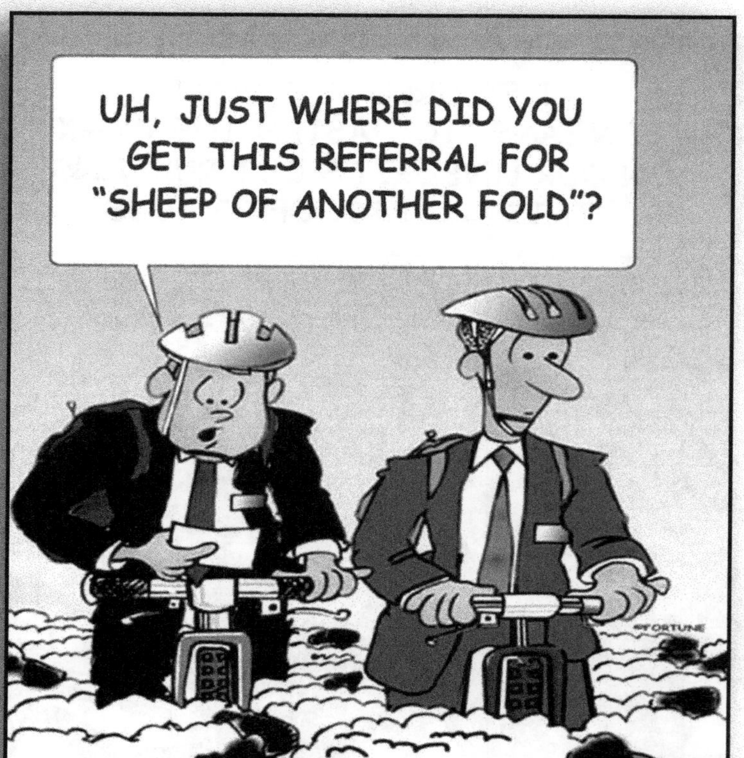
UH, JUST WHERE DID YOU GET THIS REFERRAL FOR "SHEEP OF ANOTHER FOLD"?
©FORTUNE

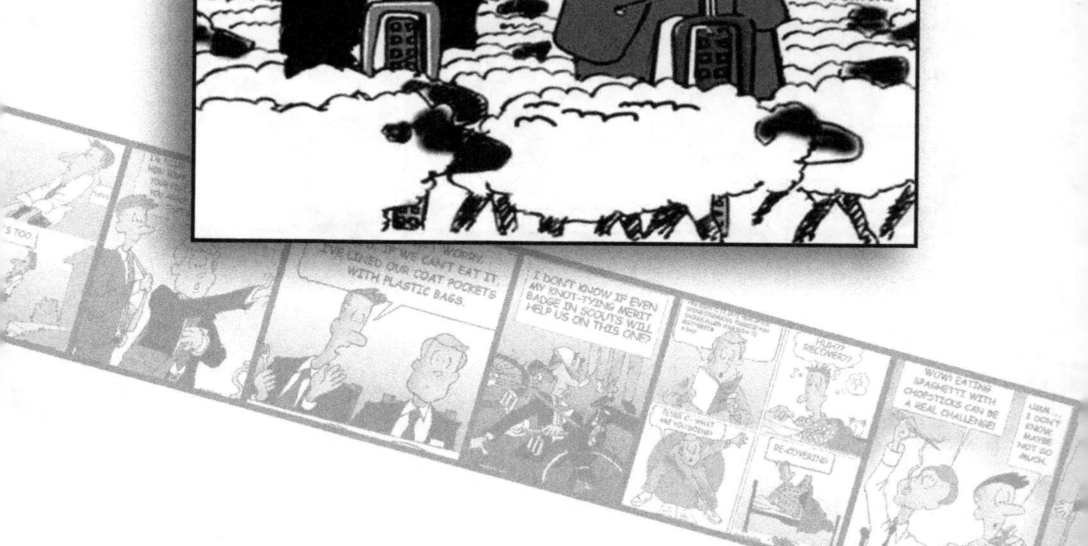
WITH PLASTIC BAGS.
I DON'T KNOW IF EVEN MY KNOT-TYING MERIT BADGE IN SCOUTS WILL HELP US ON THIS ONE?
HUH?? RECOVER??
RE-COVERING
WOW! EATING SPAGHETTI WITH CHOPSTICKS CAN BE A REAL CHALLENGE!
UMM... I DON'T KNOW. MAYBE NOT SO MUCH.

Homesickness or Farm Sickness?

My first mission president was a wonderful man, Robert L. Backman. Several years after being released as mission president of the Northwestern States Mission, he spoke in a sacrament meeting I attended. Elder Backman related an experience he had while serving as mission president. He said:

"It was the first day in the mission field for a missionary who had been raised on a dairy farm in western Utah. He was away from home for the first time. We had completed our orientation, and I found him crying in a corner of the dining room. I put my arm around him and asked if there was anything I could do. He turned, burying his head on my shoulder, and said, 'Oh, President, I miss my cows.'" (Used by permission.)

Bruce E. Dana

Keeping an FBI Out

"Brother Steele of North Ogden, Utah, retired from the FBI and was immediately called as a mission president. While waiting for the departure date, he saw in the newspaper the announcement of a missionary farewell for a young man who would be going to the mission he would soon preside over. He and his wife decided to attend.

"When they arrived to the mission, all the missionaries had heard that the new mission president had retired from the FBI, so they were apprehensive about their future. President Steele got them together for a meeting and said, 'Now I know some of you may be nervous about me, but let me assure you, I have no knowledge of your past, only an interest in your future. . . . Well, actually, I do have some files here,' at which time he pulled a stack of file folders from his briefcase. He opened the first one and said, 'Is Elder _____ here?' When the new missionary stood, President Steele said, 'Let's see . . . You are _____ and your mom and dad are _____ and your aunt _____ said that when you were fifteen . . .' and he related what he learned about this young elder at his farewell.

"Every elder's eyes were as big as dollars for the rest of the meeting." (Used by permission.)

John Brockbank

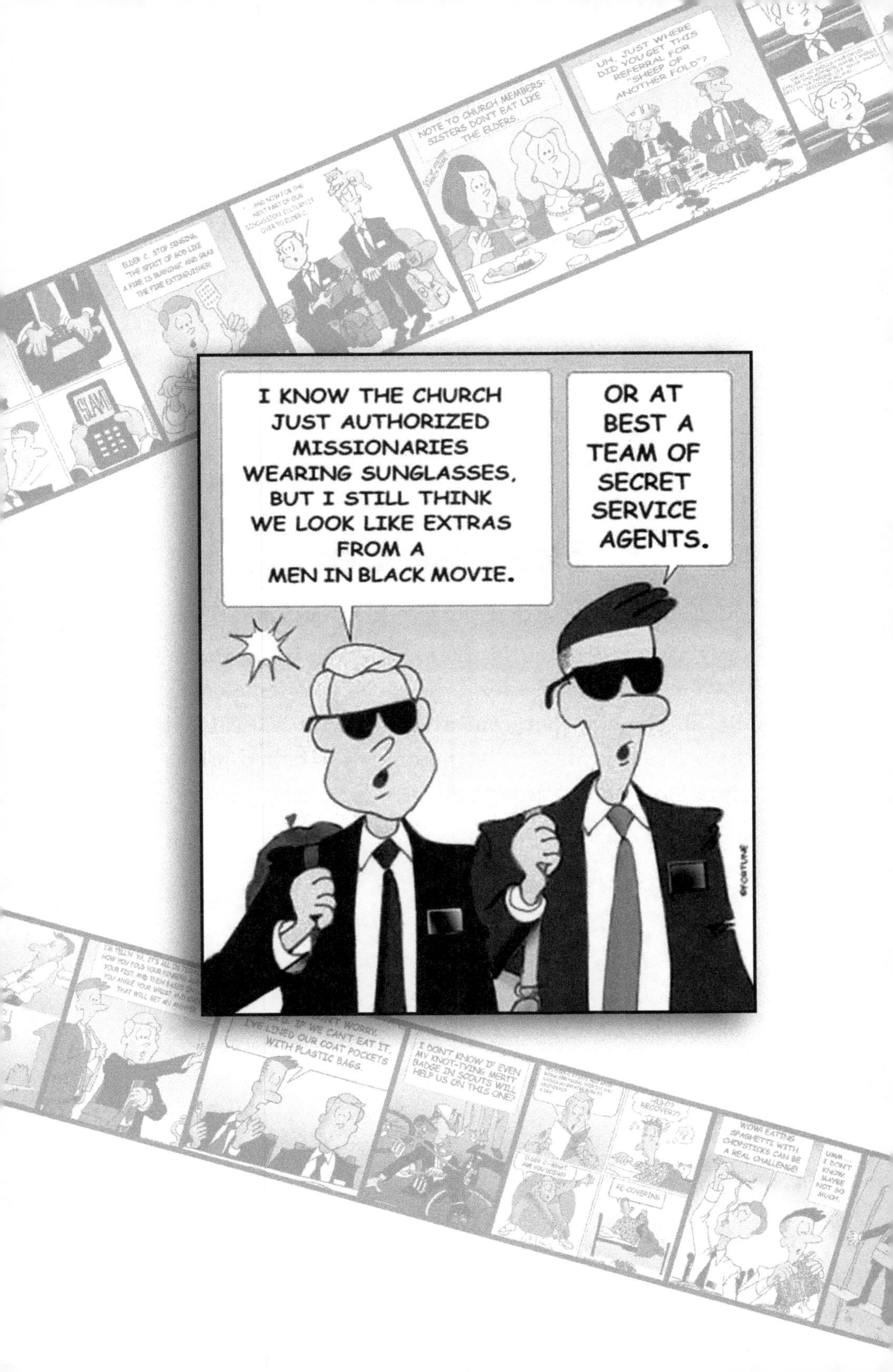
ELDER C, STOP SINGING 'THE SPIRIT OF GOD LIKE A FIRE IS BURNING' AND GRAB THE FIRE EXTINGUISHER!
NOTE TO CHURCH MEMBERS: SISTERS DON'T EAT LIKE THE ELDERS.
UH, JUST WHERE DID YOU GET THIS REFERRAL FOR "SHEEP OF ANOTHER FOLD"?
I KNOW THE CHURCH JUST AUTHORIZED MISSIONARIES WEARING SUNGLASSES, BUT I STILL THINK WE LOOK LIKE EXTRAS FROM A MEN IN BLACK MOVIE.
OR AT BEST A TEAM OF SECRET SERVICE AGENTS.
I DON'T KNOW IF EVEN MY KNOT-TYING MERIT BADGE IN SCOUTS WILL HELP US ON THIS ONE?
HUH? RECOVER??
RE-COVERING
WOW! EATING SPAGHETTI WITH CHOPSTICKS CAN BE A REAL CHALLENGE!
UMM... I DON'T KNOW. MAYBE NOT SO MUCH

Herding Cats

Shortly after Elder Paul H. Dunn was released as the president of the New England Mission, he spoke in a stake conference I attended. He said, "Someone asked me what it was like being a mission president. It was like taking two hundred priests on an overnight hike for three years."

Bruce E. Dana

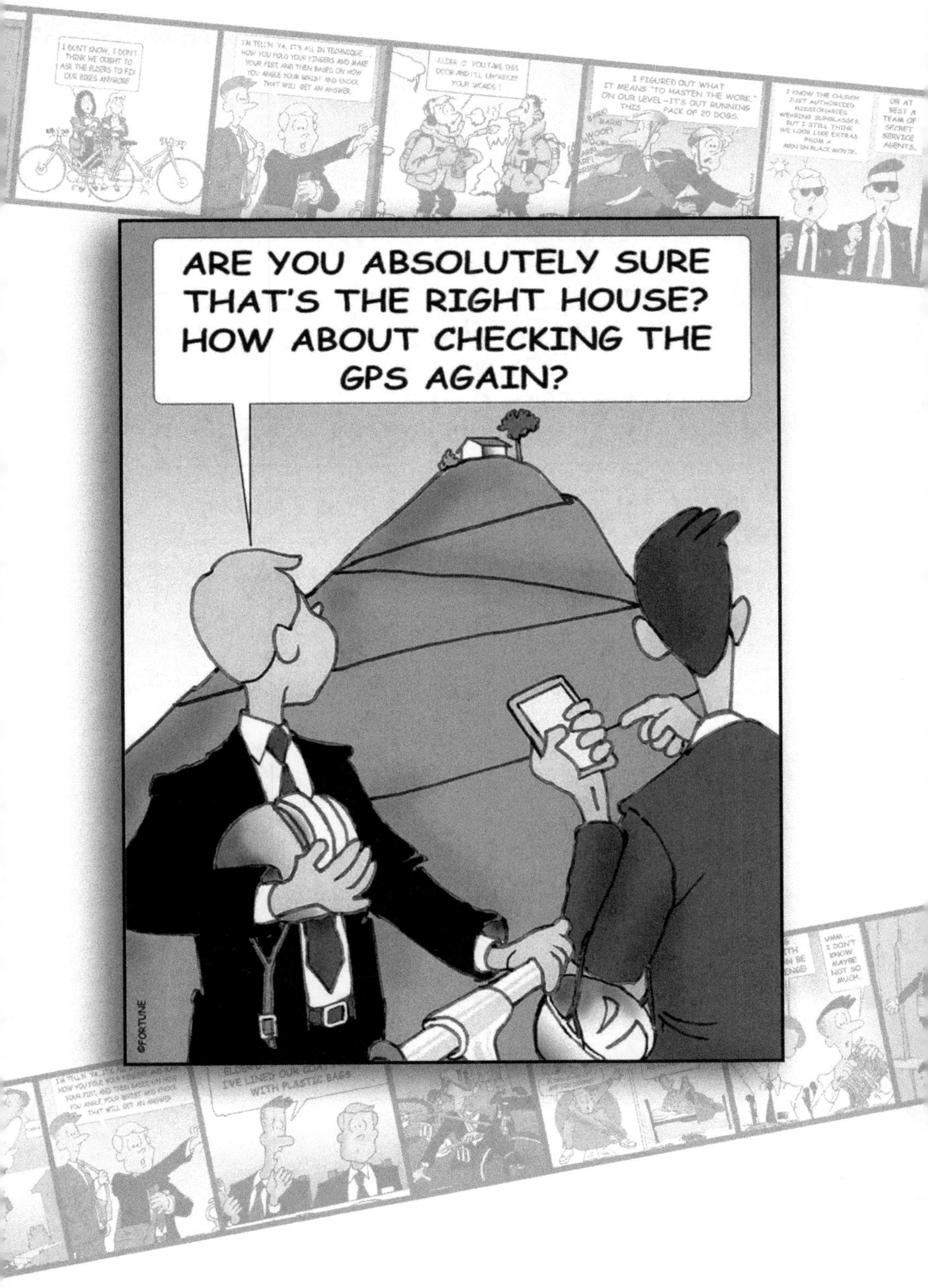

I FIGURED OUT WHAT IT MEANS "TO HASTEN THE WORK." ON OUR LEVEL—IT'S OUT RUNNING THIS PACK OF 20 DOGS.
I KNOW THE CHURCH JUST AUTHORIZED MISSIONARIES WEARING SUNGLASSES, BUT I STILL THINK WE LOOK LIKE EXTRAS FROM A MEN IN BLACK MOVIE.
OR AT BEST A TEAM OF SECRET SERVICE AGENTS.
ARE YOU ABSOLUTELY SURE THAT'S THE RIGHT HOUSE? HOW ABOUT CHECKING THE GPS AGAIN?
©FORTUNE

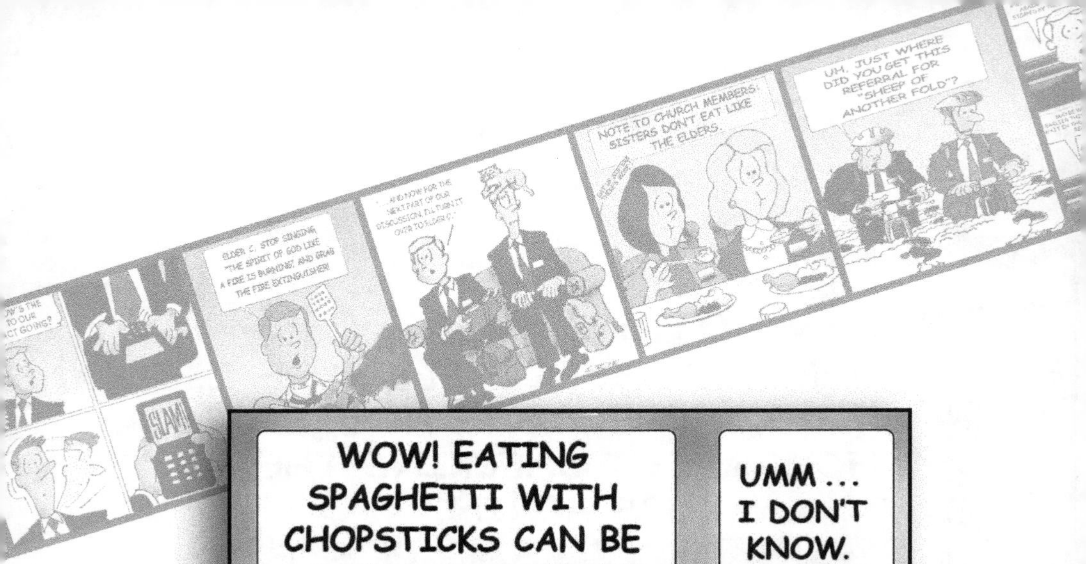
ELDER C, STOP SINGING "THE SPIRIT OF GOD LIKE A FIRE IS BURNING," AND GRAB THE FIRE EXTINGUISHER!
NOTE TO CHURCH MEMBERS: SISTERS DON'T EAT LIKE THE ELDERS.
UH, JUST WHERE DID YOU GET THIS REFERRAL FOR "SHEEP OF ANOTHER FOLD"?
SLAM!

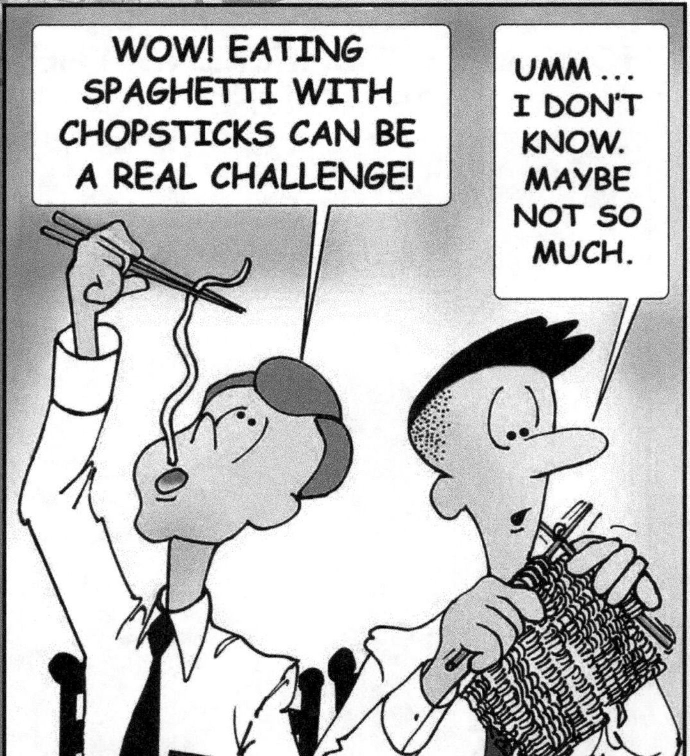
WOW! EATING SPAGHETTI WITH CHOPSTICKS CAN BE A REAL CHALLENGE!
UMM ... I DON'T KNOW. MAYBE NOT SO MUCH.
©FORTUNE

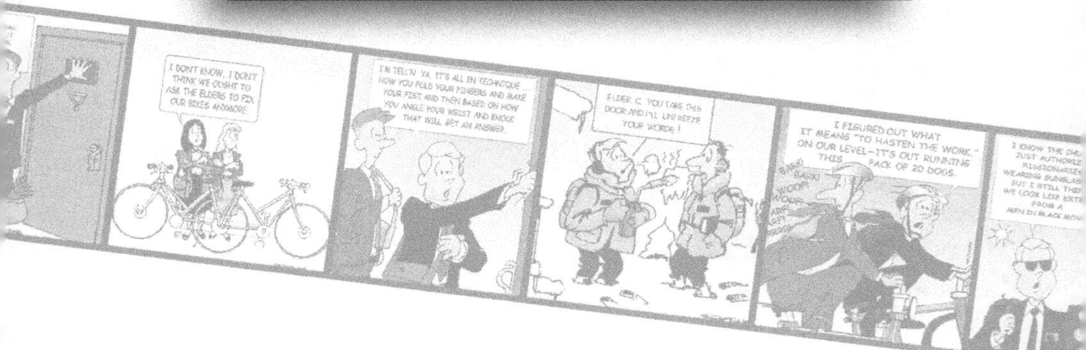
I DON'T KNOW, I DON'T THINK WE OUGHT TO ASK THE ELDERS TO FIX OUR BIKES ANYMORE.

The Right Timing Can Be Filling

The Golden Rule:
"Whatsoever ye would that men should do to you,
do ye even so to them." (Matt. 7:12)

"It was my first week in the mission field at Oakland, California. My trainer from Brazil was kind and at times a stern trainer. We went to a party hosted by a recent convert Hispanic family. Both my trainer (Elder Texiera) and I sat in awe with the large portions they gave to each of us. One plate of food could have been three plates.

"Once I got halfway through my plate, I started to slow down. Each bite felt like I was stuffing a handful of food into my stomach. I was motivated to make a good first impression for this newly baptized family, and the mother who apparently spent hours tirelessly cooking in the kitchen. I had almost finished my plate and after my final and forceful swallow, my trainer—noticing that the mother was not looking—quickly switched plates with me. His plate was nearly full."

Jared Carlson

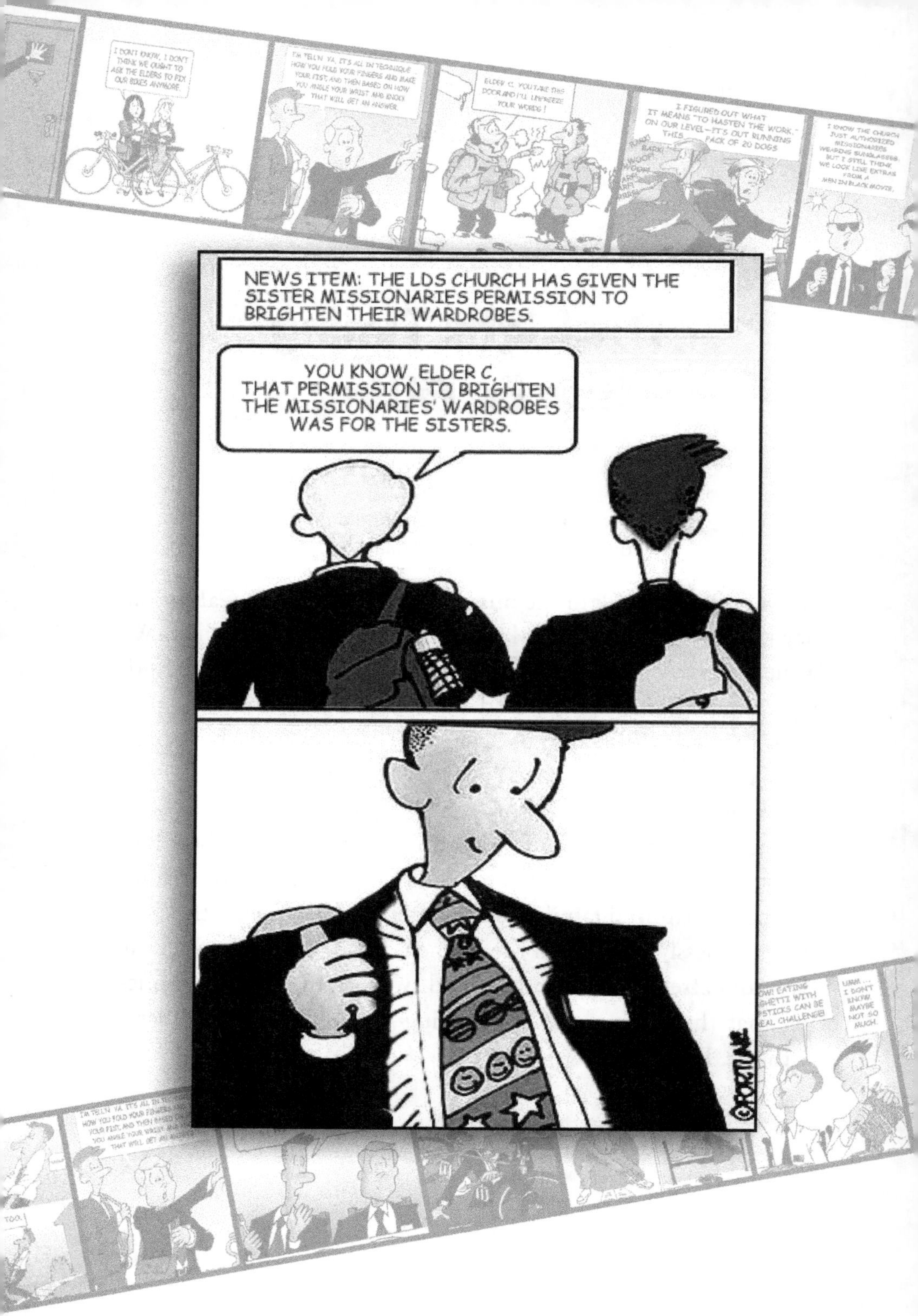
I DON'T KNOW, I DON'T THINK WE OUGHT TO ASK THE ELDERS TO FIX OUR BIKES ANYMORE.
I'M TELL'N YA, IT'S ALL IN TECHNIQUE — HOW YOU FOLD YOUR FINGERS AND MAKE YOUR FIST, AND THEN BASED ON HOW YOU ANGLE YOUR WRIST AND KNOCK THAT WILL GET AN ANSWER.
ELDER C, YOU TAKE THIS DOOR AND I'LL UNFREEZE YOUR WORDS!
I FIGURED OUT WHAT IT MEANS "TO HASTEN THE WORK." ON OUR LEVEL—IT'S OUT RUNNING THIS PACK OF 20 DOGS
I KNOW THE CHURCH JUST AUTHORIZED MISSIONARIES WEARING SUNGLASSES, BUT I STILL THINK WE LOOK LIKE EXTRAS FROM A MEN IN BLACK MOVIE.
NEWS ITEM: THE LDS CHURCH HAS GIVEN THE SISTER MISSIONARIES PERMISSION TO BRIGHTEN THEIR WARDROBES.
YOU KNOW, ELDER C, THAT PERMISSION TO BRIGHTEN THE MISSIONARIES' WARDROBES WAS FOR THE SISTERS.
UMM... I DON'T KNOW. MAYBE NOT SO MUCH.

Look on the Bright Side

A missionary serving in France received a package from some of his fraternity brothers in Arizona. It contained what appeared to be a very plain and ordinary necktie, suitable for wearing on a mission. One evening, when Elder Philips and his companion were visiting a very proper family, in the middle of a spiritual discussion, the lights suddenly went out. It was pitch black—except for Elder Philips's tie, on which gleamed in florescent colors the words "KISS ME!"

Behold!
A Voice of Thunder

"My companion, Elder Painter, and I were serving in Peabody, Kansas. This was a rural town of approximately 2,000 people. It had rained all day, and my companion and I approached a home and knocked on the front door. A lady answered, and we introduced ourselves and told her we were representatives from The Church of Jesus Christ of Latter-day Saints and had an important message to give her. At that moment a super loud clap of thunder [sounded] directly above the house. All of us jumped. Immediately Elder Painter raised his right arm up and with his index pointing toward the sound said, 'And we speak with authority!'"

Harvey Brown

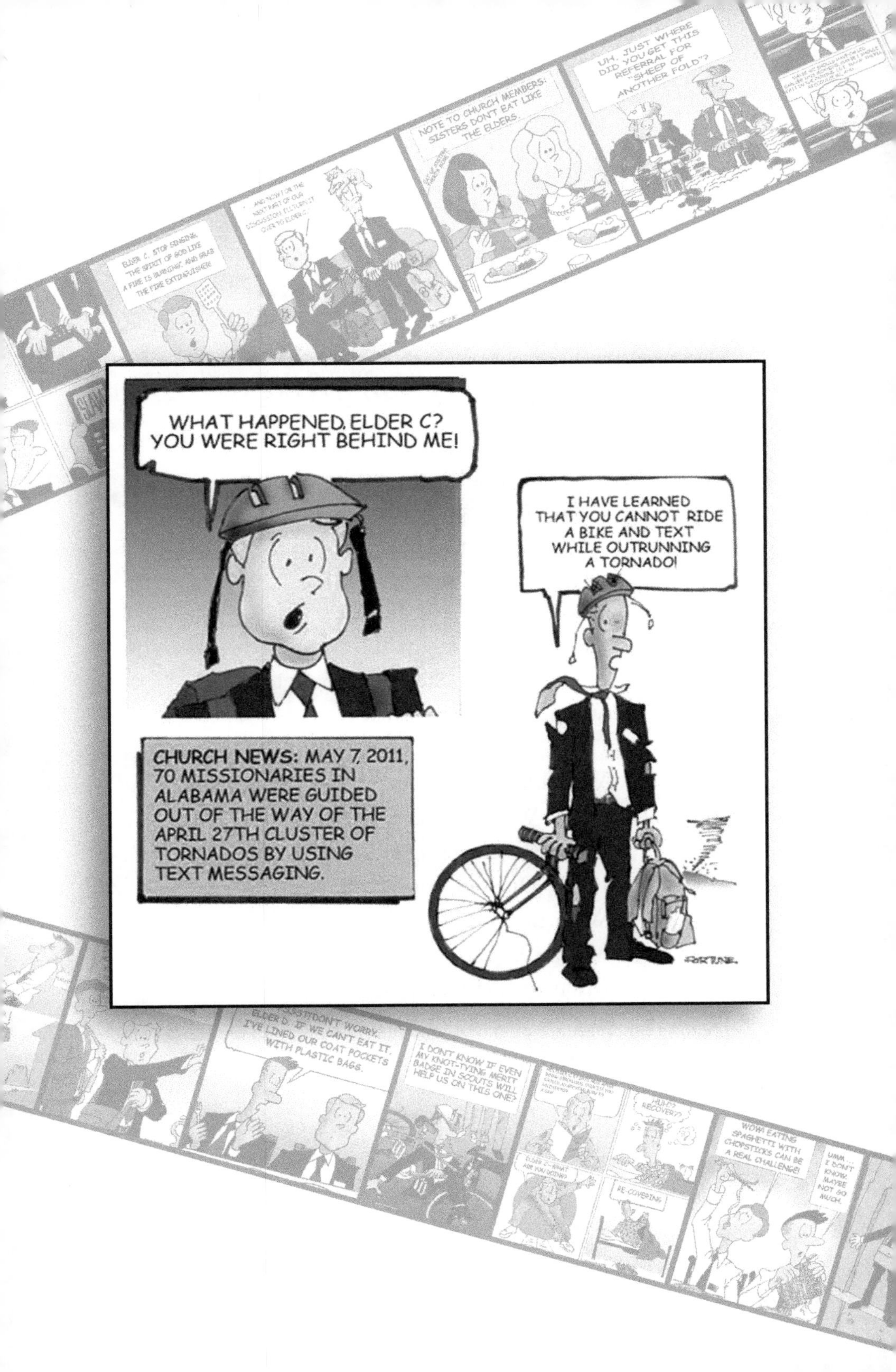
WHAT HAPPENED, ELDER C? YOU WERE RIGHT BEHIND ME!
I HAVE LEARNED THAT YOU CANNOT RIDE A BIKE AND TEXT WHILE OUTRUNNING A TORNADO!
CHURCH NEWS: MAY 7, 2011, 70 MISSIONARIES IN ALABAMA WERE GUIDED OUT OF THE WAY OF THE APRIL 27TH CLUSTER OF TORNADOS BY USING TEXT MESSAGING.
FORTUNE
NOTE TO CHURCH MEMBERS: SISTERS DON'T EAT LIKE THE ELDERS.
UH, JUST WHERE DID YOU GET THIS REFERRAL FOR "SHEEP OF ANOTHER FOLD"?
ELDER C, STOP SINGING "THE SPIRIT OF GOD LIKE A FIRE IS BURNING" AND GRAB THE FIRE EXTINGUISHER!
SLAM
ELDER D, IF WE CAN'T EAT IT, I'VE LINED OUR COAT POCKETS WITH PLASTIC BAGS.
I DON'T KNOW IF EVEN MY KNOT-TYING MERIT BADGE IN SCOUTS WILL HELP US ON THIS ONE?
HUH? RECOVER??
RE-COVERING
WOW! EATING SPAGHETTI WITH CHOPSTICKS CAN BE A REAL CHALLENGE!
UMM... I DON'T KNOW. MAYBE NOT SO MUCH.

A Missionary Poem

MISSIONARY CHRISTMAS

'Twas the night before Christmas,
    And all through the mission,
Each elder was tracting,
    At least we were wishing.
Me in my old suit,
    The elder in his too,
Sat down by the mailbox
    For our checks to come through.
When out on the street
    There arose such a clatter
We all looked to see
    What was the matter.
It was the traveling elders
    Dressed in missionary array
Who came to tract
    On this white Christmas day.
My heart skipped a beat,
    And my mind had a thought:
Tracting on Christmas
    Wasn't so hot!

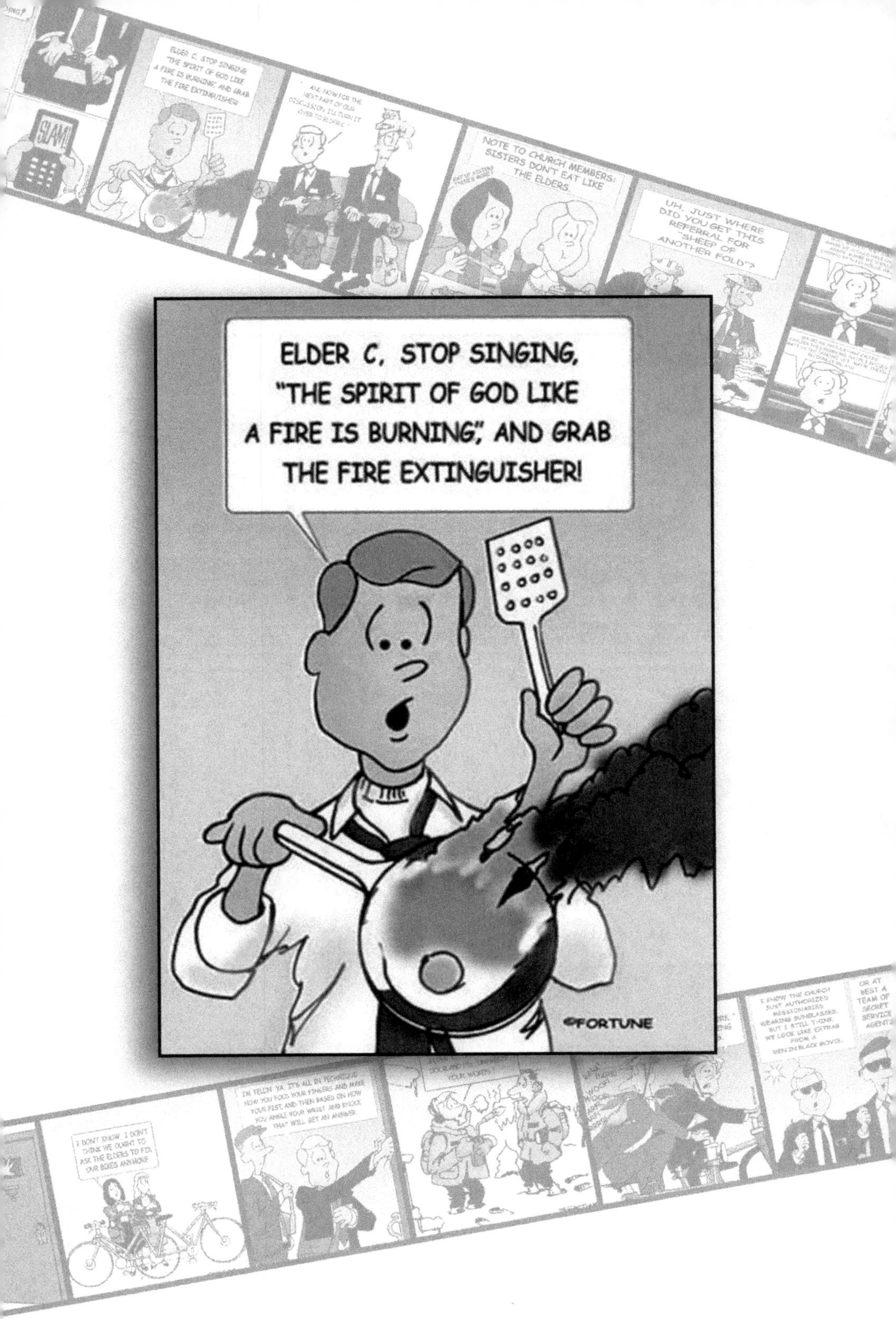
NOTE TO CHURCH MEMBERS: SISTERS DON'T EAT LIKE THE ELDERS.
UH, JUST WHERE DID YOU GET THIS REFERRAL FOR "SHEEP OF ANOTHER FOLD"?
ELDER C, STOP SINGING, "THE SPIRIT OF GOD LIKE A FIRE IS BURNING", AND GRAB THE FIRE EXTINGUISHER!
©FORTUNE
I KNOW THE CHURCH JUST AUTHORIZES MISSIONARIES WEARING SUNGLASSES, BUT I STILL THINK WE LOOK LIKE EXTRAS FROM A MEN IN BLACK MOVIE.
OR AT BEST A TEAM OF SECRET SERVICE AGENTS
I'M TELLIN' YA. IT'S ALL IN TECHNIQUE. HOW YOU FOLD YOUR FINGERS AND MAKE YOUR FIST, AND THEN BASED ON HOW YOU ANGLE YOUR WRIST AND KNOCK THAT WILL GET AN ANSWER.
I DON'T KNOW. I DON'T THINK WE OUGHT TO ASK THE ELDERS TO FIX OUR BIKES ANYMORE

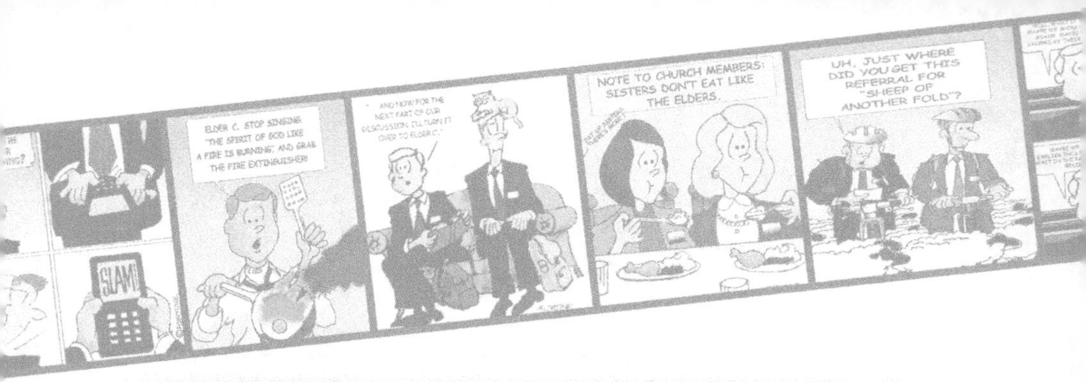
SLAM!
ELDER C. STOP SINGING "THE SPIRIT OF GOD LIKE A FIRE IS BURNING," AND GRAB THE FIRE EXTINGUISHER!
...AND NOW FOR THE NEXT PART OF OUR DISCUSSION. I'LL TURN IT OVER TO ELDER C.
NOTE TO CHURCH MEMBERS: SISTERS DON'T EAT LIKE THE ELDERS.
UH, JUST WHERE DID YOU GET THIS REFERRAL FOR "SHEEP OF ANOTHER FOLD"?

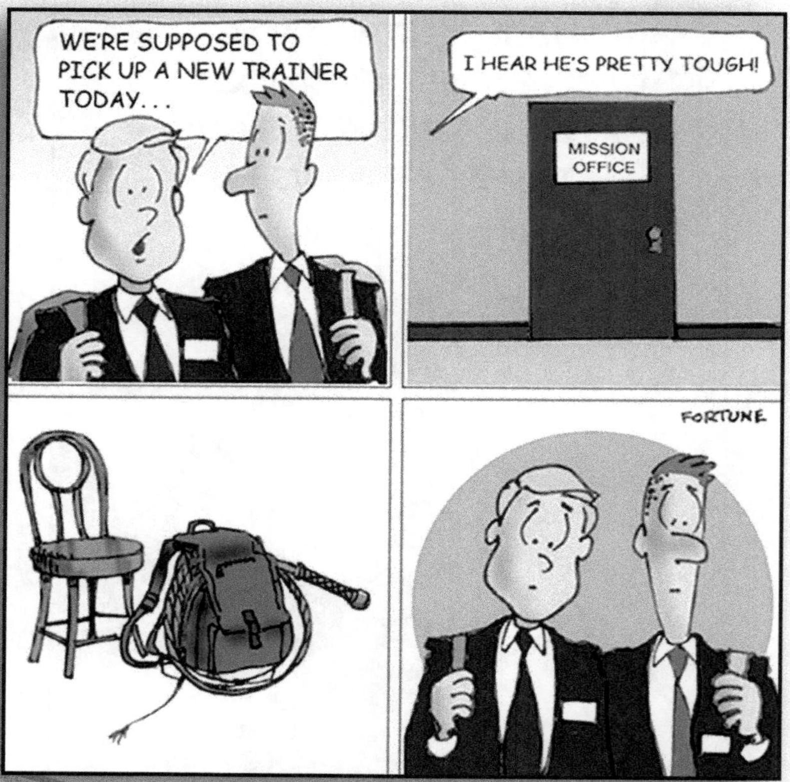
WE'RE SUPPOSED TO PICK UP A NEW TRAINER TODAY...
I HEAR HE'S PRETTY TOUGH!
MISSION OFFICE
FORTUNE

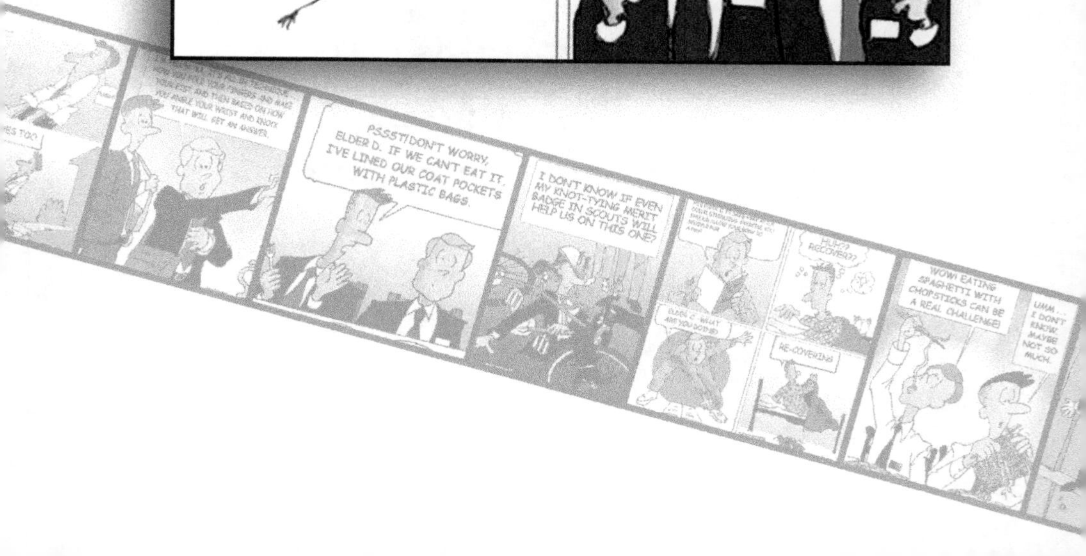
PSSST! DON'T WORRY, ELDER D. IF WE CAN'T EAT IT, I'VE LINED OUR COAT POCKETS WITH PLASTIC BAGS.
I DON'T KNOW IF EVEN MY KNOT-TYING MERIT BADGE IN SCOUTS WILL HELP US ON THIS ONE!
HUH?? RECOVER??
RE-COVERING!
WOW! EATING SPAGHETTI WITH CHOPSTICKS CAN BE A REAL CHALLENGE!
UMM... I DON'T KNOW. MAYBE NOT SO MUCH.

"Take No Thought... What Ye Shall Eat or Drink"

"I was a greenie in the west coast of Scotland nearly fifty years ago. My trainer and I were invited to dinner at a non-member's home, and they gave us a drink they said was cider. In my mind, I was thinking it must be apple cider. This refreshment was called Bulmers Togona and could be purchased at any fish and chip place. I'd never had this drink and thought it had a nasty taste; therefore, I only took a sip of it. My trainer did not seem to mind the taste and, in fact, had several glasses during the meal. On the way to our dig (apartment), my companion was exceptionally happy and laughed a lot. Later on, my trainer and I discovered that this drink contained at least 3 percent alcohol. Oops!"

Dave Montgomery

Confusing Relationships

Sisters Stevens and Allen stopped at a member's house and asked if they could have a cold drink of water. While visiting, Amy, the member's six-year-old daughter, proudly announced, "My sister had a baby, but she did not tell me if it's a boy or girl, so I don't know if I'm an aunt or uncle."

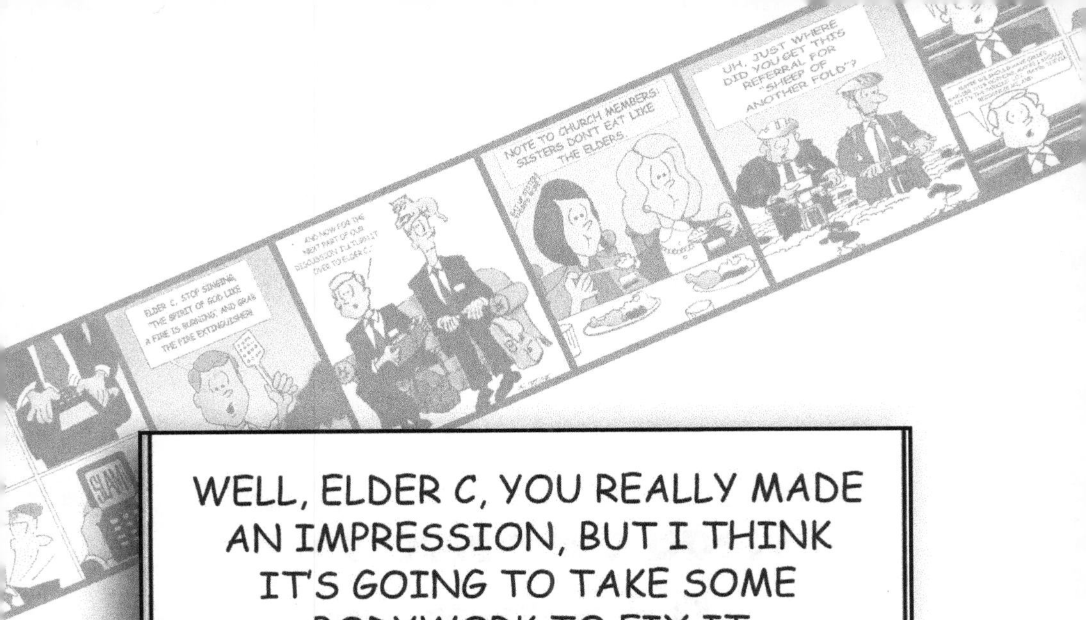
ELDER C, STOP SINGING "THE SPIRIT OF GOD LIKE A FIRE IS BURNING," AND GRAB THE FIRE EXTINGUISHER.
AND NOW FOR THE NEXT PART OF OUR DISCUSSION I'LL TURN IT OVER TO ELDER C.
NOTE TO CHURCH MEMBERS: SISTERS DON'T EAT LIKE THE ELDERS.
UH, JUST WHERE DID YOU GET THIS REFERRAL FOR "SHEEP OF ANOTHER FOLD"?

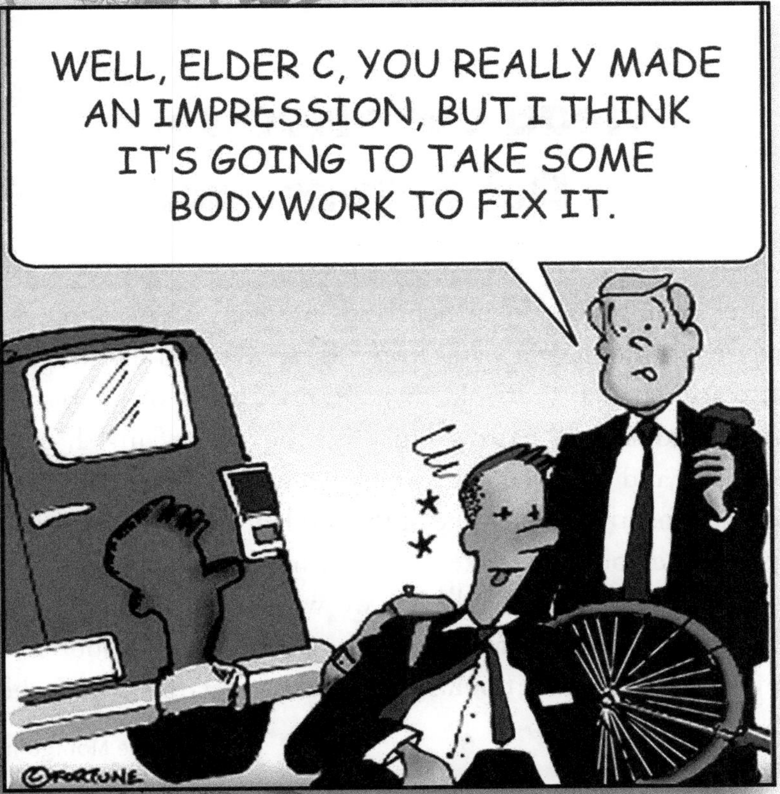
WELL, ELDER C, YOU REALLY MADE AN IMPRESSION, BUT I THINK IT'S GOING TO TAKE SOME BODYWORK TO FIX IT.
©FORTUNE

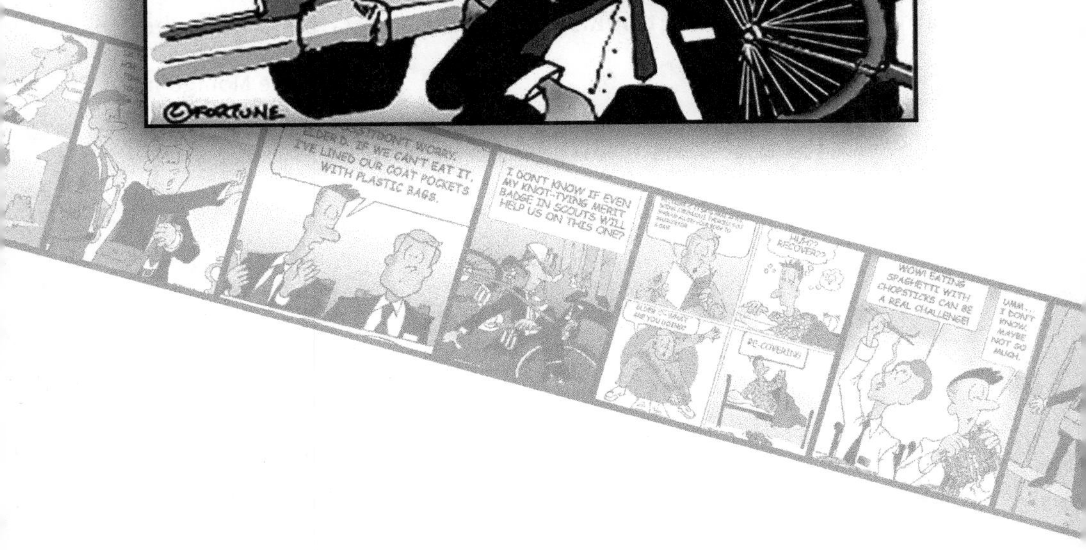
ELDER D, IF WE CAN'T EAT IT, I'VE LINED OUR COAT POCKETS WITH PLASTIC BAGS.
I DON'T KNOW IF EVEN MY KNOT-TYING MERIT BADGE IN SCOUTS WILL HELP US ON THIS ONE?
HUH? RECOVER??
RE-COVERING
WOW! EATING SPAGHETTI WITH CHOPSTICKS CAN BE A REAL CHALLENGE!
UMM... I DON'T KNOW. MAYBE NOT SO MUCH.

Head over Heels on a Door Approach

"Later on my mission in Scotland, my companion and I were tracting homes near a water front. These were old dwellings that were around 300 years old. It had rained most of the day, and we entered a dark, narrow stairway. The soles of my shoes had no tread, and I slipped and tumbled down the stairs and hit my head against the door of one of the residences. The women inside opened the door and looked down at me. While blood was running from my head, I told her we were missionaries from the Church and had an important message for her. Without saying anything, she shut the door. Not one of my best door approaches."

Dave Montgomery

It's All Relative

Elders Wilson and Hancock lived in a housing complex. One of the tenants was an older man who belonged to the Jewish faith. Over the next two weeks, the elders and this man exchanged small talk. One day, the elders purposely visited with this man, Ben Edersheim. After nearly a half hour of visiting, Elder Hancock started to tell Mr. Edersheim of all the great things that his lineage had accomplished over the years. Almost too proudly, he said, "Did you know that one of my relatives signed the Declaration of Independence?"

"That's wonderful, indeed," remarked Mr. Edersheim. Then, with a smile on his face, he softly said, "Did you know that one of my relatives wrote the Ten Commandments?"

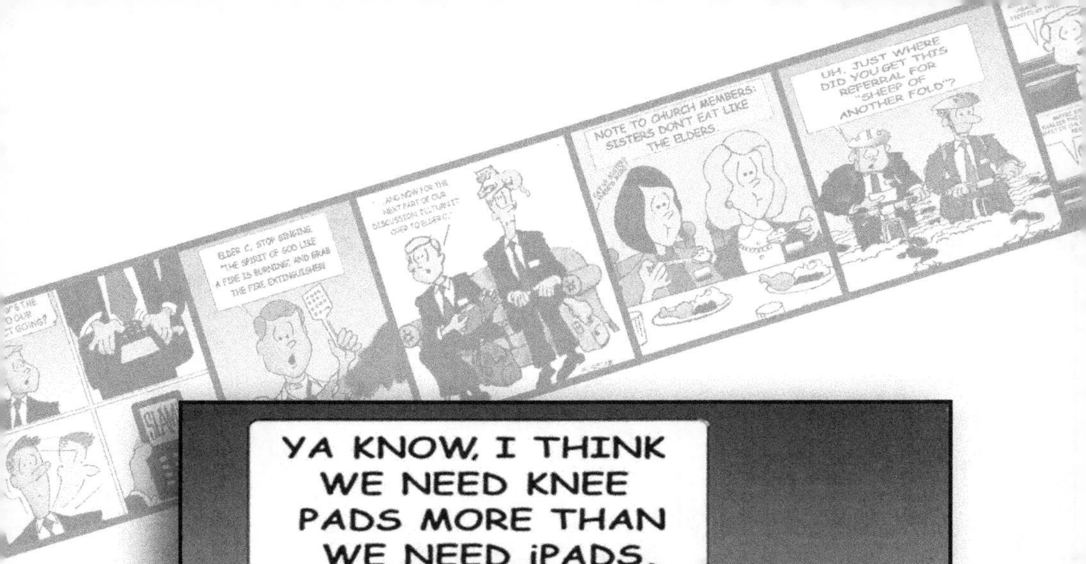
ELDER C. STOP SINGING "THE SPIRIT OF GOD LIKE A FIRE IS BURNING" AND GRAB THE FIRE EXTINGUISHER!
...AND NOW FOR THE NEXT PART OF OUR DISCUSSION, I'LL TURN IT OVER TO ELDER C.
NOTE TO CHURCH MEMBERS: SISTERS DON'T EAT LIKE THE ELDERS.
UH, JUST WHERE DID YOU GET THIS REFERRAL FOR "SHEEP OF ANOTHER FOLD"?

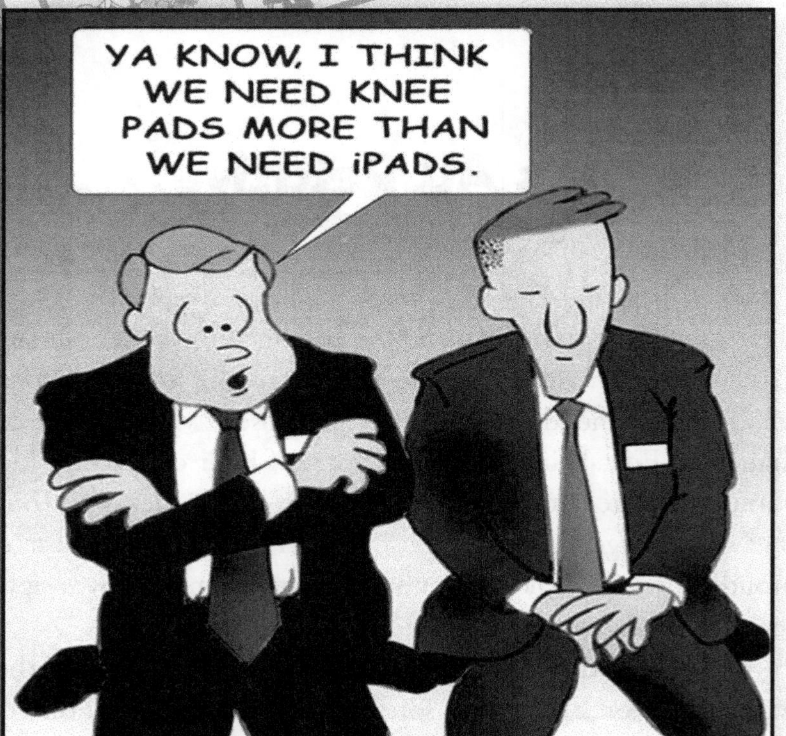
YA KNOW, I THINK WE NEED KNEE PADS MORE THAN WE NEED iPADS.
©FORTUNE

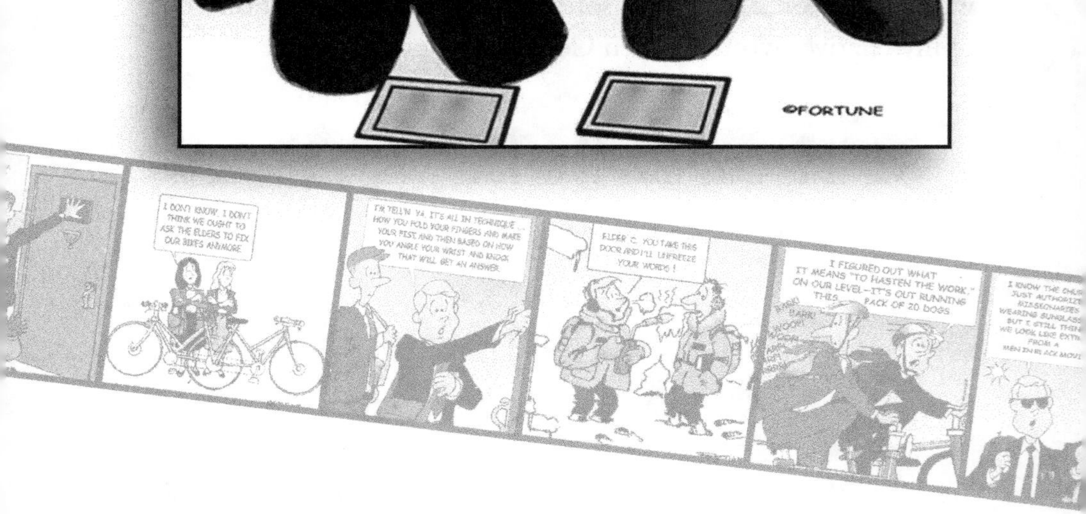
I DON'T KNOW. I DON'T THINK WE OUGHT TO ASK THE ELDERS TO FIX OUR BIKES ANYMORE.
I'M TELL'N YA, IT'S ALL IN TECHNIQUE... HOW YOU FOLD YOUR FINGERS AND MAKE YOUR FIST AND THEN BASED ON HOW YOU ANGLE YOUR WRIST AND KNOCK THAT WILL GET AN ANSWER.
ELDER C. YOU TAKE THIS DOOR AND I'LL UNFREEZE YOUR WORDS!

A Prayer without a Leg to Stand On

"[I] attended a district meeting with my companion. It was a good, uplifting meeting. I was asked to say the closing prayer. When I knelt down, I developed a severe leg cramp. While the other elders were kneeling with their eyes closed, I quickly stood up. I was in so much pain, I couldn't say anything. Soon the elders were slowly opening their eyes, wondering why I wasn't saying anything. I quickly said, 'Amen!' and started to hop around. Don't know if the Lord was laughing, but the elders were."

Dave Montgomery

No Good Deed Goes Unpunished

With other missionaries, Sisters Fry and Rivers were helping paint a church house for a non-LDS congregation. Storm clouds gathered, and it felt like it was going to rain. Knowing that their paint cans were nearly empty, these two sisters decided to quickly add paint thinner. They had just finished painting the steeple when it began to rain hard. The next day, both sisters looked at the steeple. To their dismay, the paint was nearly washed away. While speaking with the minister, they explained what had happened. With a smile on his face, he instructed Sister Fry and Sister Rivers, "Repaint, repaint, and thin no more!"

Mary Higgins

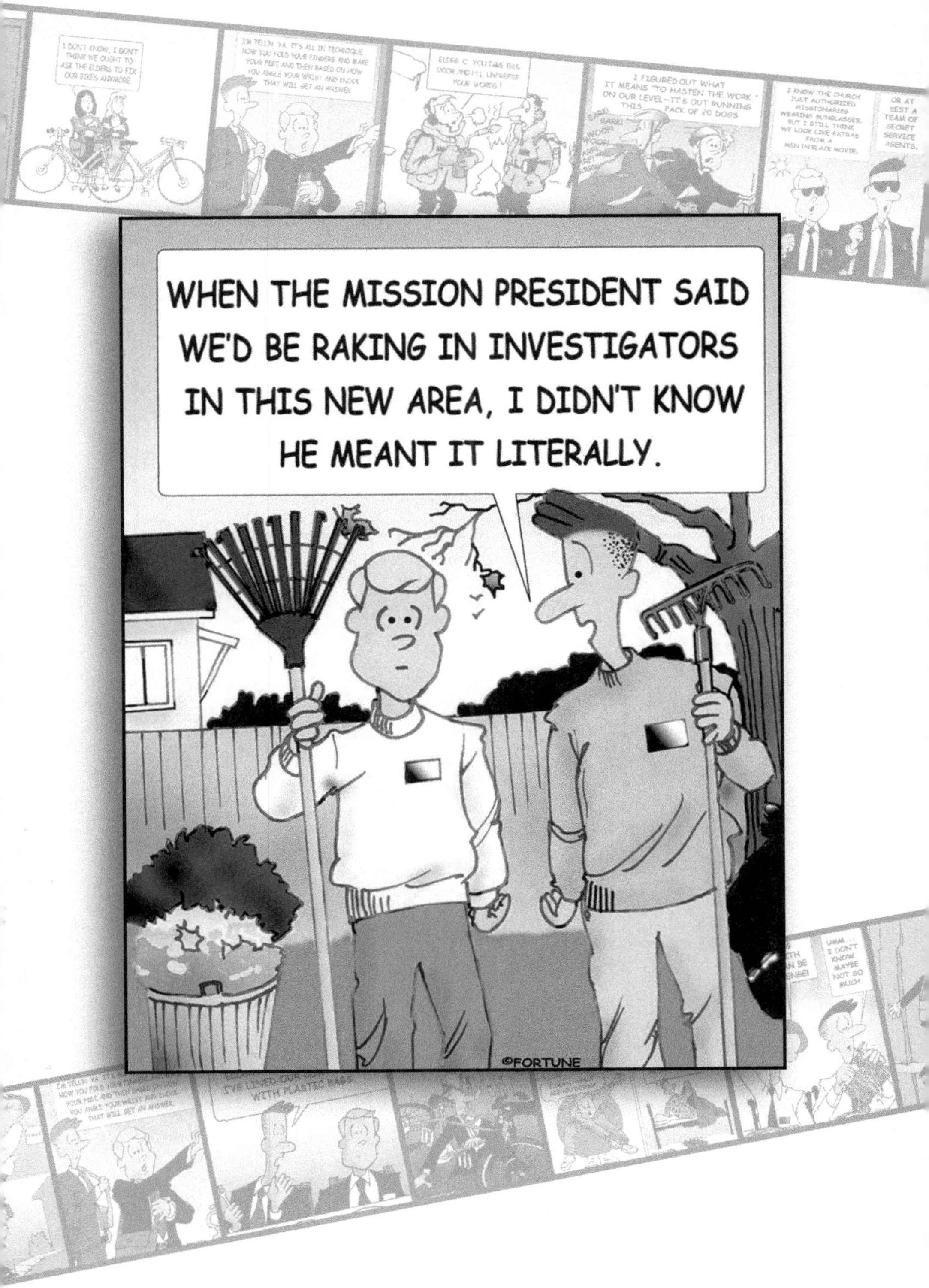
WHEN THE MISSION PRESIDENT SAID WE'D BE RAKING IN INVESTIGATORS IN THIS NEW AREA, I DIDN'T KNOW HE MEANT IT LITERALLY.
©FORTUNE

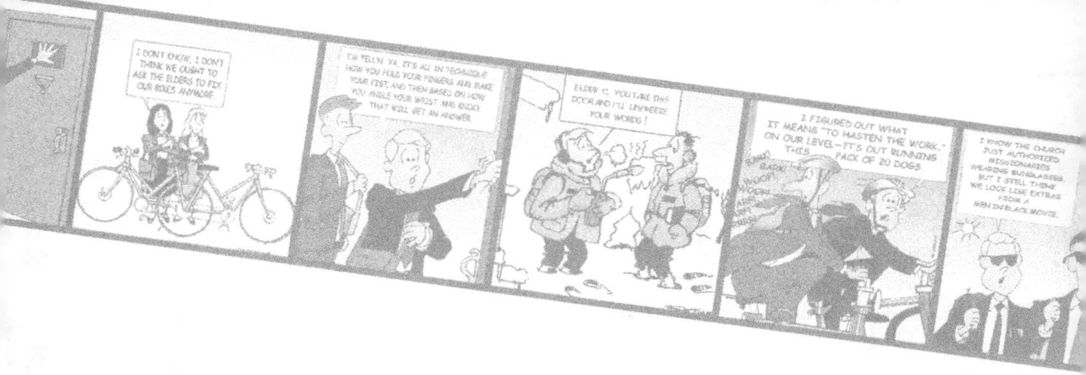
I DON'T KNOW, I DON'T THINK WE OUGHT TO ASK THE ELDERS TO FIX OUR BIKES ANYMORE.
I'M TELL'N YA, IT'S ALL IN TECHNIQUE. HOW YOU FOLD YOUR FINGERS AND MAKE YOUR FIST, AND THEN BASED ON HOW YOU ANGLE YOUR WRIST AND KNOCK THAT WILL GET AN ANSWER.
ELDER C. YOU TAKE THIS DOOR AND I'LL UNFREEZE YOUR WORDS!
I FIGURED OUT WHAT IT MEANS "TO HASTEN THE WORK." ON OUR LEVEL—IT'S OUT RUNNING THIS PACK OF 20 DOGS
BARK! BARK! WOOF!
I KNOW THE CHURCH JUST AUTHORIZED MISSIONARIES WEARING SUNGLASSES, BUT I STILL THINK WE LOOK LIKE EXTRAS FROM A MEN IN BLACK MOVIE.

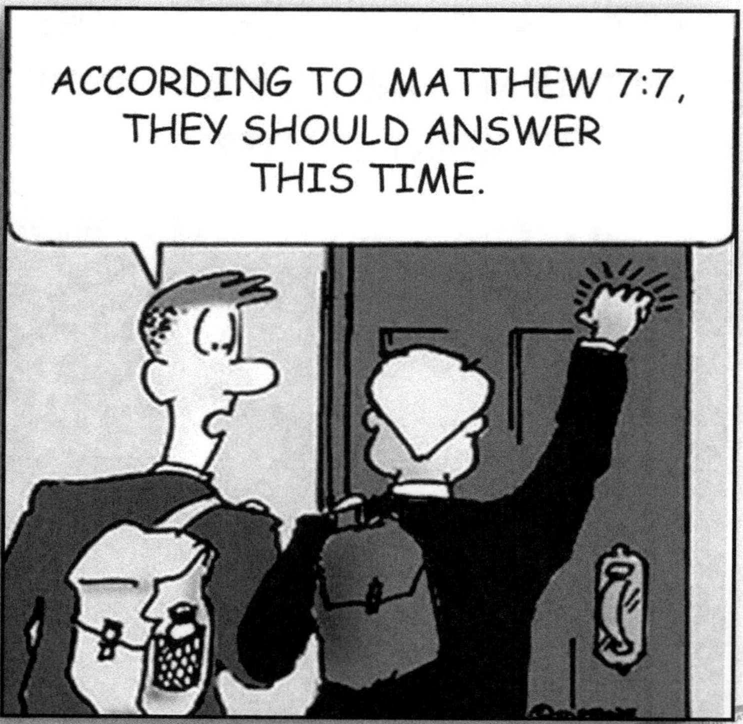
ACCORDING TO MATTHEW 7:7, THEY SHOULD ANSWER THIS TIME.

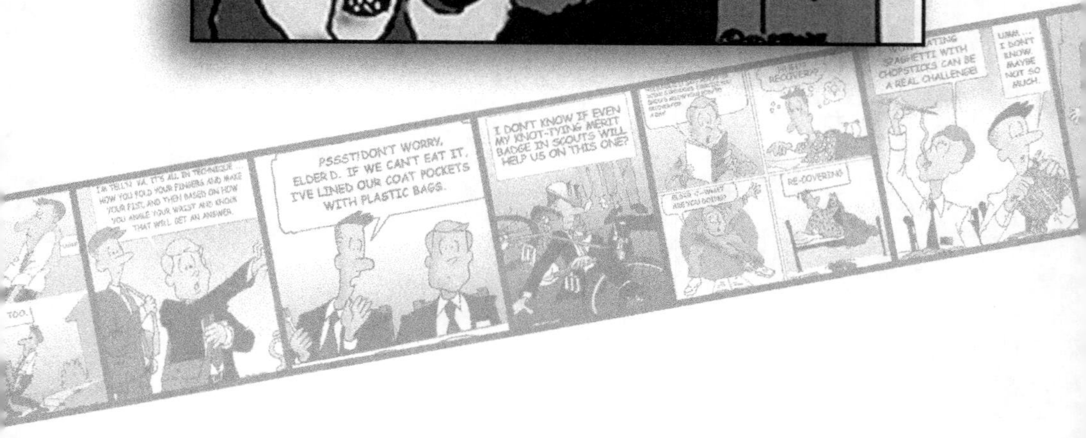
I'M TELL'N YA, IT'S ALL IN TECHNIQUE... HOW YOU FOLD YOUR FINGERS AND MAKE YOUR FIST, AND THEN BASED ON HOW YOU ANGLE YOUR WRIST AND KNOCK THAT WILL GET AN ANSWER.
PSSST! DON'T WORRY, ELDER D. IF WE CAN'T EAT IT, I'VE LINED OUR COAT POCKETS WITH PLASTIC BAGS.
I DON'T KNOW IF EVEN MY KNOT-TYING MERIT BADGE IN SCOUTS WILL HELP US ON THIS ONE?
RE-COVERING
SPAGHETTI WITH CHOPSTICKS CAN BE A REAL CHALLENGE!
UMM... I DON'T KNOW. MAYBE NOT SO MUCH.

Nobody but Us Chickens

"While serving in Southern Japan, I and my companion knocked on the door of a home. A young girl, probably 6 years of age, opened the door. I introduced myself and my companion, and asked if her parents were home. She responded, 'Let me go and check.' She came back shortly and said, 'My mom and dad said they are not here.'"

Val Gunnell

Two Wrong Turns
Don't Make It Right

Sisters Tomlinson and Rodriguez were visiting in the home of the Todd family, who were members of the Church. A young daughter, Jennifer, was telling the sisters about the lesson she had learned in Primary class on Sunday. She said, "My Primary teacher told how Lot's wife looked back at Sodom and was turned into a pillar of salt."

To the mother's chagrin, another daughter, Sarah, who was two years older than Jennifer, excitedly exclaimed, "My mother looked back once while she was driving the car, and she turned into a power pole!"

Mary Tomlinson

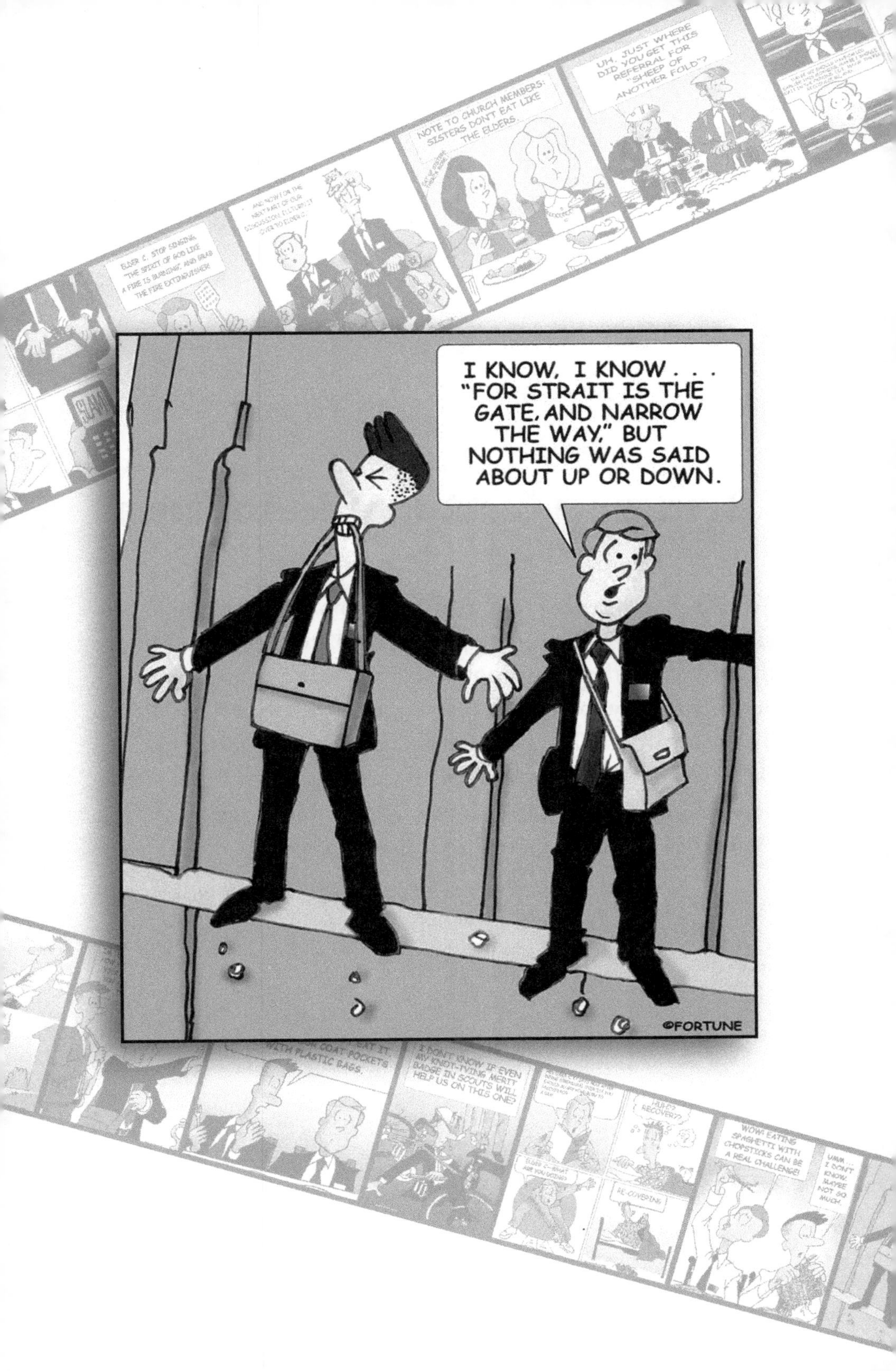
ELDER C, STOP SINGING "THE SPIRIT OF GOD LIKE A FIRE IS BURNING" AND GRAB THE FIRE EXTINGUISHER.
NOTE TO CHURCH MEMBERS: SISTERS DON'T EAT LIKE THE ELDERS.
UH, JUST WHERE DID YOU GET THIS REFERRAL FOR "SHEEP OF ANOTHER FOLD"?
I KNOW, I KNOW . . . "FOR STRAIT IS THE GATE, AND NARROW THE WAY," BUT NOTHING WAS SAID ABOUT UP OR DOWN.
©FORTUNE
I DON'T KNOW IF EVEN MY KNOT-TYING MERIT BADGE IN SCOUTS WILL HELP US ON THIS ONE!
RE-COVERING
WOW! EATING SPAGHETTI WITH CHOPSTICKS CAN BE A REAL CHALLENGE!
UMM... I DON'T KNOW. MAYBE NOT SO MUCH.

Bridging Cultural Relations

"While [I was] serving in Japan, my companion was anxious to race me on his bike to our apartment. There was a small bridge that led to a park where people liked to gather. It was getting dark outside, and my companion rode up and down the bridge fast. To his great surprise, he saw a man walking his dog as they neared the bridge. My companion had no choice but to ride his bike between them. After these three came tumbling together, it was discovered that the man had a leash attached to his dog."

Roger Nelson

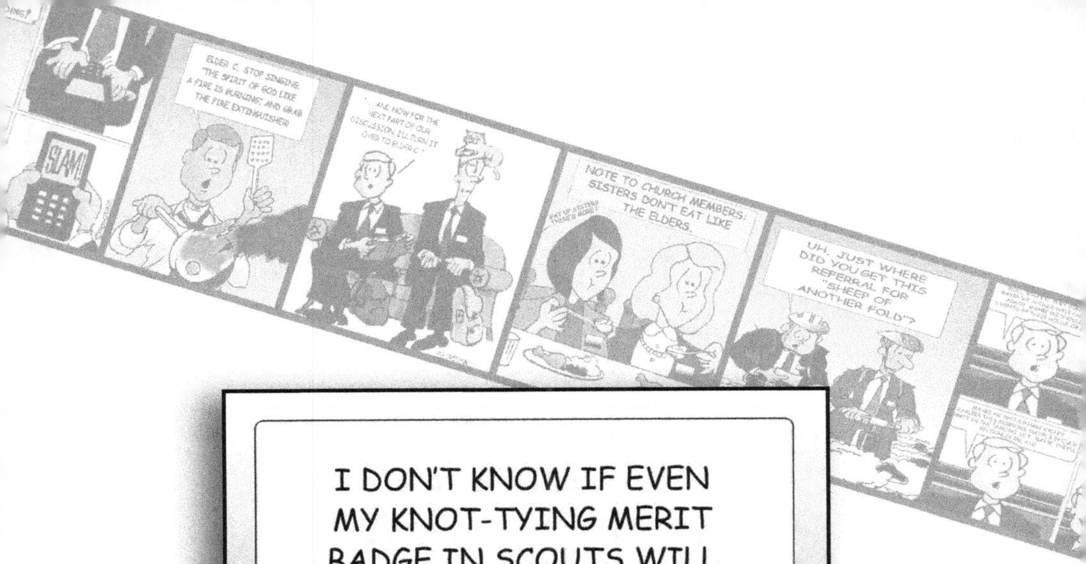
ELDER C, STOP SINGING "THE SPIRIT OF GOD LIKE A FIRE IS BURNING" AND GRAB THE FIRE EXTINGUISHER!
SLAM!
NOTE TO CHURCH MEMBERS: SISTERS DON'T EAT LIKE THE ELDERS.
UH, JUST WHERE DID YOU GET THIS REFERRAL FOR "SHEEP OF ANOTHER FOLD"?

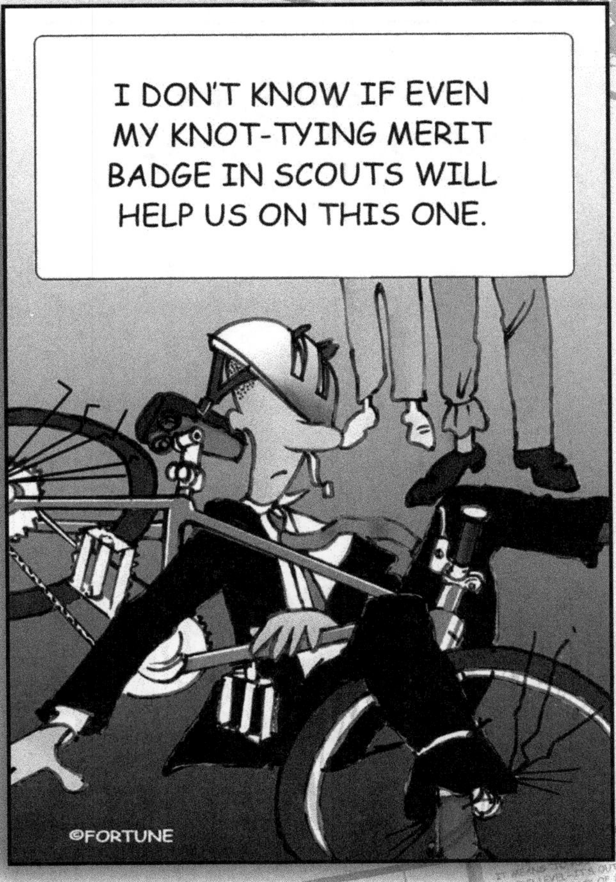
I DON'T KNOW IF EVEN MY KNOT-TYING MERIT BADGE IN SCOUTS WILL HELP US ON THIS ONE.
©FORTUNE

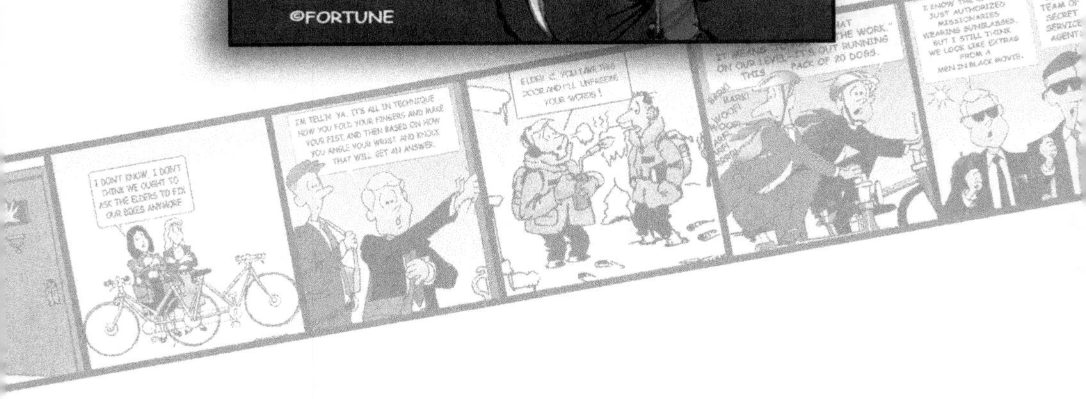
I DON'T KNOW, I DON'T THINK WE OUGHT TO ASK THE ELDERS TO FIX OUR BIKES ANYMORE.
I'M TELL'N YA, IT'S ALL IN TECHNIQUE. HOW YOU FOLD YOUR FINGERS AND MAKE YOUR FIST, AND THEN BASED ON HOW YOU ANGLE YOUR WRIST AND KNOCK THAT WILL GET AN ANSWER.
I KNOW THE CHURCH JUST AUTHORIZED MISSIONARIES WEARING SUNGLASSES, BUT I STILL THINK WE LOOK LIKE EXTRAS FROM A MEN IN BLACK MOVIE.
OR AT BEST A TEAM OF SECRET SERVICE AGENTS.

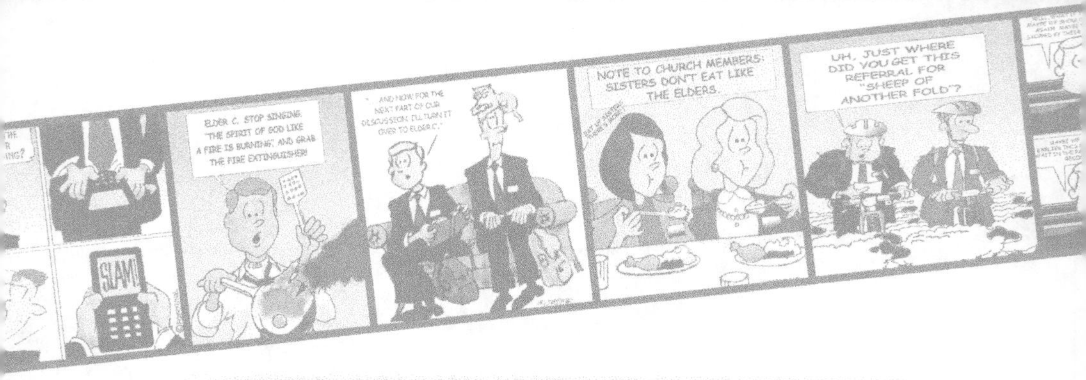
ELDER C. STOP SINGING "THE SPIRIT OF GOD LIKE A FIRE IS BURNING," AND GRAB THE FIRE EXTINGUISHER!
SLAM!
NOTE TO CHURCH MEMBERS: SISTERS DON'T EAT LIKE THE ELDERS.
UH, JUST WHERE DID YOU GET THIS REFERRAL FOR "SHEEP OF ANOTHER FOLD"?

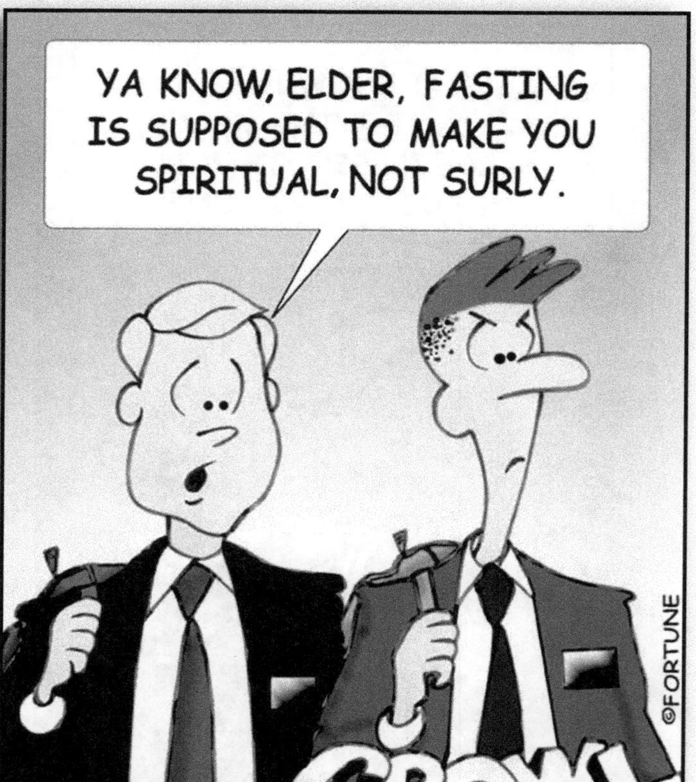
YA KNOW, ELDER, FASTING IS SUPPOSED TO MAKE YOU SPIRITUAL, NOT SURLY.
GROWL
©FORTUNE

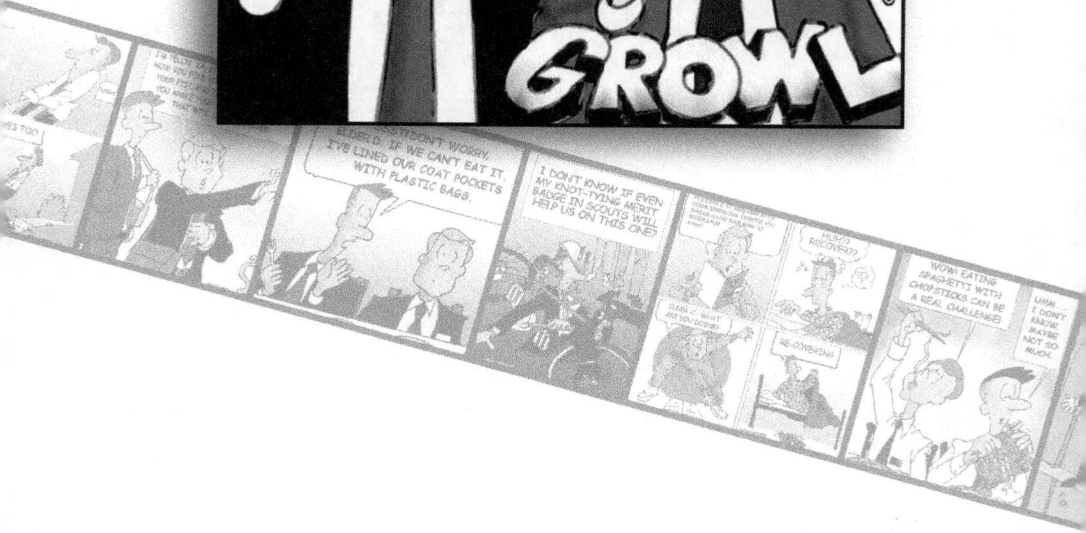
IF WE CAN'T EAT IT, I'VE LINED OUR COAT POCKETS WITH PLASTIC BAGS.
I DON'T KNOW IF EVEN MY KNOT-TYING MERIT BADGE IN SCOUTS WILL HELP US ON THIS ONE?
HUH?? RECOVER??
RE-COVERING
WOW! EATING SPAGHETTI WITH CHOPSTICKS CAN BE A REAL CHALLENGE!
UMM... I DON'T KNOW. MAYBE NOT SO MUCH.

A Sobering Thought

"While [I was] serving in Tacoma, Washington, nearly fifty years ago, it was nearing midnight when the telephone rang. I answered it, and a man who was drunk asked, 'Is this John?'

"Being sleepy, I said, 'No,' and hung the phone up. Five minutes later, the same thing happened. Again, I responded the same way. Ten minutes later, the phone rang again. It was this same man. This time I said, 'This is Elder Dana. I'm a missionary for The Church of Jesus Christ of Latter-day Saints; would you like to know more about the Mormons?'

"This man hung up and never called again. Either I startled him or sobered him up."

Bruce E. Dana

Not Crying over Spilled Milk, Just Mad

"While serving in Brownstown, Washington, on the Yakima Indian Reservation, my companion, Elder Sweeney, and I were blessed to receive free milk from a member family. We were able to go to the farm and retrieve the glass bottles of milk from a cooler. We decided to get two gallons. As I was walking to our car, I accidentally hit the two glass jars together. Both bottles broke and milk went everywhere, including on my suit and shoes. Needless to say, I was upset and embarrassed. My companion kept his composure until he said, 'Don't cry over spilled milk.' He then laughed heartily."

Bruce E. Dana

A Humbling Stumble

"While serving in this same area, my companion and I were walking in a rural area, and I did not see a piece of wood on the ground in front of me. I tripped and nearly fell down. Trying to justify my action, I said to my companion, 'They tell us to always look up.'

"My companion and friend replied, 'Sometimes, Elder Dana, you have to look down to be humble.'"

Bruce E. Dana

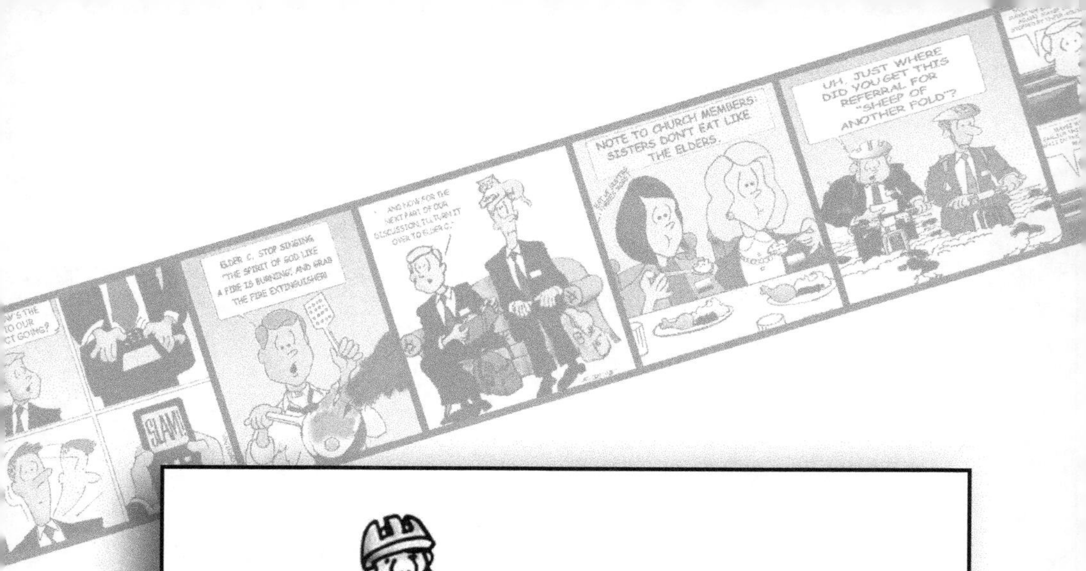
SLAM!
ELDER C, STOP SINGING "THE SPIRIT OF GOD LIKE A FIRE IS BURNING," AND GRAB THE FIRE EXTINGUISHER!
...AND NOW FOR THE NEXT PART OF OUR DISCUSSION, I'LL TURN IT OVER TO ELDER C.
NOTE TO CHURCH MEMBERS: SISTERS DON'T EAT LIKE THE ELDERS.
UH, JUST WHERE DID YOU GET THIS REFERRAL FOR "SHEEP OF ANOTHER FOLD"?

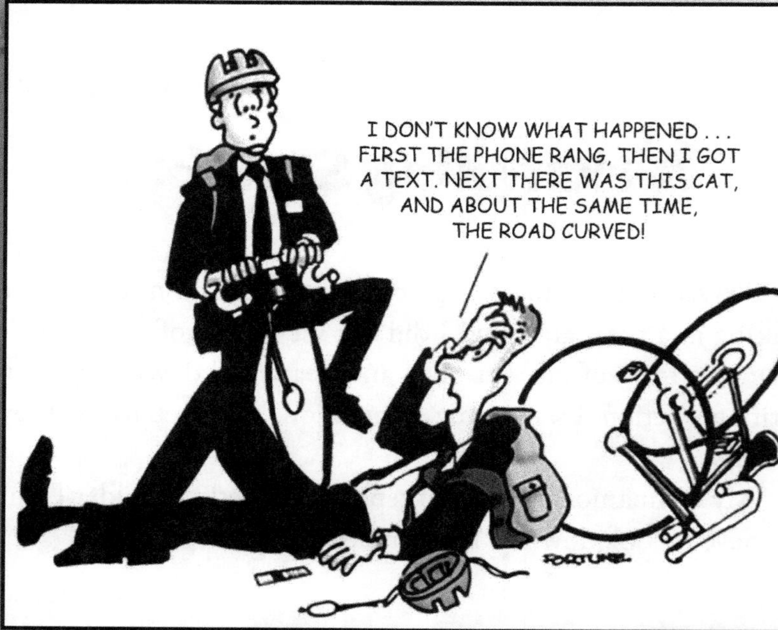
I DON'T KNOW WHAT HAPPENED . . .
FIRST THE PHONE RANG, THEN I GOT
A TEXT. NEXT THERE WAS THIS CAT,
AND ABOUT THE SAME TIME,
THE ROAD CURVED!

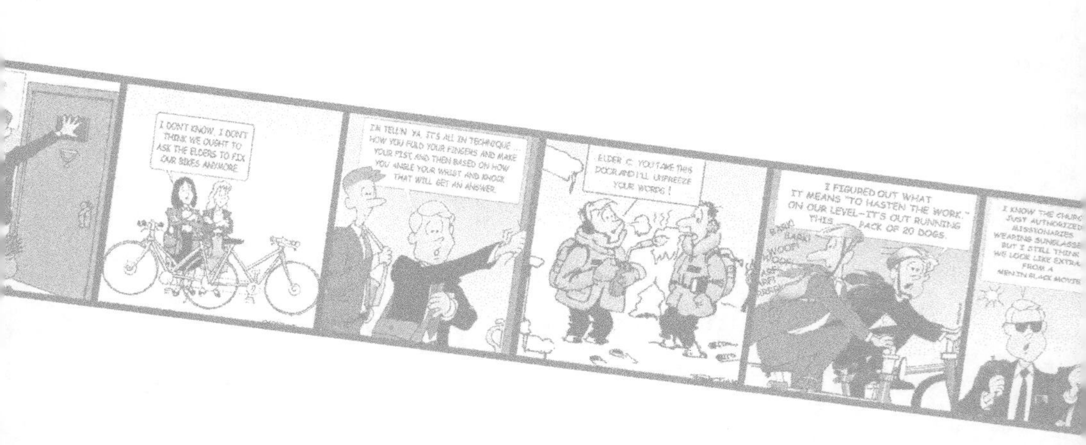
I DON'T KNOW. I DON'T THINK WE OUGHT TO ASK THE ELDERS TO FIX OUR BIKES ANYMORE.
I'M TELL'N YA, IT'S ALL IN TECHNIQUE... HOW YOU FOLD YOUR FINGERS AND MAKE YOUR FIST, AND THEN BASED ON HOW YOU ANGLE YOUR WRIST AND KNOCK THAT WILL GET AN ANSWER.
ELDER C: YOU TAKE THIS DOOR AND I'LL UNFREEZE YOUR WORDS!
I FIGURED OUT WHAT IT MEANS "TO HASTEN THE WORK" ON OUR LEVEL—IT'S OUT RUNNING THIS... PACK OF 20 DOGS.

The Gift of Tongues

Sisters Evans and Ruvalcaba were tracting in Mexico City. To their great surprise, they met an American member family who was visiting the city. After visiting with this family, Sister Ruvalcaba said to the four-year-old son, "Hasta la vista."

Not knowing Spanish, the young lad answered back, "Happy Easter to you too!"

Rebecca Evans

To Carry One Another's Burdens

Elder Fry confided with his new companion, Elder Turner: "In my previous district, my companion and I were asked to help move three families. However, due to one reason or another, we arrived when most of the move was done. My district leader was not real happy and called us 'blisters.'"

Curious, Elder Turner asked, "Why did he call you that?"

"He said we were blisters because we showed up when all the work was done."

SHARING THE GOSPEL AND THE ROAD

A Case of Mistaken Identity

Sisters Royal and Ashton were asked by the bishop to ride in the car of an older sister in the ward who had a doctor's appointment.

To the sisters' great alarm, this woman tailgated a man in a busy boulevard. Then she quickly turned into the next lane and tailgated another car. Because the light turned yellow, this woman slammed on her brakes and honked the horn. She opened her window and leaned her head out, screaming in frustration at the car in front of her, for she had missed her chance to get through the intersection. As she was yelling, she noticed a very serious-looking police officer standing next to her car window.

The officer ordered her to pull her car over to the side of the road. A tow truck was called, and the car was impounded. Then he took the woman and the two sisters to a police station, where they were escorted to a holding area.

After about an hour, the arresting officer said to the woman, "I'm very sorry for this mistake. Because you had a 'Choose the Right' license plate holder, 'Families are forever' bumper sticker, and a chrome-plated Angel Moroni emblem on the trunk, I assumed you had stolen the car."

Nothing to Sneeze At

Spring was in the air. Flowers were starting to bloom, and trees were beginning to bud. Elders Tidwell and Bramwell were visiting a Gospel Doctrine class with a couple who had recently gotten married. This couple was helpful in referring these elders to non-member friends who were interested in knowing more about the Church. During this class, Elder Tidwell was experiencing mild allergies and his eyes were watering. After the class, Sister Curtis told the elders, "When I was younger, I experienced what I thought was hay fever. My mother took me to a specialist, and after doing tests, he discovered I was allergic to my kitten. Sadly, my parents had no choice but to give my pet away." With a smile on her face, she added, "Maybe, Elder Tidwell, you're allergic to your companion?"

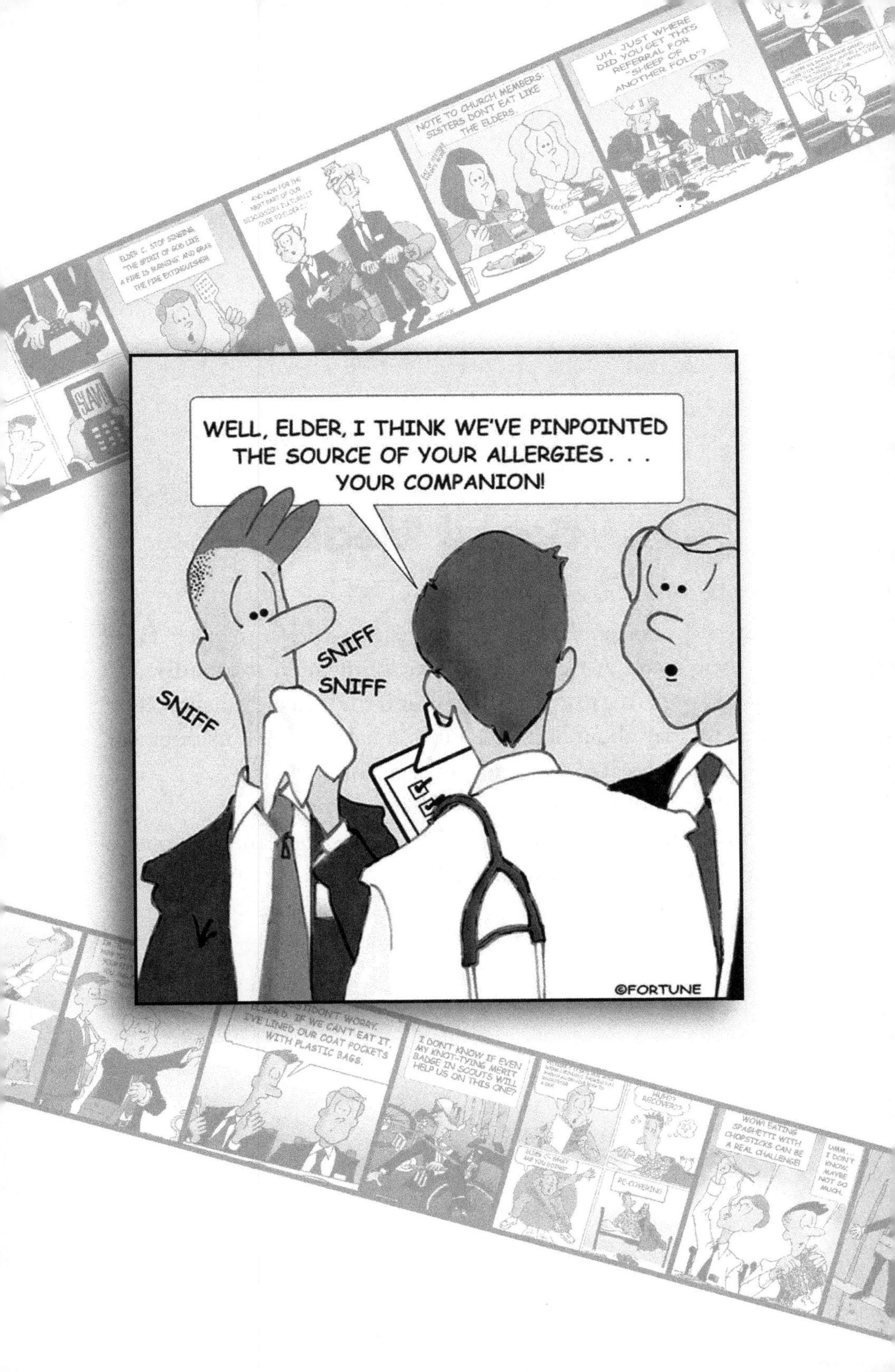
ELDER C, STOP SINGING "THE SPIRIT OF GOD LIKE A FIRE IS BURNING," AND GRAB THE FIRE EXTINGUISHER!
AND NOW FOR THE NEXT PART OF OUR DISCUSSION I'LL TURN IT OVER TO ELDER C.
NOTE TO CHURCH MEMBERS: SISTERS DON'T EAT LIKE THE ELDERS.
UH, JUST WHERE DID YOU GET THIS REFERRAL FOR "SHEEP OF ANOTHER FOLD"?
SLAM
WELL, ELDER, I THINK WE'VE PINPOINTED THE SOURCE OF YOUR ALLERGIES . . . YOUR COMPANION!
SNIFF
SNIFF
SNIFF
©FORTUNE
DON'T WORRY. IF WE CAN'T EAT IT, I'VE LINED OUR COAT POCKETS WITH PLASTIC BAGS.
I DON'T KNOW IF EVEN MY KNOT-TYING MERIT BADGE IN SCOUTS WILL HELP US ON THIS ONE?
HUH? RECOVER??
RE-COVERING
WOW! EATING SPAGHETTI WITH CHOPSTICKS CAN BE A REAL CHALLENGE!
UMM... I DON'T KNOW. MAYBE NOT SO MUCH.

Social Media

Sisters Stevens and Arnold were visiting with a member family at their home. A teenage daughter, Emily, told the family, "The bishop wants me to give a fifteen-minute talk in sacrament meeting next Sunday about how social media helps us find investigators."

"That's great, dear," replied her Mom.

"But, Mom, I can't talk for fifteen minutes!"

Her mother smiled and said, "Perhaps you can take your cell phone to the podium with you."

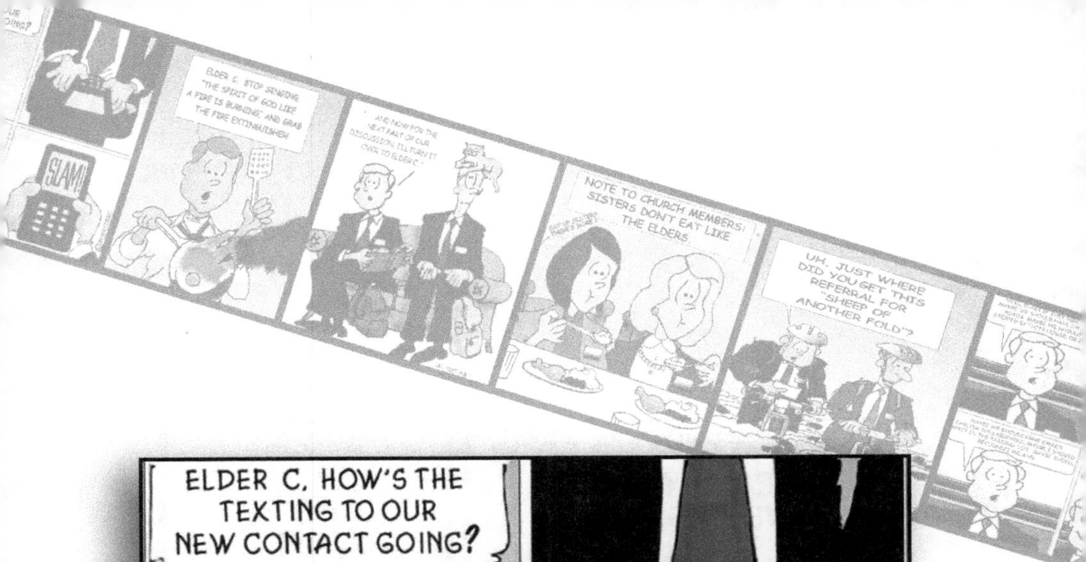

ELDER C. STOP SINGING "THE SPIRIT OF GOD LIKE A FIRE IS BURNING" AND GRAB THE FIRE EXTINGUISHER!
AND NOW FOR THE NEXT PART OF OUR DISCUSSION, I'LL TURN IT OVER TO ELDER C.
NOTE TO CHURCH MEMBERS: SISTERS DON'T EAT LIKE THE ELDERS.
UH, JUST WHERE DID YOU GET THIS REFERRAL FOR "SHEEP OF ANOTHER FOLD"?

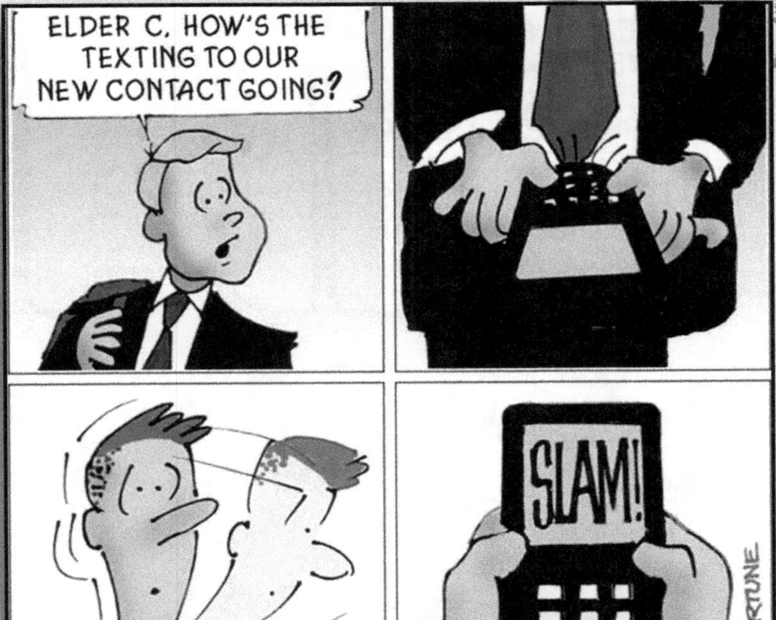

ELDER C, HOW'S THE TEXTING TO OUR NEW CONTACT GOING?
SLAM!
© FORTUNE

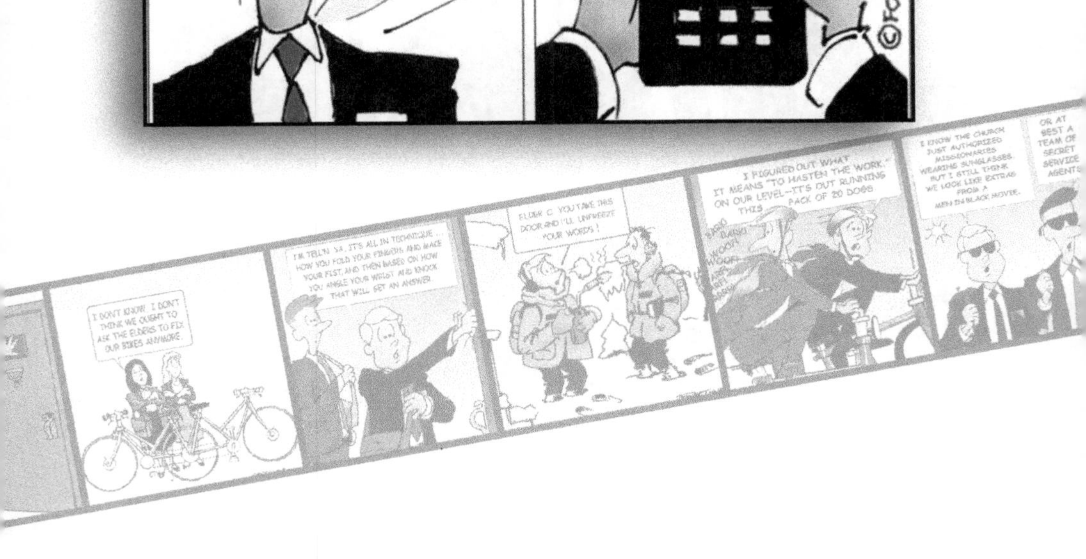

I DON'T KNOW. I DON'T THINK WE OUGHT TO ASK THE ELDERS TO FIX OUR BIKES ANYMORE.
I'M TELL'N SA, IT'S ALL IN TECHNIQUE... HOW YOU FOLD YOUR FINGERS AND MAKE YOUR FIST, AND THEN BASED ON HOW YOU ANGLE YOUR WRIST AND KNOCK THAT WILL GET AN ANSWER.
ELDER C. YOU TAKE THIS DOOR AND I'LL UNFREEZE YOUR WORDS!
I FIGURED OUT WHAT IT MEANS "TO HASTEN THE WORK" ON OUR LEVEL—IT'S OUT RUNNING THIS PACK OF 20 DOGS
I KNOW THE CHURCH JUST AUTHORIZED MISSIONARIES WEARING SUNGLASSES, BUT I STILL THINK WE LOOK LIKE EXTRAS FROM A MEN IN BLACK MOVIE.
OR AT BEST A TEAM OF SECRET SERVICE AGENTS

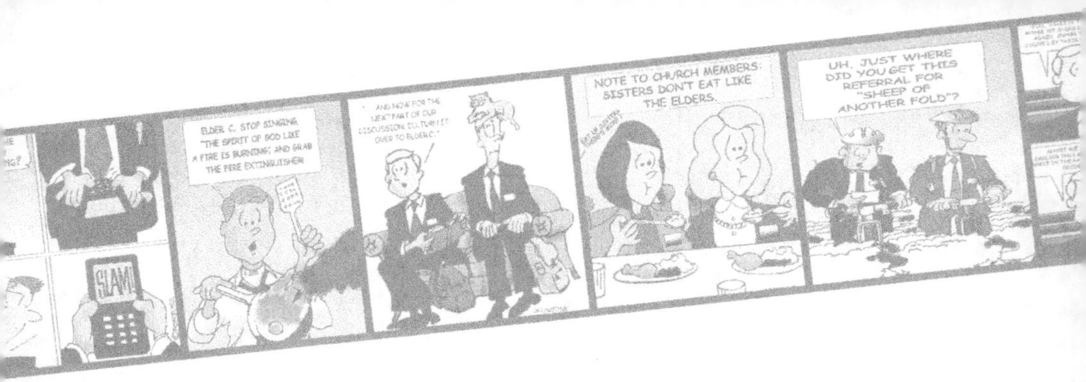
ELDER C, STOP SINGING "THE SPIRIT OF GOD LIKE A FIRE IS BURNING," AND GRAB THE FIRE EXTINGUISHER!
SLAM!
NOTE TO CHURCH MEMBERS: SISTERS DON'T EAT LIKE THE ELDERS.
UH, JUST WHERE DID YOU GET THIS REFERRAL FOR "SHEEP OF ANOTHER FOLD"?

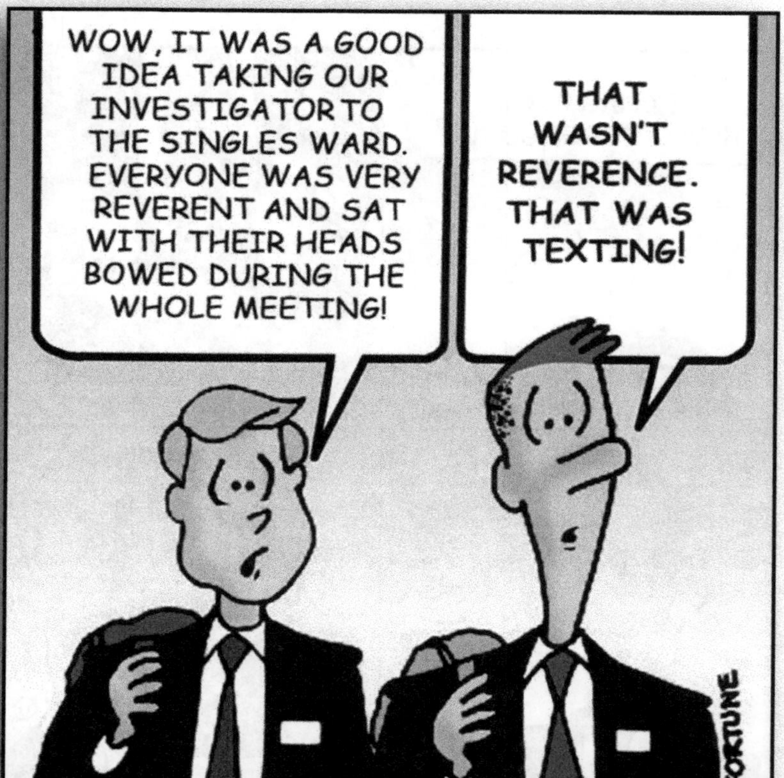
WOW, IT WAS A GOOD IDEA TAKING OUR INVESTIGATOR TO THE SINGLES WARD. EVERYONE WAS VERY REVERENT AND SAT WITH THEIR HEADS BOWED DURING THE WHOLE MEETING!
THAT WASN'T REVERENCE. THAT WAS TEXTING!
©FORTUNE

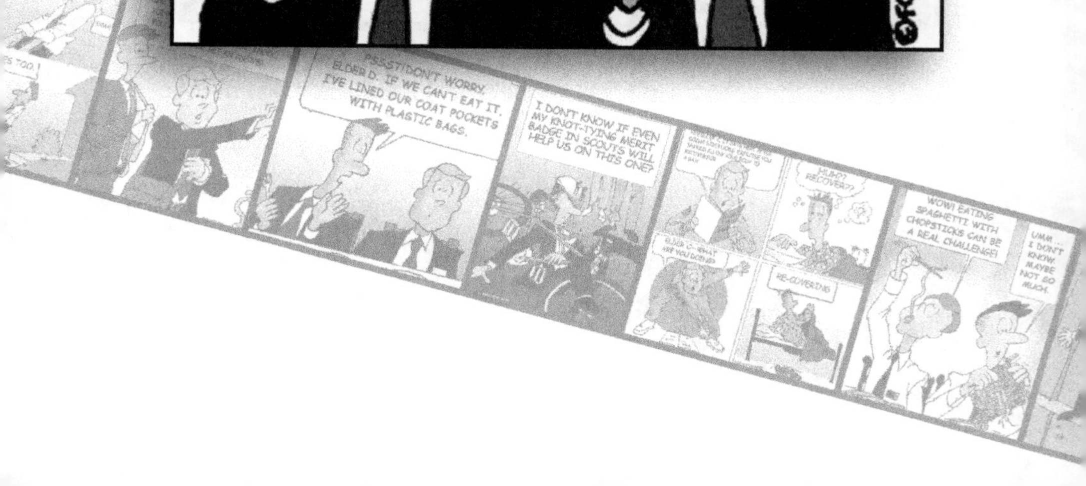
PSSST! DON'T WORRY, ELDER D. IF WE CAN'T EAT IT, I'VE LINED OUR COAT POCKETS WITH PLASTIC BAGS.
I DON'T KNOW IF EVEN MY KNOT-TYING MERIT BADGE IN SCOUTS WILL HELP US ON THIS ONE?
HUH? RECOVER??
RE-COVERING
WOW! EATING SPAGHETTI WITH CHOPSTICKS CAN BE A REAL CHALLENGE!
UMM... I DON'T KNOW. MAYBE NOT SO MUCH.

How to Avoid a DUI: Join the Church

"I served . . . in the New Zealand Wellington Mission. My companion and I were teaching a man and his wife. One day, this man asked my companion and me to go with him to catch an eel. We consented. He drove his vehicle and we took ours. On our way to the ocean, he stopped at a pub to get a flagon of beer. When we were ready to leave, I asked this man, 'Do you want us to follow you home?'

"'No, I know the way home.'

"Well, he was pulled over for a burned-out taillight and also got a ticket for a DUI. Later he said, 'Mormons don't drink; I will join the Church.'"

Carl Cordingley

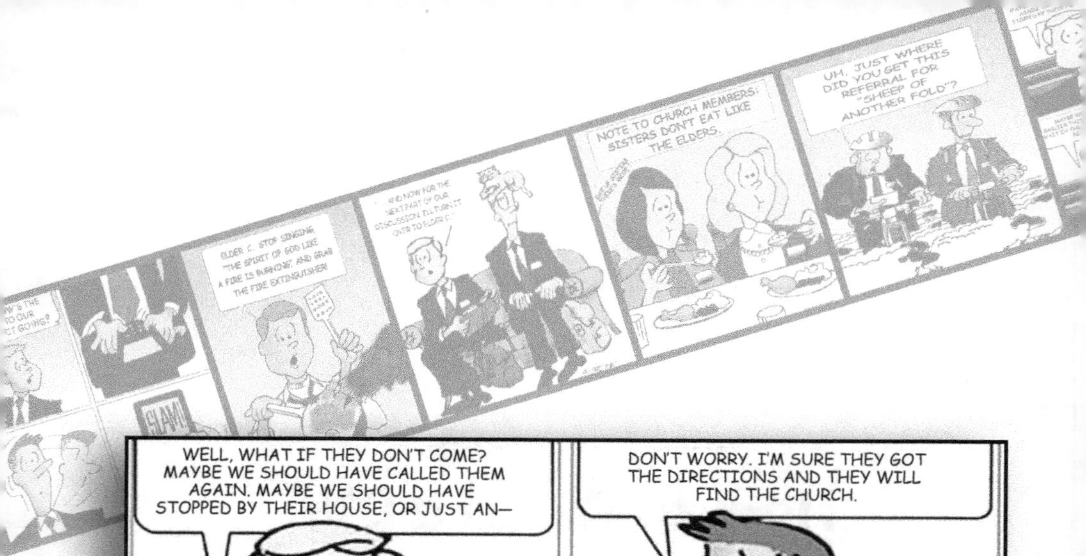
ELDER C. STOP SINGING "THE SPIRIT OF GOD LIKE A FIRE IS BURNING," AND GRAB THE FIRE EXTINGUISHER!
AND NOW FOR THE NEXT PART OF OUR DISCUSSION I'LL TURN IT OVER TO ELDER C.
NOTE TO CHURCH MEMBERS: SISTERS DON'T EAT LIKE THE ELDERS.
UH, JUST WHERE DID YOU GET THIS REFERRAL FOR "SHEEP OF ANOTHER FOLD"?

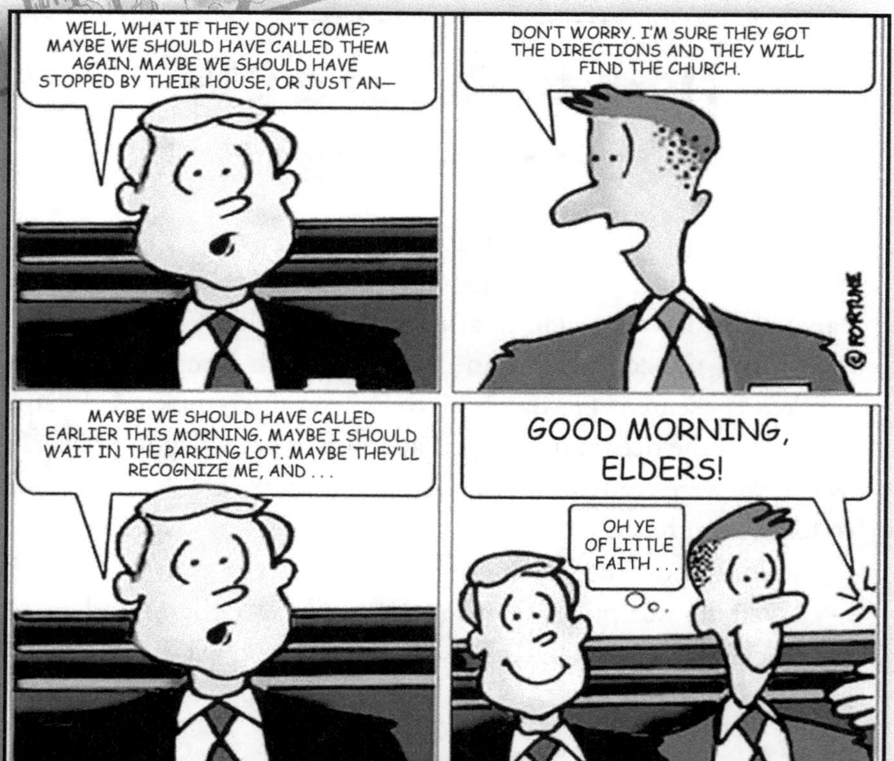
WELL, WHAT IF THEY DON'T COME? MAYBE WE SHOULD HAVE CALLED THEM AGAIN. MAYBE WE SHOULD HAVE STOPPED BY THEIR HOUSE, OR JUST AN—
DON'T WORRY. I'M SURE THEY GOT THE DIRECTIONS AND THEY WILL FIND THE CHURCH.
© FORTUNE
MAYBE WE SHOULD HAVE CALLED EARLIER THIS MORNING. MAYBE I SHOULD WAIT IN THE PARKING LOT. MAYBE THEY'LL RECOGNIZE ME, AND . . .
GOOD MORNING, ELDERS!
OH YE OF LITTLE FAITH . . .

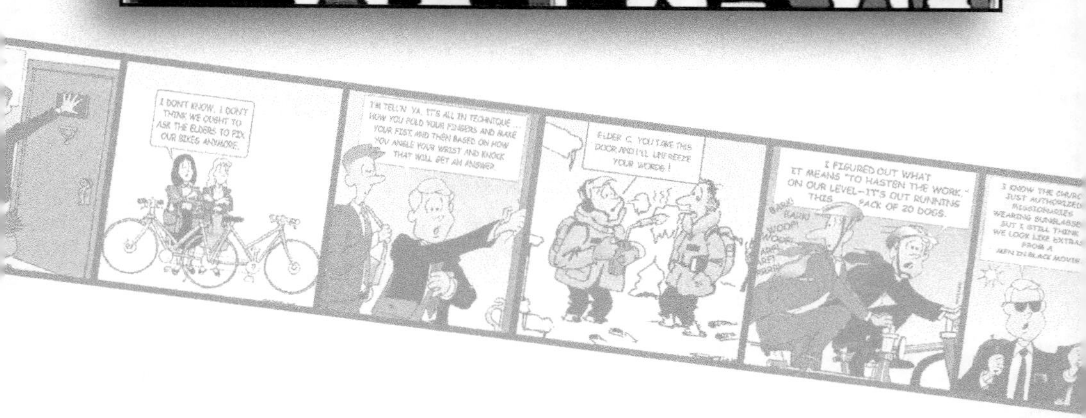
I DON'T KNOW, I DON'T THINK WE OUGHT TO ASK THE ELDERS TO FIX OUR BIKES ANYMORE.
I FIGURED OUT WHAT IT MEANS "TO HASTEN THE WORK" ON OUR LEVEL—IT'S OUT RUNNING THIS PACK OF 20 DOGS.

Mormons Have a Prophet Too?

"We were talking to various people about the teachings of the Church. While visiting with a man, I said, 'My companion and I are missionaries for The Church of Jesus Christ of Latter-day Saints, and we believe we have a prophet.'

"To our great surprise, this man declared, 'You better watch out for those Mormons. They think they have a prophet too.'"

Carl Cordingley

Lack of Faith or Cell Phone?

Elders Taggart and Roundy were traveling by car to a referral in a rural location. Elder Taggart observed, "It is amazing that cell phones have a GPS installed in them. And, in my opinion, the GPS is the modern version of the Liahona, which an individual worked by faith."

Having no success in finding the referral, Elder Roundy teased, "You're saying we are lost because you left your cell phone in the apartment; therefore, you lack the modern version of faith?"

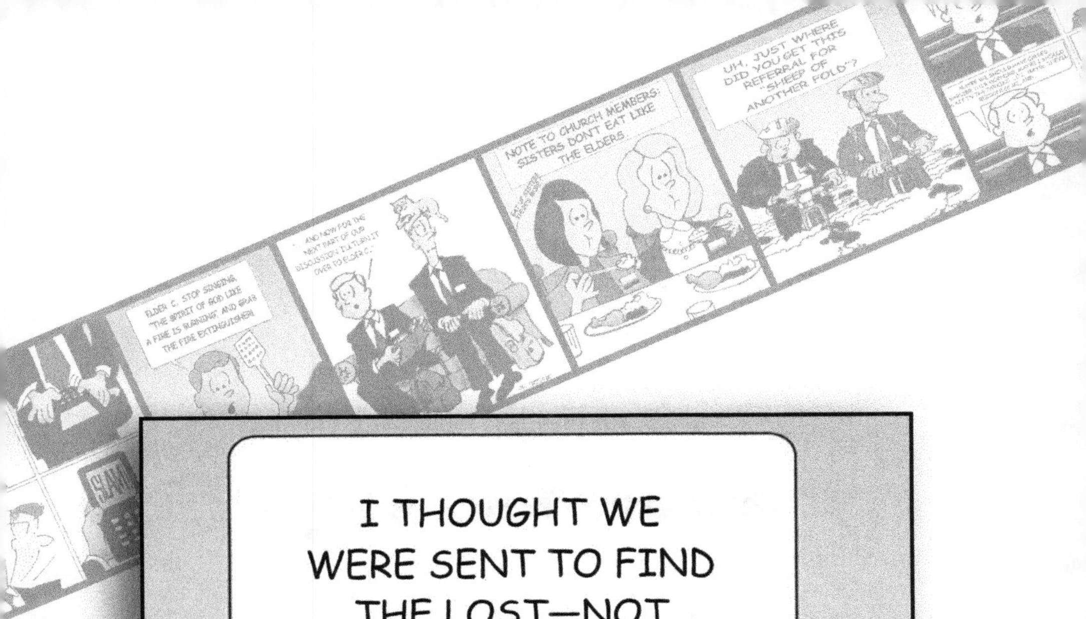
ELDER C. STOP SINGING "THE SPIRIT OF GOD LIKE A FIRE IS BURNING," AND GRAB THE FIRE EXTINGUISHER.
AND NOW FOR THE NEXT PART OF OUR DISCUSSION I'LL TURN IT OVER TO ELDER C.
NOTE TO CHURCH MEMBERS: SISTERS DON'T EAT LIKE THE ELDERS.
UH, JUST WHERE DID YOU GET THIS REFERRAL FOR "SHEEP OF ANOTHER FOLD"?

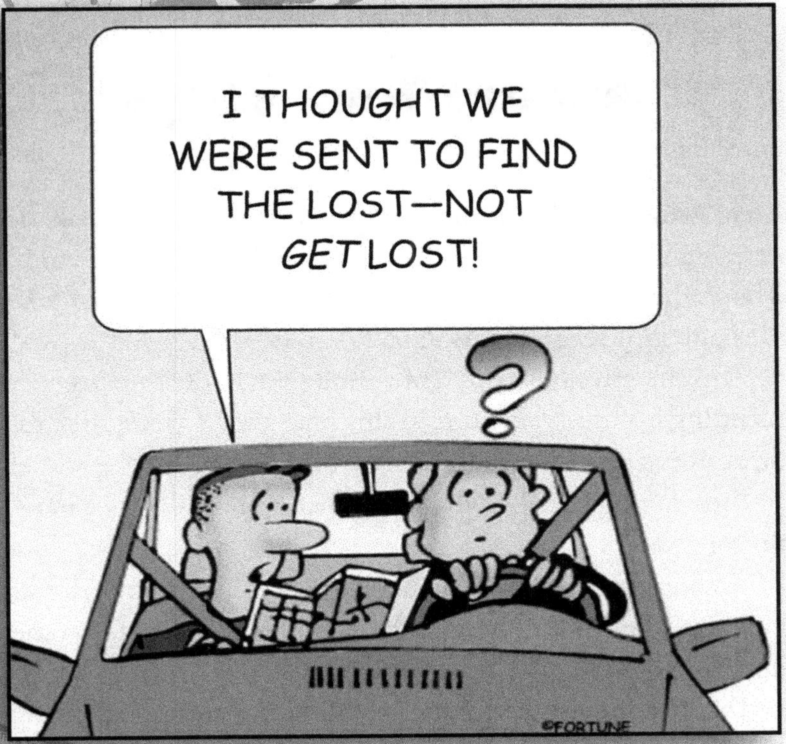
I THOUGHT WE WERE SENT TO FIND THE LOST—NOT *GET* LOST!
©FORTUNE

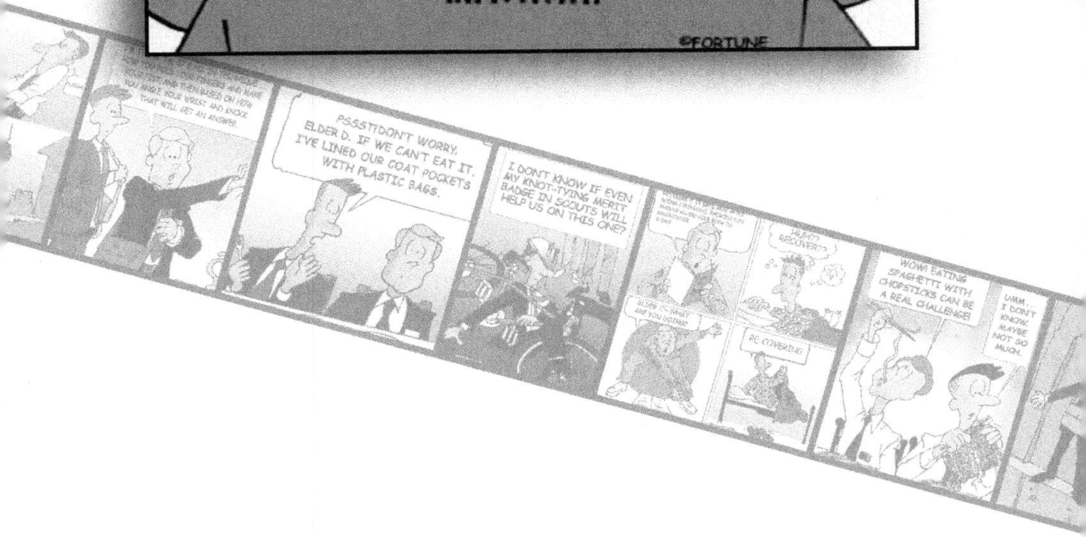
PSSST! DON'T WORRY, ELDER D. IF WE CAN'T EAT IT, I'VE LINED OUR COAT POCKETS WITH PLASTIC BAGS.
I DON'T KNOW IF EVEN MY KNOT-TYING MERIT BADGE IN SCOUTS WILL HELP US ON THIS ONE?
HUH? RECOVER??
RE-COVERING
WOW! EATING SPAGHETTI WITH CHOPSTICKS CAN BE A REAL CHALLENGE!
UMM... I DON'T KNOW. MAYBE NOT SO MUCH.

Amend Your Ways

Sisters Allred and Robinson were visiting with the bishop. They expressed concern for the inactive husband of an active wife. The bishop advised the sisters to be patient. He then related a story that happened several years ago:

"This inactive husband was a good man but felt no urgency in amending his lifestyle. I said to this husband, 'I would like to see you active in the Church and enjoy the blessings of the gospel.'

"The man replied, 'I will come to church when I get straightened out.'

"I continued to visit this man over the years, and the same story was told: 'Well, when I get straightened out, I'll come to Church.'"

The bishop said to the sisters, "Looking at the casket in the front of the chapel, I said to myself, 'This man is finally in a church, and he surely was straightened out!'"

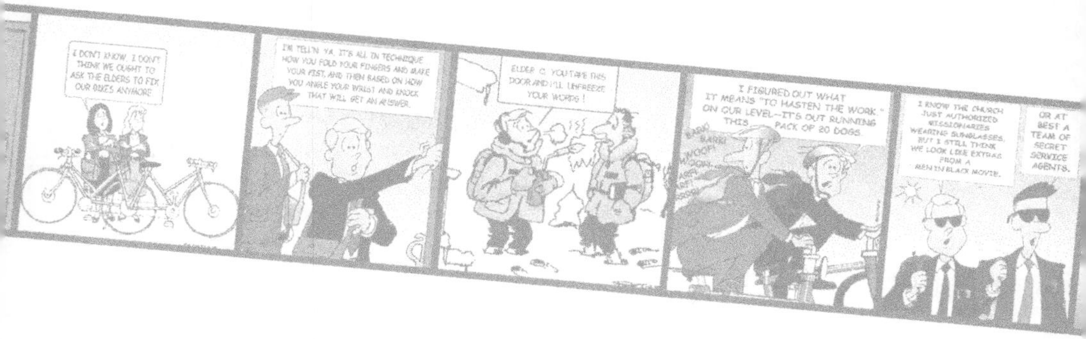
I DON'T KNOW. I DON'T THINK WE OUGHT TO ASK THE ELDERS TO FIX OUR BIKES ANYMORE.
I'M TELL'N YA, IT'S ALL IN TECHNIQUE HOW YOU FOLD YOUR FINGERS AND MAKE YOUR FIST, AND THEN BASED ON HOW YOU ANGLE YOUR WRIST AND KNOCK THAT WILL GET AN ANSWER.
ELDER C. YOU TAKE THIS DOOR AND I'LL UNFREEZE YOUR WORDS!
I FIGURED OUT WHAT IT MEANS "TO HASTEN THE WORK" ON OUR LEVEL--IT'S OUT RUNNING THIS PACK OF 20 DOGS.
BARK! BARK!
WOOF!
I KNOW THE CHURCH JUST AUTHORIZED MISSIONARIES WEARING SUNGLASSES, BUT I STILL THINK WE LOOK LIKE EXTRAS FROM A MEN IN BLACK MOVIE.
OR AT BEST A TEAM OF SECRET SERVICE AGENTS.

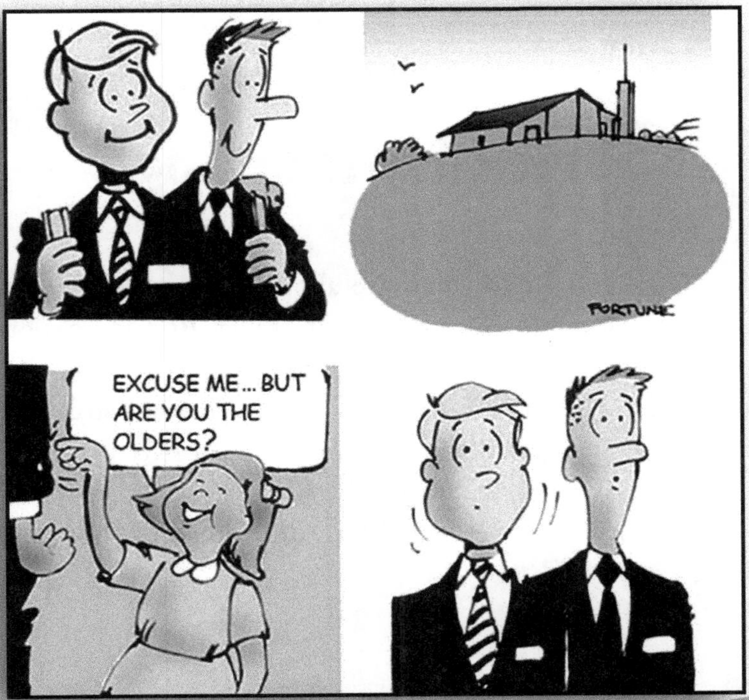
FORTUNE
EXCUSE ME... BUT ARE YOU THE OLDERS?

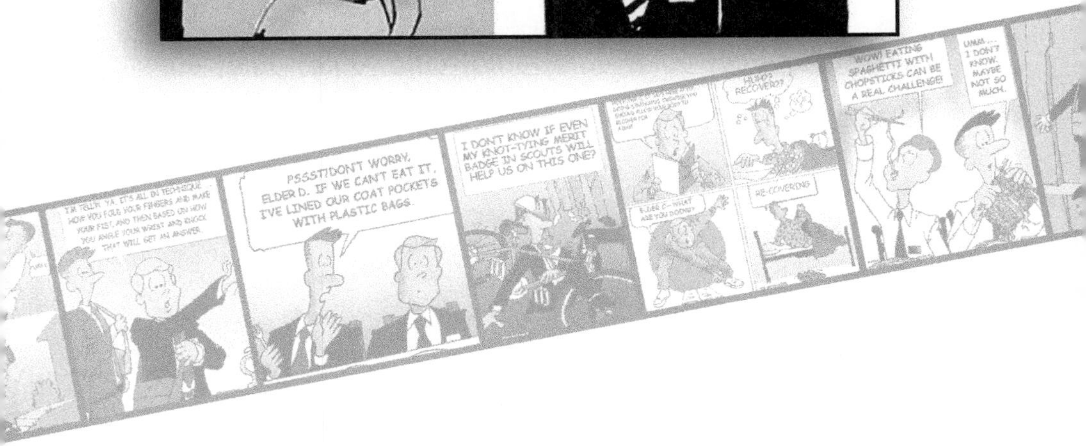
I'M TELL'N YA, IT'S ALL IN TECHNIQUE HOW YOU FOLD YOUR FINGERS AND MAKE YOUR FIST, AND THEN BASED ON HOW YOU ANGLE YOUR WRIST AND KNOCK THAT WILL GET AN ANSWER.
PSSST! DON'T WORRY, ELDER D. IF WE CAN'T EAT IT, I'VE LINED OUR COAT POCKETS WITH PLASTIC BAGS.
I DON'T KNOW IF EVEN MY KNOT-TYING MERIT BADGE IN SCOUTS WILL HELP US ON THIS ONE?
HUH? RECOVER??
ELDER C--WHAT ARE YOU DOING?
RE-COVERING
WOW! EATING SPAGHETTI WITH CHOPSTICKS CAN BE A REAL CHALLENGE!
UMM... I DON'T KNOW. MAYBE NOT SO MUCH.

Trick-or-Tracting

Elders Hyer and Rodriquez were about to have evening prayer on Halloween night. As they knelt, Elder Rodriquez noticed that Elder Hyer's backpack was stuffed with Halloween candy. When Elder Hyer had gone on a split with the ward mission leader that evening, while at the trunk-or-treat party, the parents gave him candy as a gift to the elders. Not knowing this, Elder Rodriquez suspiciously asked, "Elder, did you go trick-or-tracting tonight?"

For Crying Out Loud

Elders Scott and Fry arrived late for sacrament meeting and could only find seating in the stage located in the gym that this particular ward had designated for fussy or crying babies, referred to as the 'Cry Room.' Elder Fry stated, "It is my opinion that babies are closer to heaven more than anything on this earth."

Annoyed by the sound, Elder Scott replied, "Unless it is close to this Cry Room."

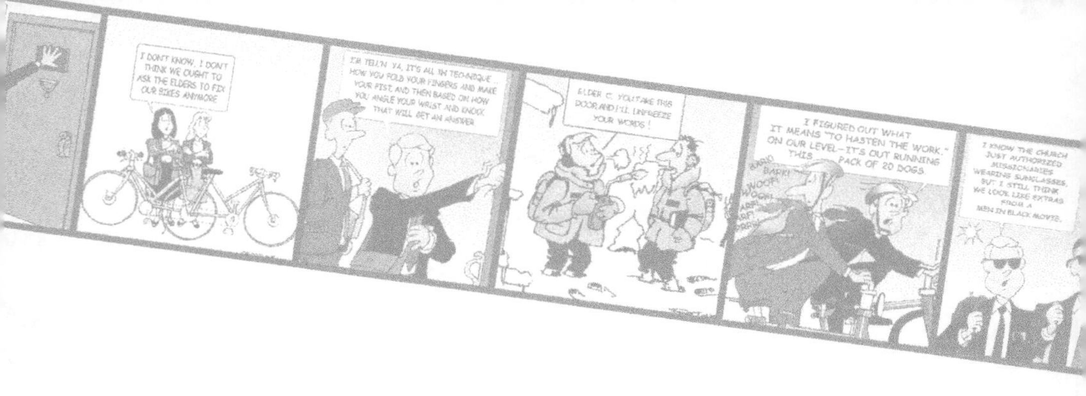
I DON'T KNOW. I DON'T THINK WE OUGHT TO ASK THE ELDERS TO FIX OUR BIKES ANYMORE
I'M TELL'N YA, IT'S ALL IN TECHNIQUE... HOW YOU FOLD YOUR FINGERS AND MAKE YOUR FIST, AND THEN BASED ON HOW YOU ANGLE YOUR WRIST AND KNOCK THAT WILL GET AN ANSWER
ELDER C. YOU TAKE THIS DOOR AND I'LL UNFREEZE YOUR WORDS!
I FIGURED OUT WHAT IT MEANS "TO HASTEN THE WORK." ON OUR LEVEL—IT'S OUT RUNNING THIS PACK OF 20 DOGS.
I KNOW THE CHURCH JUST AUTHORIZED MISSIONARIES WEARING SUNGLASSES, BUT I STILL THINK WE LOOK LIKE EXTRAS FROM A MEN IN BLACK MOVIE.

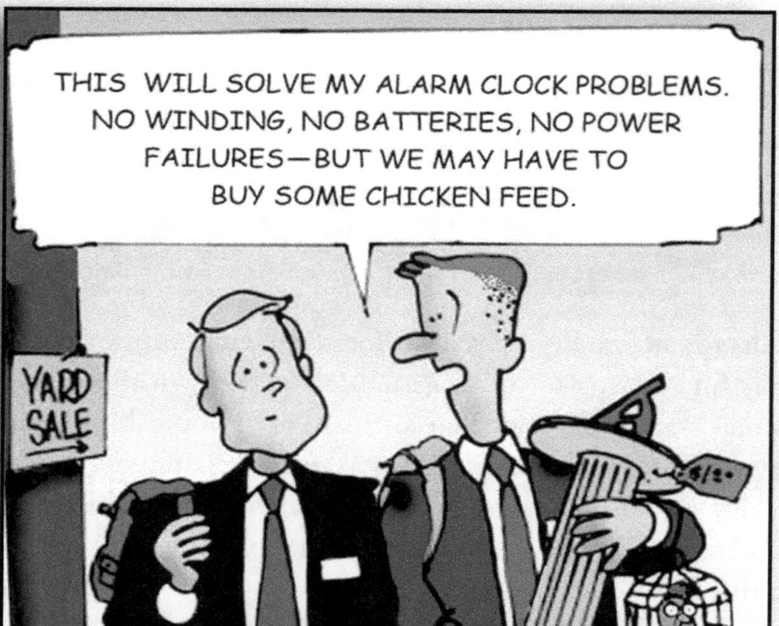
THIS WILL SOLVE MY ALARM CLOCK PROBLEMS. NO WINDING, NO BATTERIES, NO POWER FAILURES—BUT WE MAY HAVE TO BUY SOME CHICKEN FEED.
YARD SALE
©FORTUNE

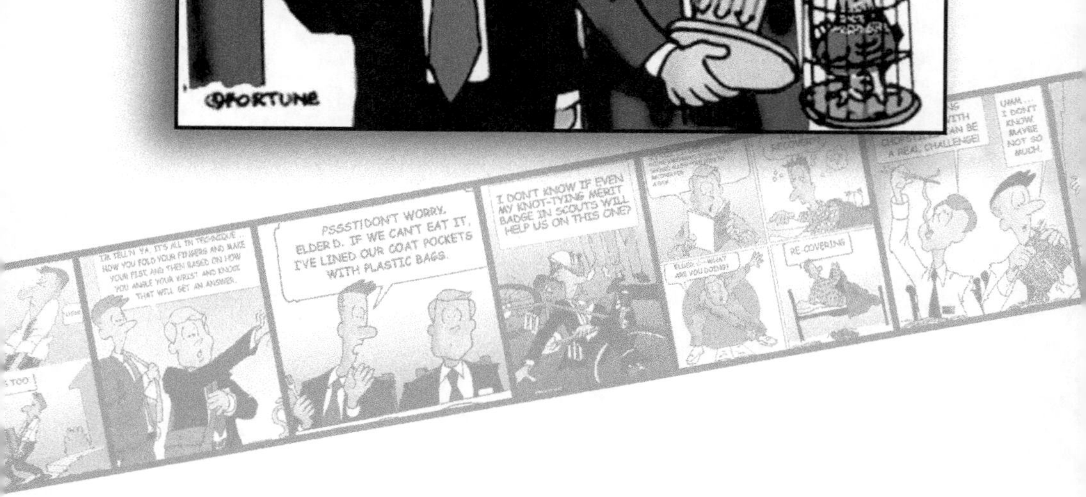
I'M TELL'N YA, IT'S ALL IN TECHNIQUE... HOW YOU FOLD YOUR FINGERS AND MAKE YOUR FIST, AND THEN BASED ON HOW YOU ANGLE YOUR WRIST AND KNOCK THAT WILL GET AN ANSWER.
PSSST! DON'T WORRY, ELDER D. IF WE CAN'T EAT IT, I'VE LINED OUR COAT POCKETS WITH PLASTIC BAGS.
I DON'T KNOW IF EVEN MY KNOT-TYING MERIT BADGE IN SCOUTS WILL HELP US ON THIS ONE?
RE-COVERING
A REAL CHALLENGE!
UMM... I DON'T KNOW. MAYBE NOT SO MUCH.

Finding the Seat of
the Problem

Sisters Stevens and Smith had just come from an appointment. They sat down in their car, and Sister Smith wanted to make a few phone calls before going to another appointment. At that same moment, the cell phone began to ring. Puzzled, Sister Smith quickly looked through her purse and then the back seat. Still not knowing where the sound was coming from, she turned to Sister Stevens in a panic and asked, "Where is the phone?"

They discovered that when Sister Smith entered the car, the phone fell out of her purse and she accidentally sat on it. All Sister Stevens could do was shake her head and laugh.

Lost Sleep in Translation

"Retire to thy bed early, . . . arise early, that your bodies
and your minds may be invigorated." (D&C 88:124)

Sisters Rachel and Simmons had a long night of investigator appointments. The next morning, Sister Simmons tried unsuccessfully to awaken her companion. Finally, shaking the covers, Sister Simmons stated, "The scripture says early to bed and early to rise . . ."

Far from under the covers came the sleepy reply of Sister Rachel: "How do you know it has been translated correctly?"

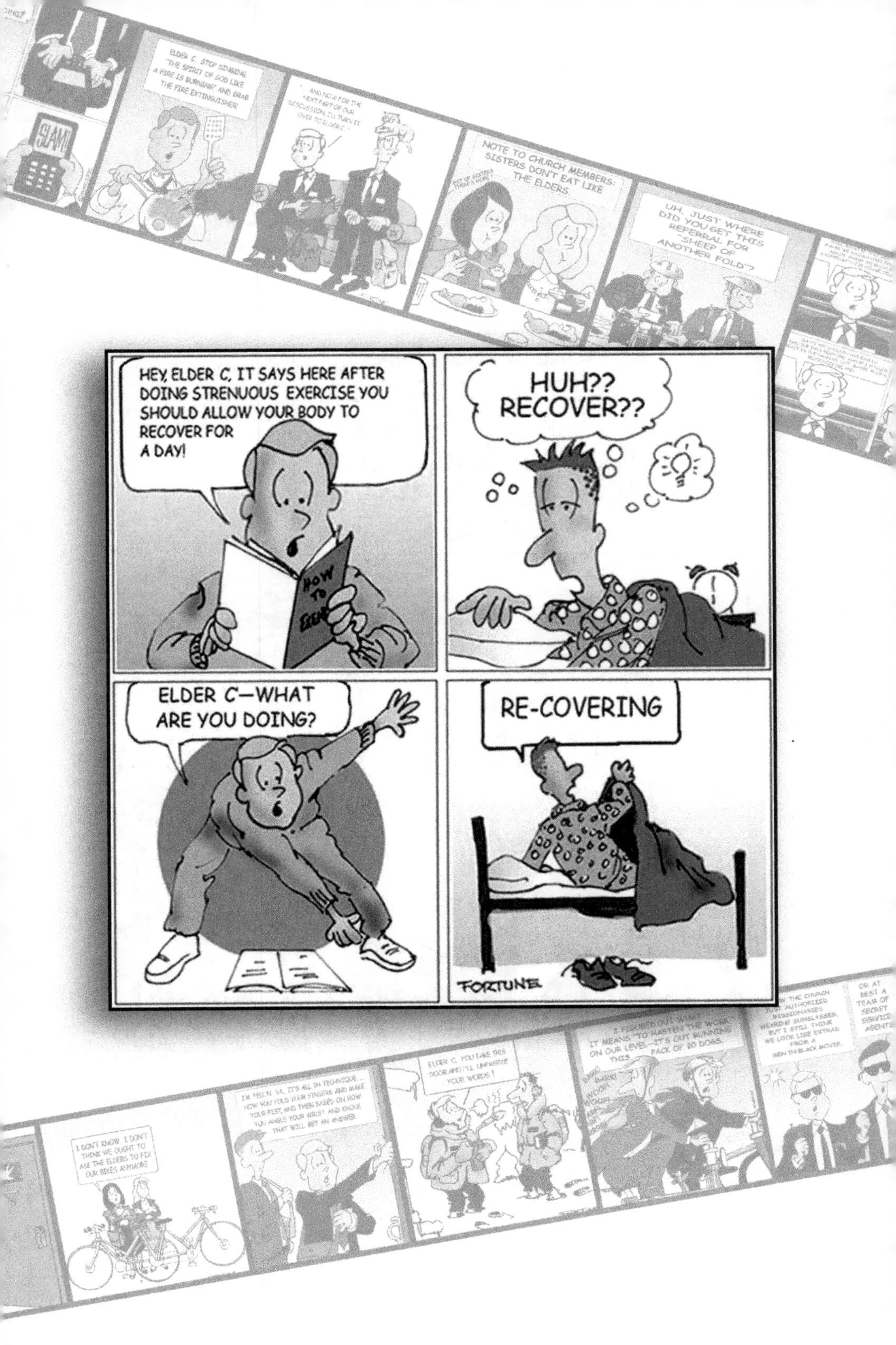
ELDER C. STOP SINGING "THE SPIRIT OF GOD LIKE A FIRE IS BURNING!" AND GRAB THE FIRE EXTINGUISHER!
SLAM!
AND NOW FOR THE NEXT PART OF OUR DISCUSSION, I'LL TURN IT OVER TO ELDER C.
NOTE TO CHURCH MEMBERS: SISTERS DON'T EAT LIKE THE ELDERS.
UH, JUST WHERE DID YOU GET THIS REFERRAL FOR "SHEEP OF ANOTHER FOLD"?
HEY, ELDER C, IT SAYS HERE AFTER DOING STRENUOUS EXERCISE YOU SHOULD ALLOW YOUR BODY TO RECOVER FOR A DAY!
HOW TO
HUH?? RECOVER??
ELDER C—WHAT ARE YOU DOING?
RE-COVERING
FORTUNE
I DON'T KNOW. I DON'T THINK WE OUGHT TO ASK THE ELDERS TO FIX OUR BIKES ANYMORE
I'M TELLIN' YA, IT'S ALL IN TECHNIQUE ... HOW YOU FOLD YOUR FINGERS AND MAKE YOUR FIST, AND THEN BASED ON HOW YOU ANGLE YOUR WRIST AND KNOCK THAT WILL GET AN ANSWER.
ELDER C, YOU TAKE THIS DOOR AND I'LL UNFREEZE YOUR WORDS!
I FIGURED OUT WHAT IT MEANS "TO HASTEN THE WORK ON OUR LEVEL"—IT'S OUT RUNNING THIS PACK OF 20 DOGS.
BARK! BARK!
OR AT BEST A TEAM OF SECRET SERVICE AGENTS

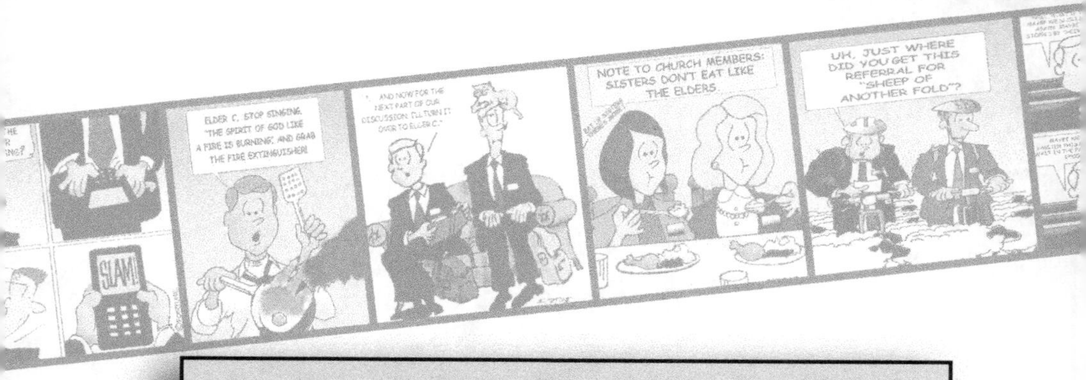
SLAM!
ELDER C, STOP SINGING "THE SPIRIT OF GOD LIKE A FIRE IS BURNING," AND GRAB THE FIRE EXTINGUISHER!
NOTE TO CHURCH MEMBERS: SISTERS DON'T EAT LIKE THE ELDERS.
UH, JUST WHERE DID YOU GET THIS REFERRAL FOR "SHEEP OF ANOTHER FOLD"?

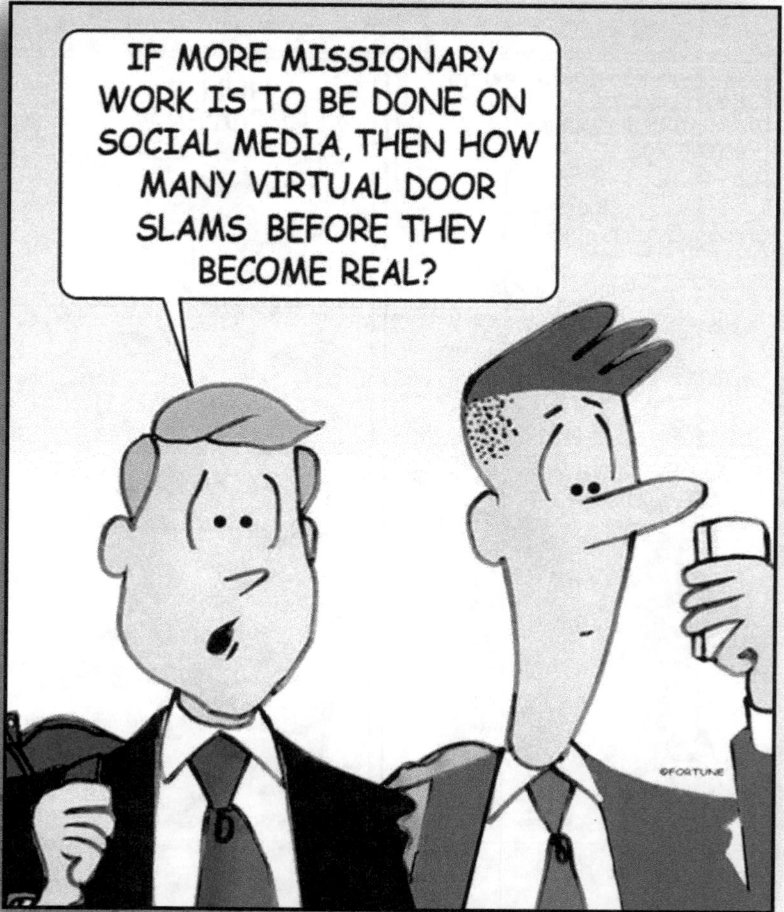
IF MORE MISSIONARY WORK IS TO BE DONE ON SOCIAL MEDIA, THEN HOW MANY VIRTUAL DOOR SLAMS BEFORE THEY BECOME REAL?
©FORTUNE

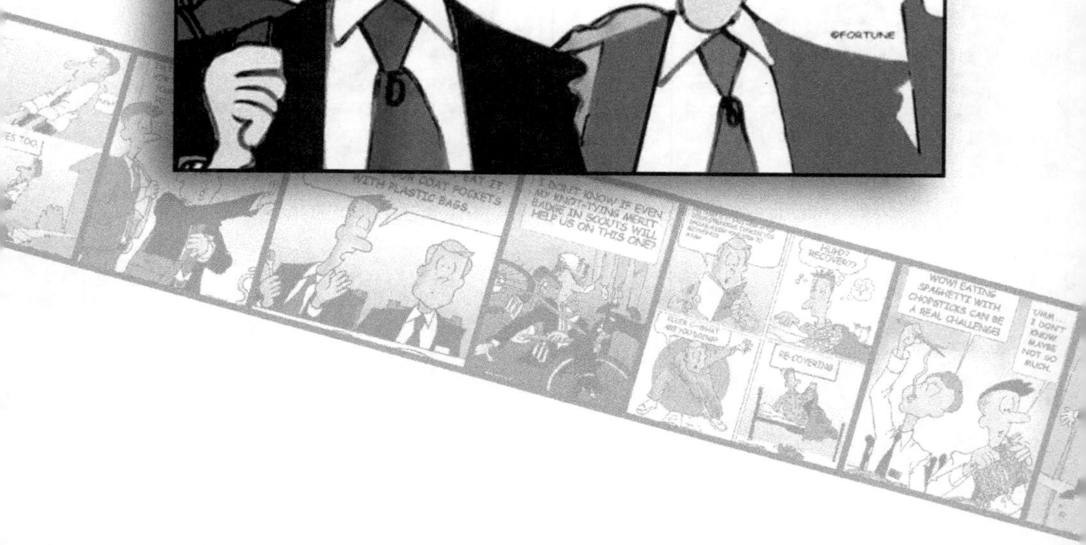
WITH PLASTIC BAGS.
I DON'T KNOW IF EVEN MY KNOT-TYING MERIT BADGE IN SCOUTS WILL HELP US ON THIS ONE?
HUH? RECOVER??
RE-COVERING
WOW! EATING SPAGHETTI WITH CHOPSTICKS CAN BE A REAL CHALLENGE!
UMM... I DON'T KNOW MAYBE NOT SO MUCH.

A Virtual Wreck

"While [I was] serving as a greenie in my first area in Virginia Beach, my trainer and I had a question. We decided to make a telephone call to our district leader and ask him if he knew the answer. My trainer dialed the number, and after a few rings, she heard his voice. 'Hello. This is Elder Grac.'

"My trainer asked him the question. We could hear windy noises on his end of the phone, signifying to us that he was riding his bike while on the phone. Bad idea. Moments later, [while he was] answering our question, we heard a loud bang!

"My trainer asked, 'Are you okay?'

"He replied slowly, 'Man, I just fell off of my bike. I'm so embarrassed.'

"The lesson: Don't text and drive, and more importantly, don't talk and ride, even on the Lord's errand."

Tara Poulsen

Give Me a Book Where the Buffalo Roam

"While [I was] serving . . . in British Columbia, Canada, in 1972, my companion, Elder Peterson, and I were assigned to the little town of Duncan, located on Vancouver Island.

"We walked up to one door [and] knocked on it, and a kindly gentleman in his mid-[fifties] answered the door.

"[Elder Peterson] asked the man, 'Have you ever read the Book of Mormon?' [to] which the man quickly replied, 'Yes, I have read it many times and am not interested in hearing what it has to say.'

"Upon hearing this, Elder Peterson quickly responded, 'Oh, so you have read the Book of Mormon? How did you like the part about Brigham Young riding across the plains on the back of a buffalo to Utah?'

"This gentleman's response, 'Well you know, it's all history.'

"*Well, I guess so*, I thought. That was the first and last time Elder Peterson (or I) ever asked that question!"

Mike Poulos

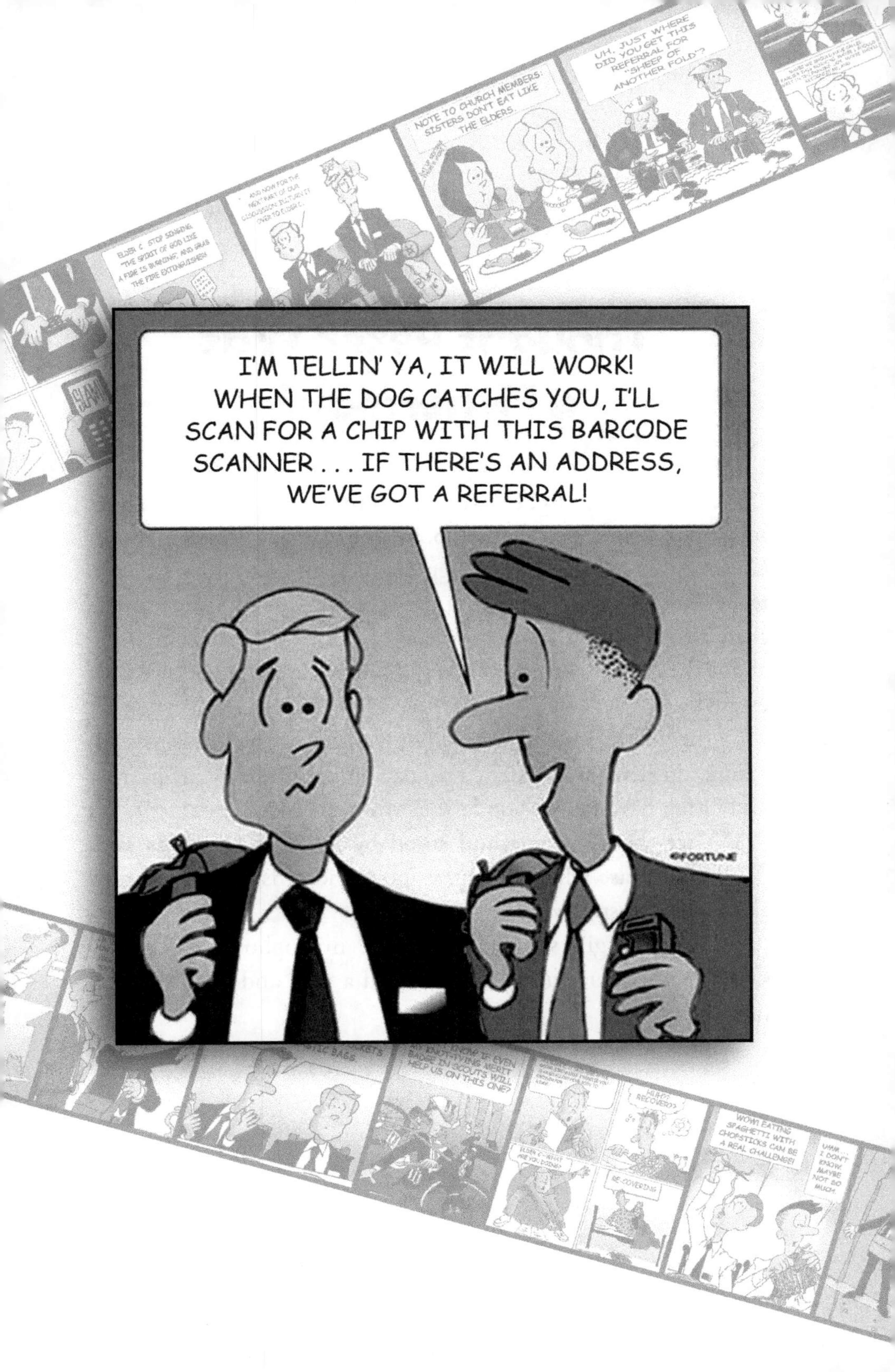
UH. JUST WHERE DID YOU GET THIS REFERRAL FOR "SHEEP OF ANOTHER FOLD"?
NOTE TO CHURCH MEMBERS: SISTERS DON'T EAT LIKE THE ELDERS.
ELDER C. STOP SINGING "THE SPIRIT OF GOD LIKE A FIRE IS BURNING," AND GRAB THE FIRE EXTINGUISHER!
I'M TELLIN' YA, IT WILL WORK! WHEN THE DOG CATCHES YOU, I'LL SCAN FOR A CHIP WITH THIS BARCODE SCANNER . . . IF THERE'S AN ADDRESS, WE'VE GOT A REFERRAL!
©FORTUNE
HUH? RECOVER??
RE-COVERING
WOW! EATING SPAGHETTI WITH CHOP-STICKS CAN BE A REAL CHALLENGE!
UMM . . . I DON'T KNOW. MAYBE NOT SO MUCH.

Thought Peter Was a Fisherman?

"Sisters Baum and Egbert were asked to speak in Primary about missionary work. Before they spoke, the Primary president, Sister Collins, was telling the children about Jesus calling twelve men to be Apostles and Peter being the senior member. Sister Collins then asked if there was anyone who could tell her something about the Apostle Peter. A little girl raised her hand and waved it excitedly.

"Thrilled to see someone so enthusiastic, Sister Collins said, 'Come up here, sweetheart. I'm glad to know that your mother and father have taught you lessons from the New Testament.'

"After the girl came and stood by her, Sister Collins said, 'Will you please tell all the other boys and girls what you know about the Apostle Peter?'

"The little girl stepped up to the microphone and clearly said, 'Peter, Peter, pumpkin eater, had a wife and couldn't keep her . . .'"

Linda Rawlings

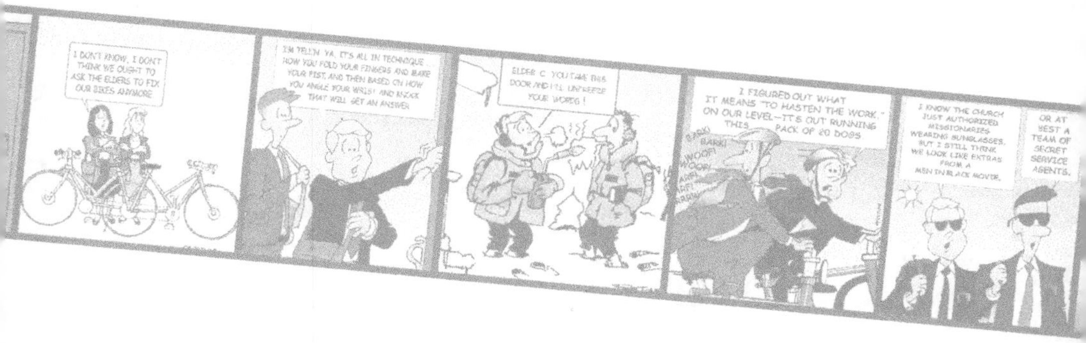
I DON'T KNOW, I DON'T THINK WE OUGHT TO ASK THE ELDERS TO FIX OUR BIKES ANYMORE.
I'M TELL'N YA, IT'S ALL IN TECHNIQUE. HOW YOU FOLD YOUR FINGERS AND MAKE YOUR FIST, AND THEN BASED ON HOW YOU ANGLE YOUR WRIST AND KNOCK THAT WILL GET AN ANSWER.
ELDER C. YOU TAKE THIS DOOR AND I'LL UNFREEZE YOUR WORDS!
I FIGURED OUT WHAT IT MEANS "TO HASTEN THE WORK" ON OUR LEVEL—IT'S OUT RUNNING THIS PACK OF 20 DOGS
I KNOW THE CHURCH JUST AUTHORIZED MISSIONARIES WEARING SUNGLASSES, BUT I STILL THINK WE LOOK LIKE EXTRAS FROM A MEN IN BLACK MOVIE.
OR AT BEST A TEAM OF SECRET SERVICE AGENTS.

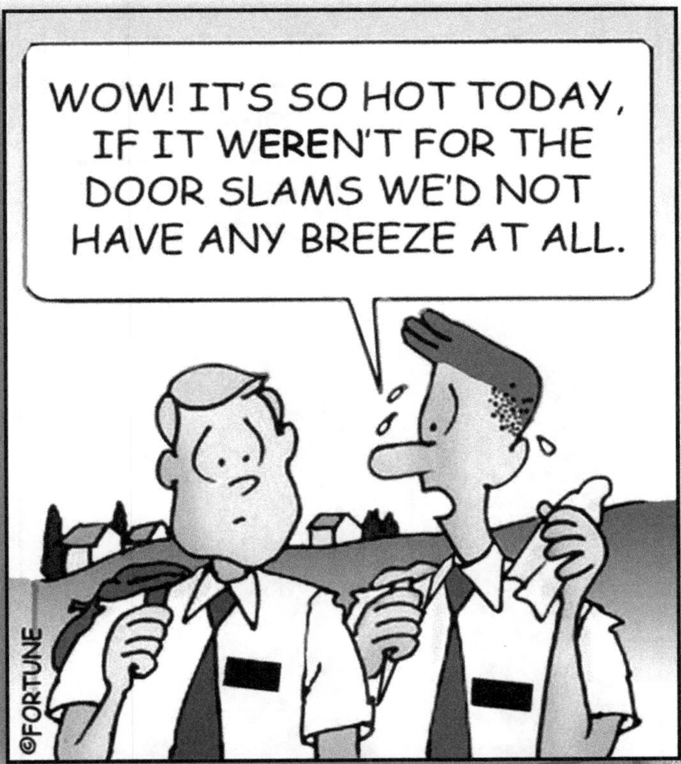
WOW! IT'S SO HOT TODAY, IF IT WEREN'T FOR THE DOOR SLAMS WE'D NOT HAVE ANY BREEZE AT ALL.
©FORTUNE

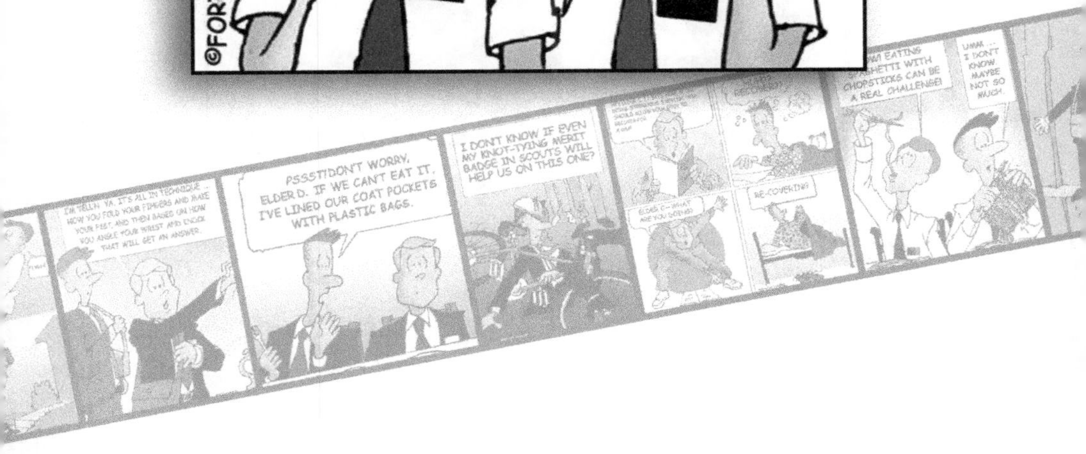
PSSST! DON'T WORRY, ELDER D. IF WE CAN'T EAT IT, I'VE LINED OUR COAT POCKETS WITH PLASTIC BAGS.
I DON'T KNOW IF EVEN MY KNOT-TYING MERIT BADGE IN SCOUTS WILL HELP US ON THIS ONE?
EATING SPAGHETTI WITH CHOPSTICKS CAN BE A REAL CHALLENGE!
UMM... I DON'T KNOW. MAYBE NOT SO MUCH.

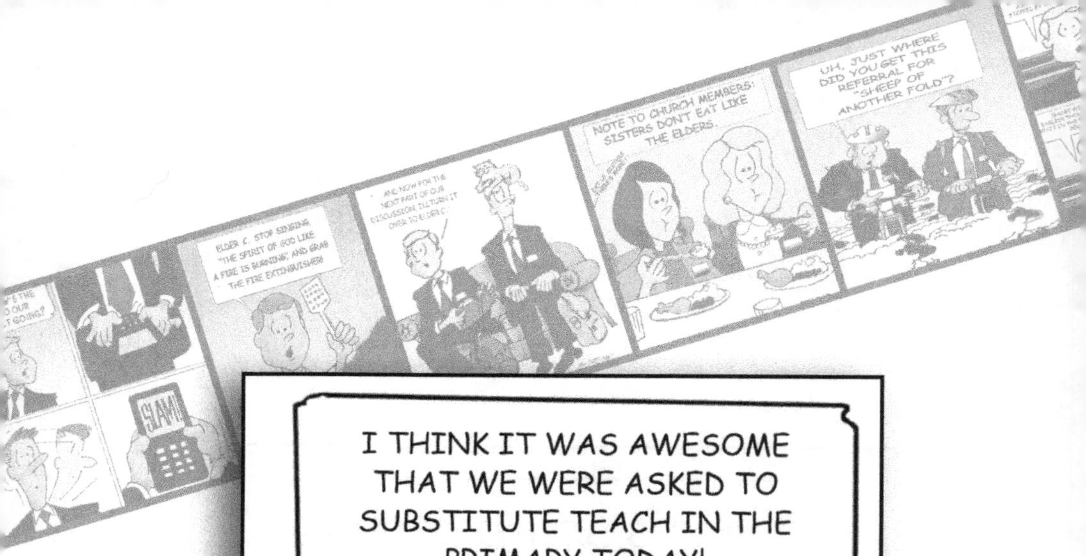
ELDER C. STOP SINGING "THE SPIRIT OF GOD LIKE A FIRE IS BURNING," AND GRAB THE FIRE EXTINGUISHER!
AND NOW FOR THE NEXT PART OF OUR DISCUSSION I'LL TURN IT OVER TO ELDER C.
NOTE TO CHURCH MEMBERS: SISTERS DON'T EAT LIKE THE ELDERS.
UH, JUST WHERE DID YOU GET THIS REFERRAL FOR "SHEEP OF ANOTHER FOLD"?
SLAM!

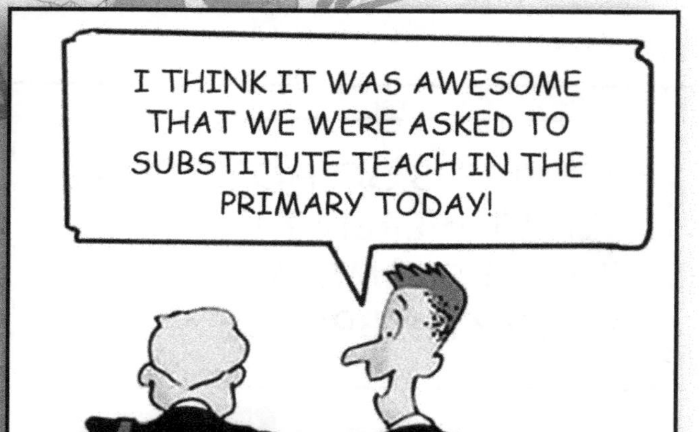
I THINK IT WAS AWESOME THAT WE WERE ASKED TO SUBSTITUTE TEACH IN THE PRIMARY TODAY!

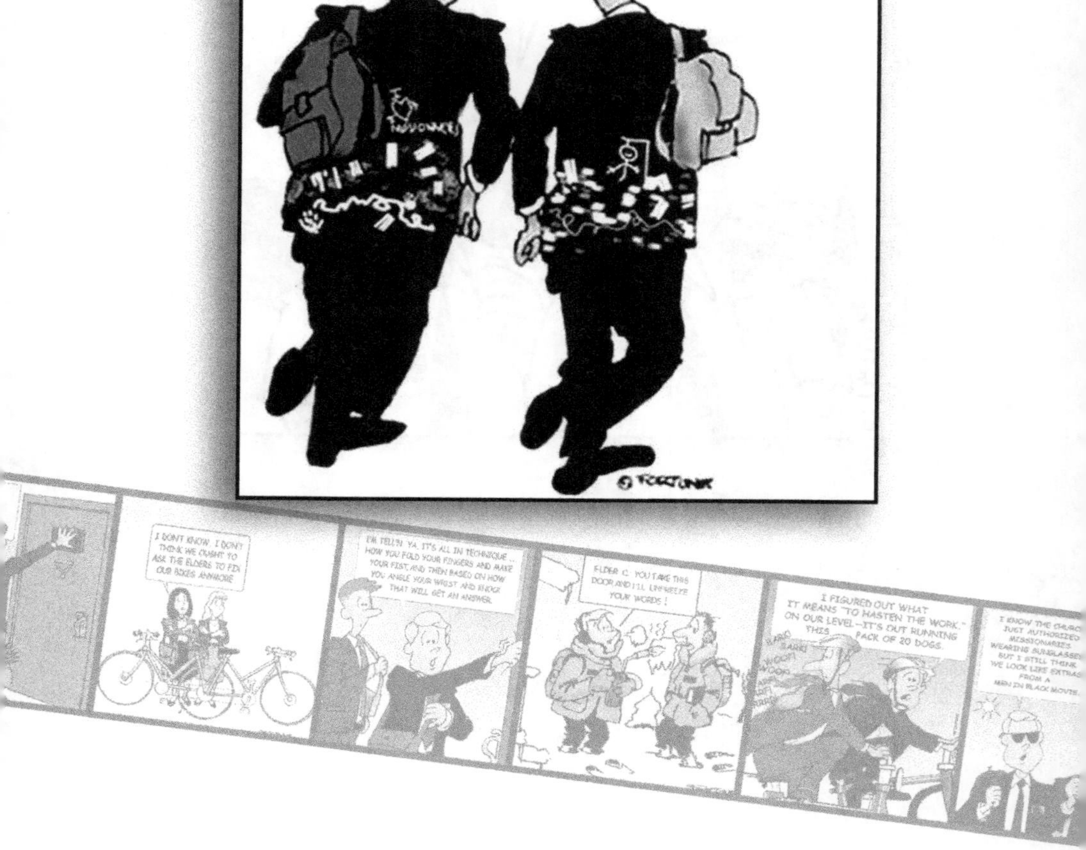
I DON'T KNOW. I DON'T THINK WE OUGHT TO ASK THE ELDERS TO FIX OUR BIKES ANYMORE
I'M TELL'N YA, IT'S ALL IN TECHNIQUE... HOW YOU FOLD YOUR FINGERS AND MAKE YOUR FIST, AND THEN BASED ON HOW YOU ANGLE YOUR WRIST AND KNOCK THAT WILL GET AN ANSWER.
ELDER C. YOU TAKE THIS DOOR AND I'LL UNFREEZE YOUR WORDS!
I FIGURED OUT WHAT IT MEANS "TO HASTEN THE WORK" ON OUR LEVEL—IT'S OUT RUNNING THIS PACK OF 20 DOGS.

Eating Your Own Words

At a three-zone conference, President Brown was giving counsel to the missionaries about thinking before speaking. To illustrate, he said, "When I was a priest in the Aaronic Priesthood, my priest advisor asked the priests, 'Who can tell me who was most upset when the prodigal son returned home after wasting his father's money on riotous living?'

"The class was quiet, until I quipped, 'The fatted calf.'

"To this day, I'm still chagrined to remember what I said. So that you will remember, I give you a short poem:

"Be careful of the words you say,

"Make them soft and sweet.

"For you never know from day to day,

"The ones you'll have to eat."

Christie Porter

Has the Devil Got a Hold on Me?

"My companion, Elder Brenchley, and I decided to visit with the stake president at his home in St. Maries, Idaho. Because it was a hot August day, we left all of the car windows down [before going inside to meet with him]. After discussing missionary activities with the stake president, we entered our car and were about to travel to our next appointment. Without our knowledge, a young kitten had climbed into the back seat. No sooner had I sat down on the passenger seat than this kitten jumped on the back of my left shoulder and dug in with his sharp claws. Super startled and slightly injured, I yelled out loudly. I seriously thought that the devil had seized me. My companion and the kitten were also startled by my yelling, and the kitten jumped out the window and ran away. My companion and I soon had a good laugh. [I] wonder if the devil had one too."

Bruce E. Dana

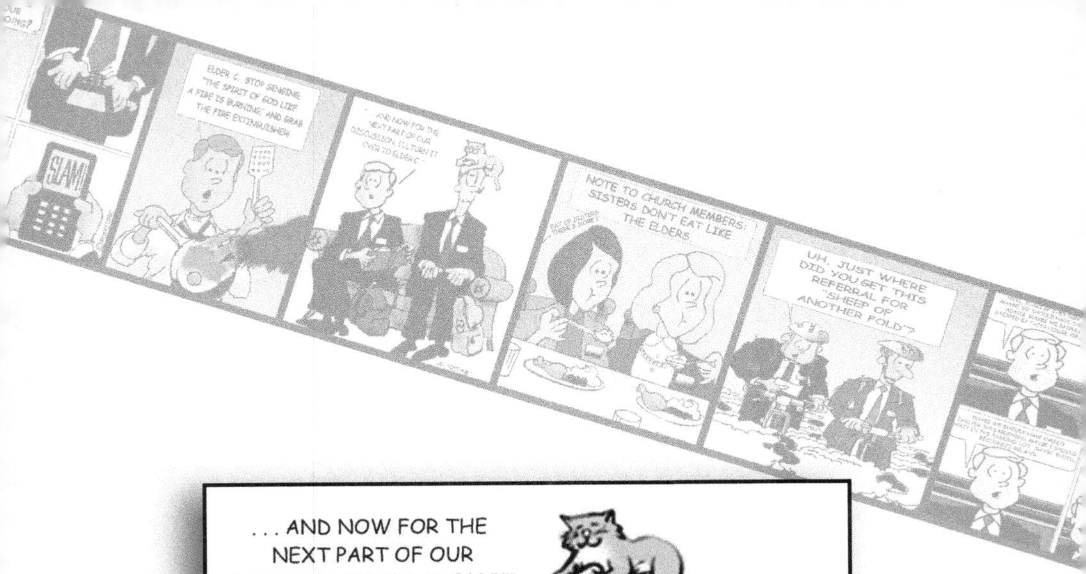
ELDER C, STOP SINGING "THE SPIRIT OF GOD LIKE A FIRE IS BURNING" AND GRAB THE FIRE EXTINGUISHER!
SLAM!
... AND NOW FOR THE NEXT PART OF OUR DISCUSSION, I'LL TURN IT OVER TO ELDER C.
NOTE TO CHURCH MEMBERS: SISTERS DON'T EAT LIKE THE ELDERS.
UH, JUST WHERE DID YOU GET THIS REFERRAL FOR "SHEEP OF ANOTHER FOLD"?

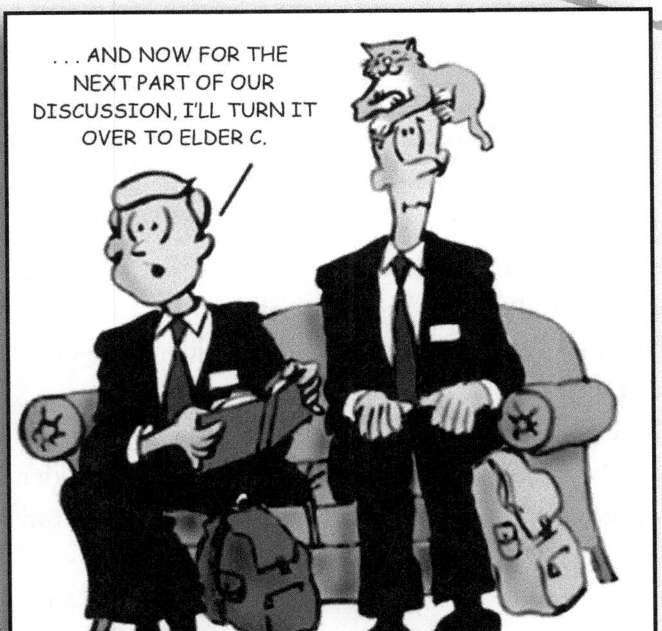
. . . AND NOW FOR THE NEXT PART OF OUR DISCUSSION, I'LL TURN IT OVER TO ELDER C.
FORTUNE

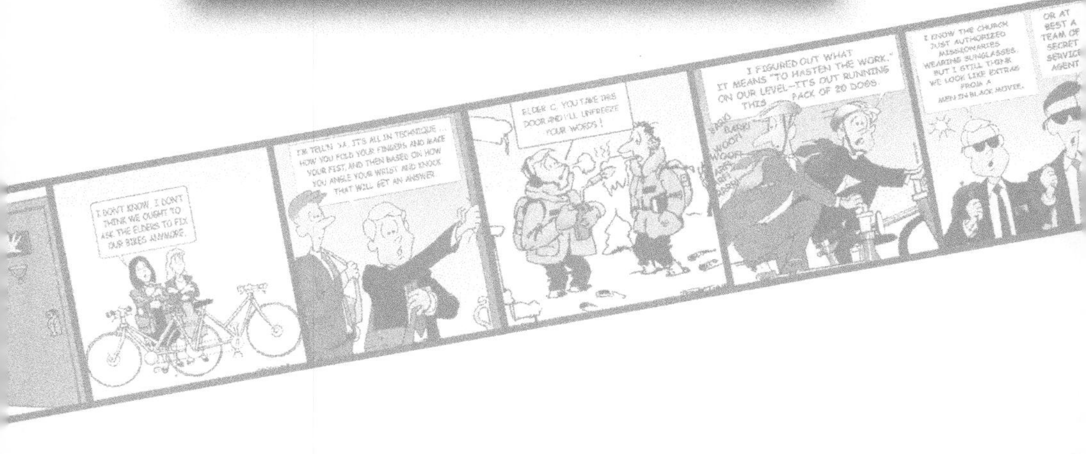
I DON'T KNOW. I DON'T THINK WE OUGHT TO ASK THE ELDERS TO FIX OUR BIKES ANYMORE.
I'M TELL'N YA, IT'S ALL IN TECHNIQUE... HOW YOU FOLD YOUR FINGERS AND MAKE YOUR FIST, AND THEN BASED ON HOW YOU ANGLE YOUR WRIST AND KNOCK THAT WILL GET AN ANSWER
ELDER C, YOU TAKE THIS DOOR AND I'LL UNFREEZE YOUR WORDS!
I FIGURED OUT WHAT IT MEANS "TO HASTEN THE WORK." ON OUR LEVEL—IT'S OUT RUNNING THIS PACK OF 20 DOGS.
I KNOW THE CHURCH JUST AUTHORIZED MISSIONARIES WEARING SUNGLASSES, BUT I STILL THINK WE LOOK LIKE EXTRAS FROM A MEN IN BLACK MOVIE.
OR AT BEST A TEAM OF SECRET SERVICE AGENT

Primary Handful

"Elders Mills and Conger were asked to speak briefly [about missionary work] to the Primary children in opening exercises. Elder Mills was 6 feet, 2 inches tall, and Elder Conger was 6 feet, 7 inches tall [and] had very large hands.

"The children had just finished singing 'I Have Two Little Hands,' when a little girl who was sitting next to Elder Conger seriously asked him, 'What happened to your little hands?'"

Trina Alberts

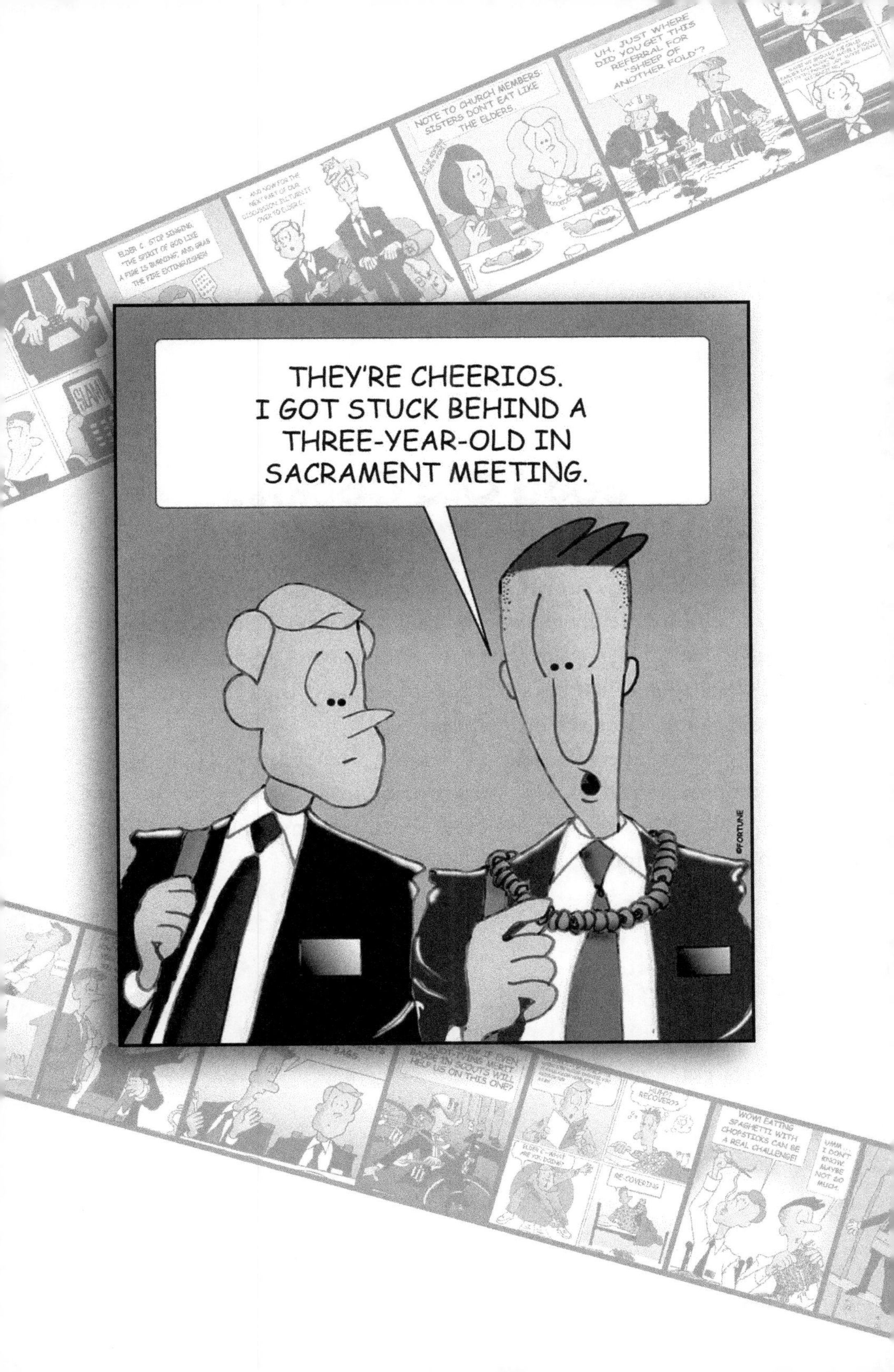
THEY'RE CHEERIOS.
I GOT STUCK BEHIND A
THREE-YEAR-OLD IN
SACRAMENT MEETING.
©FORTUNE
UH, JUST WHERE DID YOU GET THIS REFERRAL FOR "SHEEP OF ANOTHER FOLD"?
NOTE TO CHURCH MEMBERS: SISTERS DON'T EAT LIKE THE ELDERS.
ELDER C. STOP SINGING "THE SPIRIT OF GOD LIKE A FIRE IS BURNING," AND GRAB THE FIRE EXTINGUISHER
HUH? RECOVER??
RE-COVERING
WOW! EATING SPAGHETTI WITH CHOPSTICKS CAN BE A REAL CHALLENGE!
UHM... I DON'T KNOW. MAYBE NOT SO MUCH.

Good Old Cookies

"I invited Elders Brown and Michaels for supper with my family. The children really enjoyed visiting with these elders. At the end of the meal, I served chocolate chip cookies for dessert. Elder Brown took a few bites of his cookie, [and] then he turned and said to me, 'This is a little musty.'

"I was taken [a]back and almost offended, but [I] kept my composure [and asked], 'What do you mean?'

"With a smile on his face, Elder Brown answered, 'Musty have some more.'"

Elisabeth Budge

Many Are Chewin',
but Some Are Full

"My companion, Elder Winger, [and I] were invited by a member family to have dinner at their home. Sister Keller made a delicious meal. At the end of it, Elder Winger, who was from Kentucky, spoke a complimentary expression none of us had ever heard before: 'Mighty fine chewin'.' It sure made Sister Keller's day!"

Troy Wilson

Barking up the Wrong Sock

"My companion, Elder Stott, [and I] were serving a mission in Cali, Colombia. While in this country it was very important for us to eat ALL of the meal that was served. After being completely full from a previous dinner, we were asked again to eat another heavy meal at another member's home. Elder Stott and I were dreading each bite, for we knew that our stomachs couldn't take any more food. Each time we were left alone, we ripped out pages from our notebooks and wrapped the meat and stuffed it into our socks.

"Shortly after we left this member's home, we were chased by some hungry neighborhood dogs, who smelled the meat. While running for many blocks, we quickly reached down and grabbed a piece of wrapped meat from our socks and threw it toward the dogs. Gratefully, after the last piece of meat was thrown, the chase ended."

Kerry Barlow

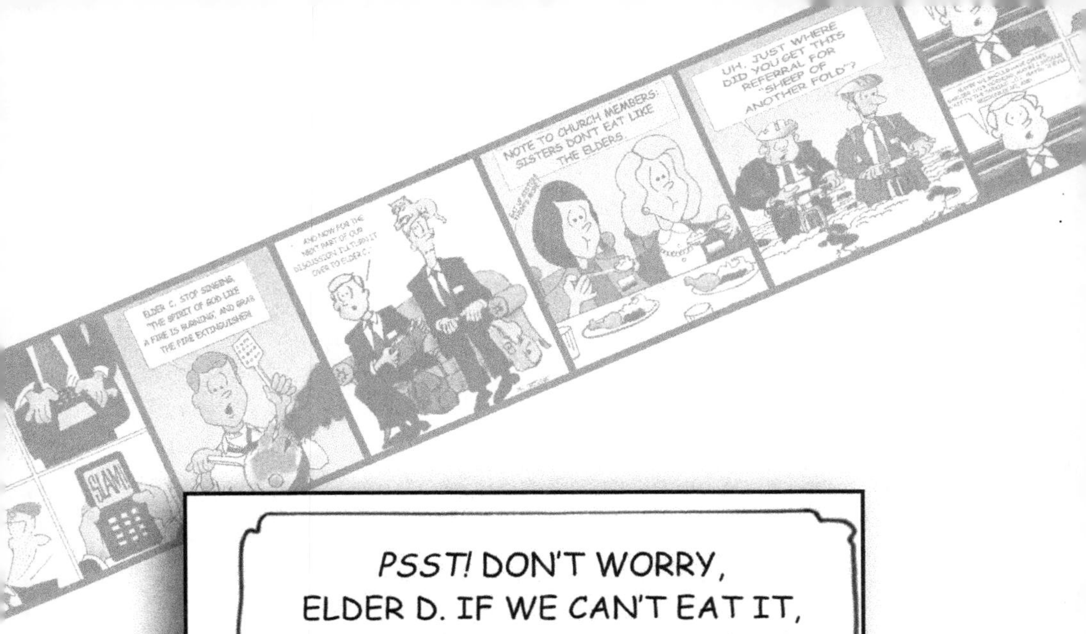
ELDER C. STOP SINGING, "THE SPIRIT OF GOD LIKE A FIRE IS BURNING," AND GRAB THE FIRE EXTINGUISHER!
SLAM
AND NOW FOR THE NEXT PART OF OUR DISCUSSION, I'LL TURN IT OVER TO ELDER C.
NOTE TO CHURCH MEMBERS: SISTERS DON'T EAT LIKE THE ELDERS.
UH, JUST WHERE DID YOU GET THIS REFERRAL FOR "SHEEP OF ANOTHER FOLD"?

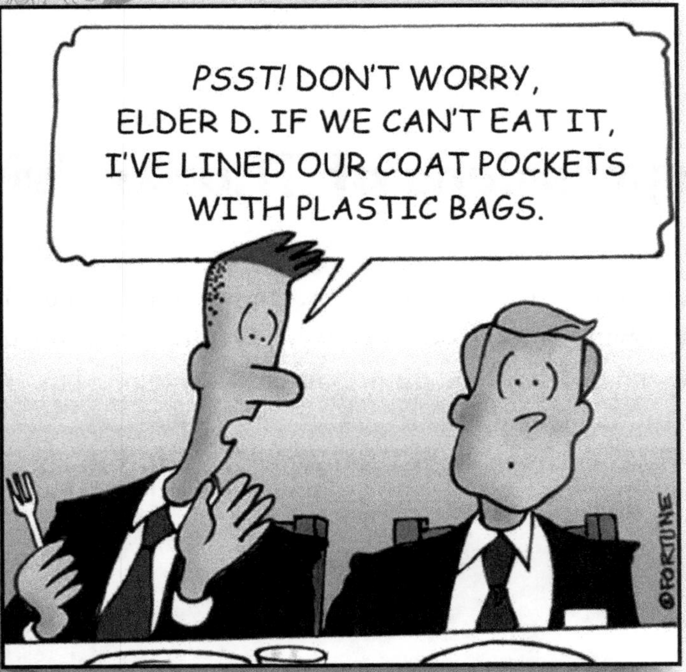
PSST! DON'T WORRY, ELDER D. IF WE CAN'T EAT IT, I'VE LINED OUR COAT POCKETS WITH PLASTIC BAGS.
©FORTUNE

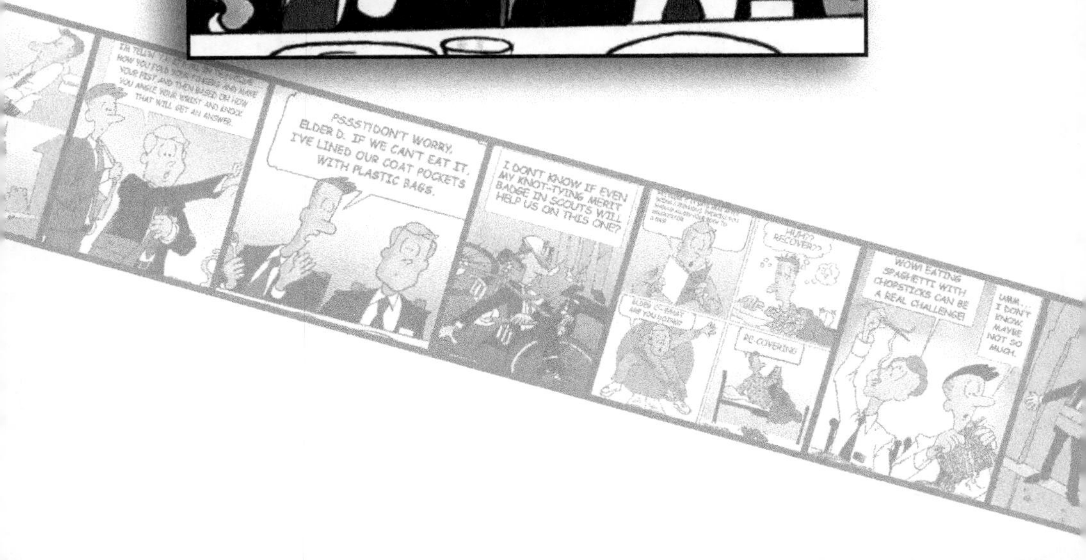
PSSST! DON'T WORRY, ELDER D. IF WE CAN'T EAT IT, I'VE LINED OUR COAT POCKETS WITH PLASTIC BAGS.
I DON'T KNOW IF EVEN MY KNOT-TYING MERIT BADGE IN SCOUTS WILL HELP US ON THIS ONE?
HUH? RECOVER??
RE-COVERING
WOW! EATING SPAGHETTI WITH CHOPSTICKS CAN BE A REAL CHALLENGE!
UMM... I DON'T KNOW. MAYBE NOT SO MUCH.

Expressions of Thanksgiving

"My companion, Sister Stephens, and I were invited to two Thanksgiving dinners, one at 1:00 p.m. and the other at 4:00 p.m. At the end of our second dinner, Sister Wilkins asked us, 'Do you want another serving?'

"My companion smiled and replied, 'I can still chew, but I can't swallow.'"

Pamela Hewitt

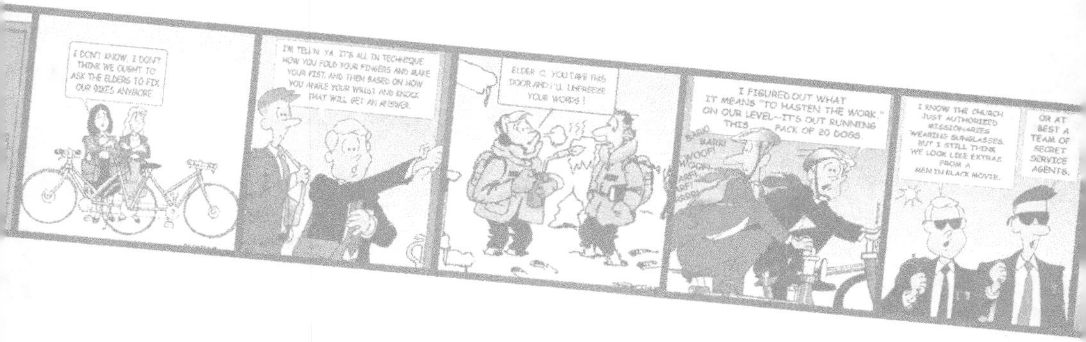
I DON'T KNOW. I DON'T THINK WE OUGHT TO ASK THE ELDERS TO FIX OUR BIKES ANYMORE.
I'M TELLIN' YA, IT'S ALL IN TECHNIQUE: HOW YOU FOLD YOUR FINGERS AND MAKE YOUR FIST, AND THEN BASED ON HOW YOU ANGLE YOUR WRIST AND KNOCK THAT WILL GET AN ANSWER.
ELDER C, YOU TAKE THIS DOOR AND I'LL UNFREEZE YOUR WORDS!
I FIGURED OUT WHAT IT MEANS "TO HASTEN THE WORK." ON OUR LEVEL—IT'S OUT RUNNING THIS PACK OF 20 DOGS.
I KNOW THE CHURCH JUST AUTHORIZED MISSIONARIES WEARING SUNGLASSES. BUT I STILL THINK WE LOOK LIKE EXTRAS FROM A MEN IN BLACK MOVIE.
OR AT BEST A TEAM OF SECRET SERVICE AGENTS.

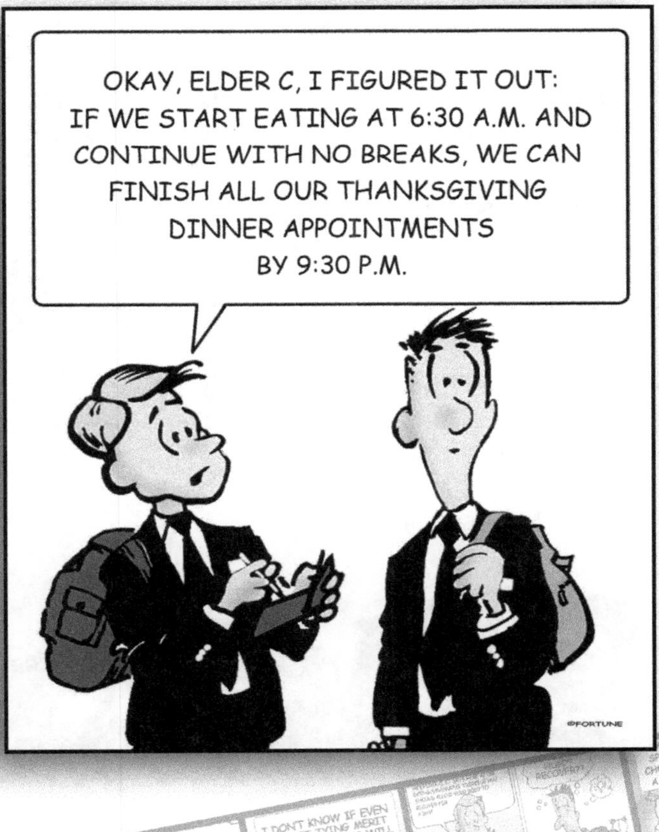
OKAY, ELDER C, I FIGURED IT OUT: IF WE START EATING AT 6:30 A.M. AND CONTINUE WITH NO BREAKS, WE CAN FINISH ALL OUR THANKSGIVING DINNER APPOINTMENTS BY 9:30 P.M.
©FORTUNE

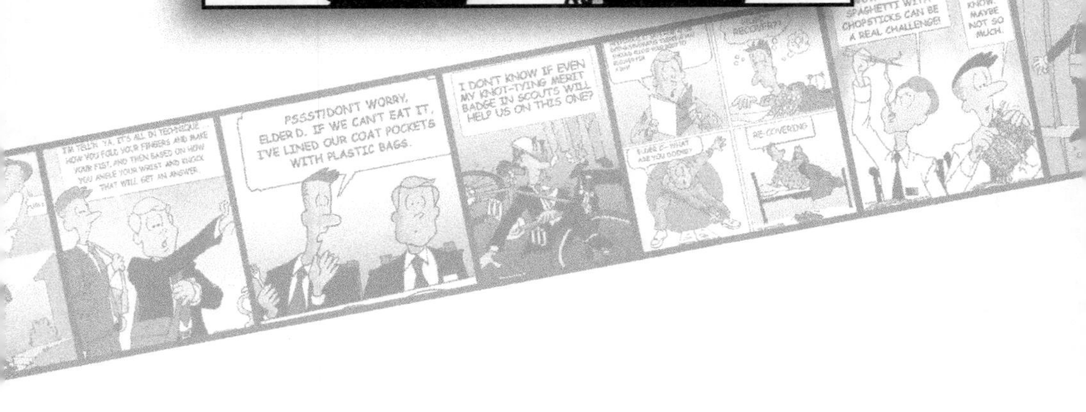
I'M TELLIN' YA, IT'S ALL IN TECHNIQUE: HOW YOU FOLD YOUR FINGERS AND MAKE YOUR FIST, AND THEN BASED ON HOW YOU ANGLE YOUR WRIST AND KNOCK THAT WILL GET AN ANSWER.
PSSST! DON'T WORRY, ELDER D. IF WE CAN'T EAT IT, I'VE LINED OUR COAT POCKETS WITH PLASTIC BAGS.
I DON'T KNOW IF EVEN MY KNOT-TYING MERIT BADGE IN SCOUTS WILL HELP US ON THIS ONE?
WOW! EATING SPAGHETTI WITH CHOPSTICKS CAN BE A REAL CHALLENGE!
UMM... I DON'T KNOW. MAYBE NOT SO MUCH.

A Focused Prayer

"My companion, Sister Douglas, became ill with pneumonia. The doctor who diagnosed the illness admitted her to one of the local hospitals. The elders and sisters in our district came to visit her on a Sunday. In addition to giving her a priesthood blessing, our kind district leader said, 'Each of us is fasting for you, and with your permission, I want to say a prayer for you.'

"Though Sister Douglas didn't feel well, she replied with her typical wit, 'I want a real specific prayer—not bless all sinners.'"

Misty Walker

And on That Note, the Door Shut

"My companion, Elder Haines, and I were proselyting in Anaheim, California. Elder Haines knocked on the front door of a residence, and a middle-aged lady answered. He told her that we were missionaries for The Church of Jesus Christ of Latter-day Saints and had a great message to give her. Politely, she said, 'I'm not interested.'

"Being persistent, Elder Haines replied, 'Elder Fisher, my companion, is a good singer; would it be okay if he at least sings you a short LDS hymn?'

"This woman replied, 'No. But let me sing you a short line from a song. 'So long, farewell, auf wiedersehen, goodbye . . .' The door suddenly shut."

Erick Fisher

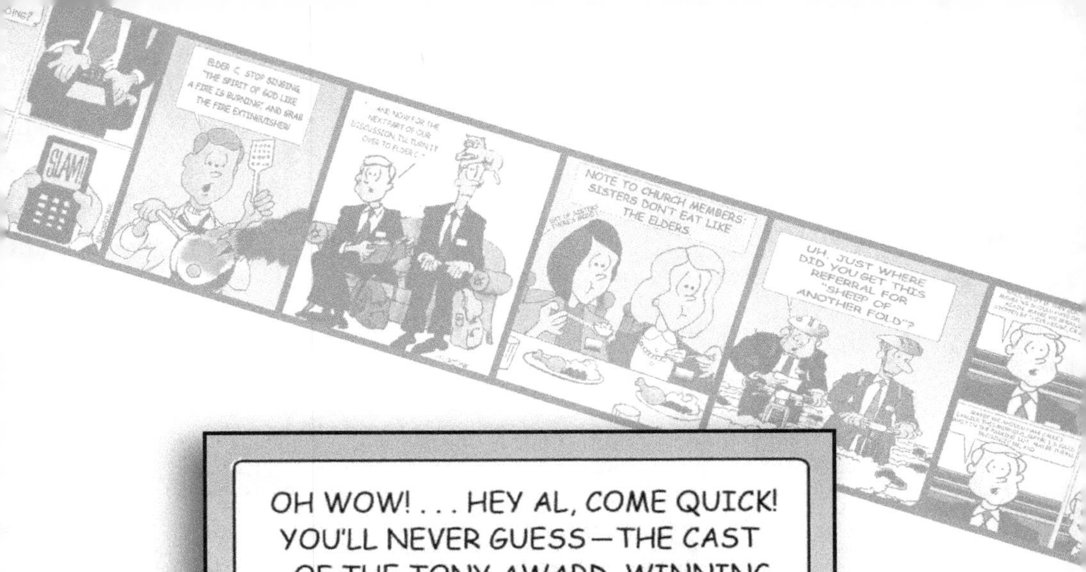
ELDER C, STOP SINGING "THE SPIRIT OF GOD LIKE A FIRE IS BURNING" AND GRAB THE FIRE EXTINGUISHER!
SLAM!
AND NOW FOR THE NEXT PART OF OUR DISCUSSION, I'LL TURN IT OVER TO ELDER C.
NOTE TO CHURCH MEMBERS: SISTERS DON'T EAT LIKE THE ELDERS.
UH, JUST WHERE DID YOU GET THIS REFERRAL FOR "SHEEP OF ANOTHER FOLD"?

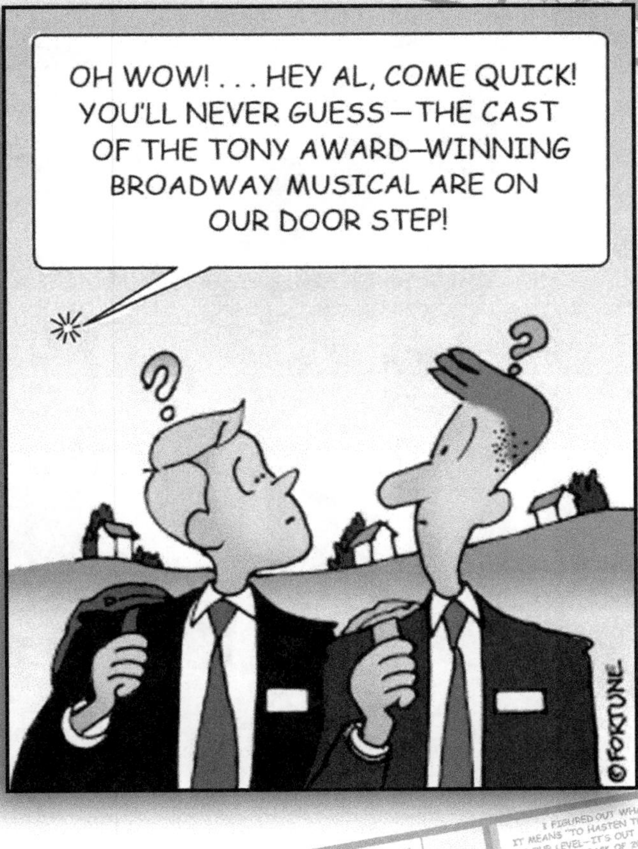
OH WOW! . . . HEY AL, COME QUICK! YOU'LL NEVER GUESS—THE CAST OF THE TONY AWARD–WINNING BROADWAY MUSICAL ARE ON OUR DOOR STEP!
©FORTUNE

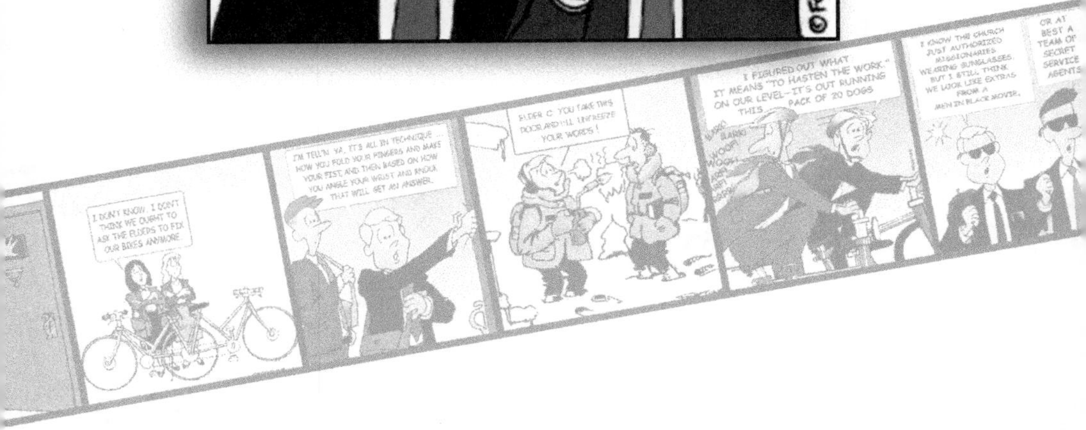
I DON'T KNOW. I DON'T THINK WE OUGHT TO ASK THE ELDERS TO FIX OUR BIKES ANYMORE.
I'M TELL'N YA, IT'S ALL IN TECHNIQUE... HOW YOU FOLD YOUR FINGERS AND MAKE YOUR FIST, AND THEN BASED ON HOW YOU ANGLE YOUR WRIST AND KNOCK THAT WILL GET AN ANSWER.
ELDER C, YOU TAKE THIS DOOR AND I'LL UNFREEZE YOUR WORDS!
I FIGURED OUT WHAT IT MEANS "TO HASTEN THE WORK." ON OUR LEVEL—IT'S OUT RUNNING THIS PACK OF 20 DOGS
I KNOW THE CHURCH JUST AUTHORIZED MISSIONARIES WEARING SUNGLASSES, BUT I STILL THINK WE LOOK LIKE EXTRAS FROM A MEN IN BLACK MOVIE.
OR AT BEST A TEAM OF SECRET SERVICE AGENTS

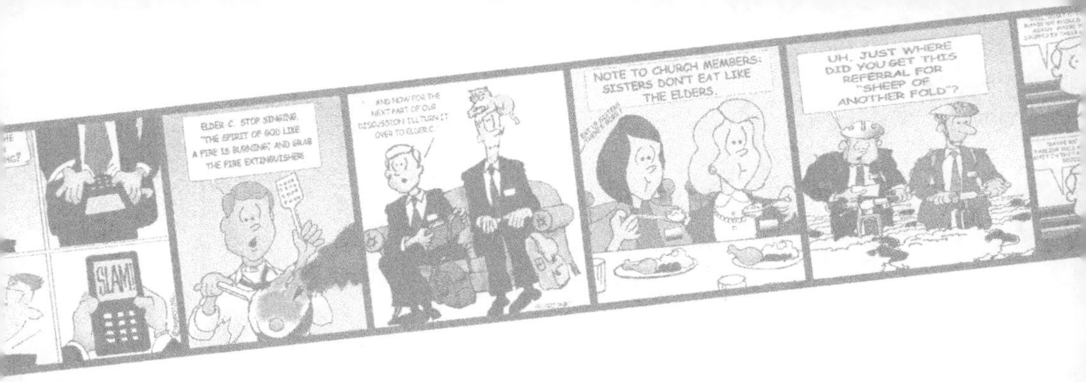
SLAM!
ELDER C. STOP SINGING, "THE SPIRIT OF GOD LIKE A FIRE IS BURNING," AND GRAB THE FIRE EXTINGUISHER!
AND NOW FOR THE NEXT PART OF OUR DISCUSSION I'LL TURN IT OVER TO ELDER C.
NOTE TO CHURCH MEMBERS: SISTERS DON'T EAT LIKE THE ELDERS.
UH, JUST WHERE DID YOU GET THIS REFERRAL FOR "SHEEP OF ANOTHER FOLD"?

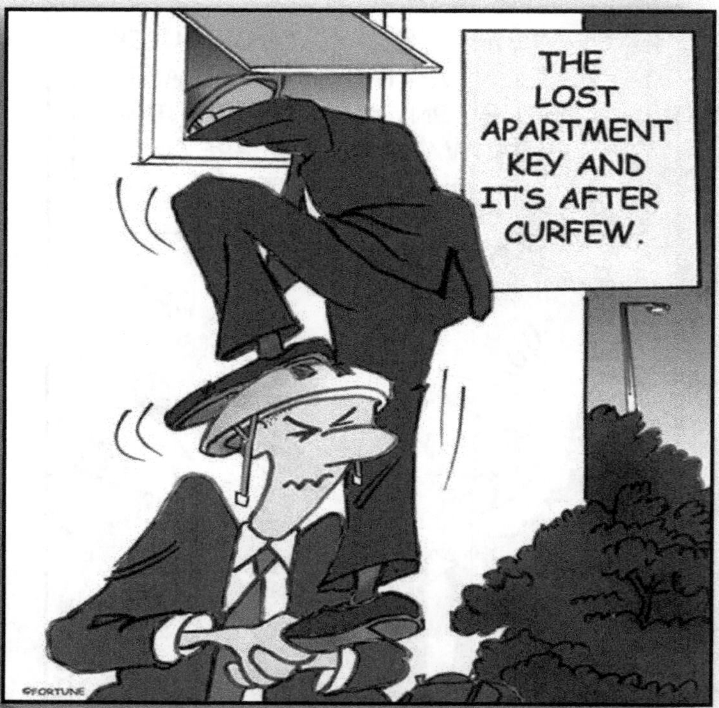
THE LOST APARTMENT KEY AND IT'S AFTER CURFEW.
©FORTUNE

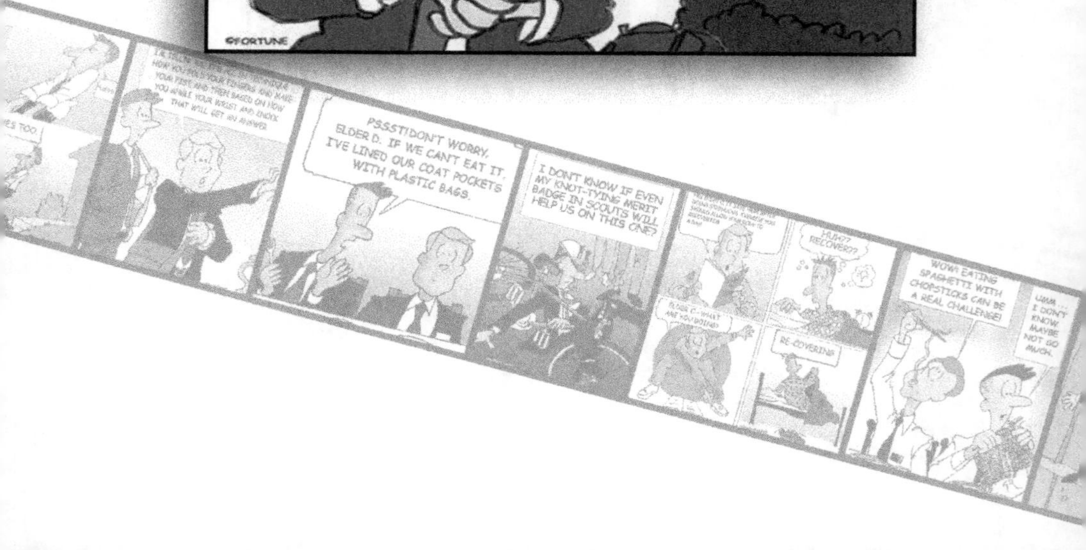
PSSST! DON'T WORRY, ELDER D. IF WE CAN'T EAT IT, I'VE LINED OUR COAT POCKETS WITH PLASTIC BAGS.
I DON'T KNOW IF EVEN MY KNOT-TYING MERIT BADGE IN SCOUTS WILL HELP US ON THIS ONE!
HUH?? RECOVER??
RE-COVERING
WOW! EATING SPAGHETTI WITH CHOPSTICKS CAN BE A REAL CHALLENGE!
UMM... I DON'T KNOW. MAYBE NOT SO MUCH.

Locked In and Locked Out

"While serving in the San Bernardino California Mission, my companion, Elder Rupp, and I were in our apartment. We began saying things to one another in a teasing way. Being feisty, I said something that appeared to make Elder Rupp upset, and he came toward me as though he [were] going to grab me. I hurried and ran into the bathroom and locked the door. He pounded on the door and told me to open it. Being small in stature, I crawled through the bathroom window and ran around to the front door. I waited outside for about 5 minutes, [and] then I hurried and opened the front door and said, 'I'm sorry.'

"Elder Rupp was surprised to see me and, while smiling, said, 'I'm not upset. However, you and I have a problem—the bathroom door is locked.'

"Both of us walked outside to the bathroom window, and while some neighbors were curiously watching us, Elder Rupp lifted me up and I crawled back through the window that I had recently exited. Oh, the dumb things that elders do at times."

Mark Bingham

Feasting on the Gospel One Bowl at a Time

"While [I was] serving my mission in Germany, my companion, Elder Schmitt, and I were in the middle of a lesson with two new investigators, Juan and Mario. We were in the kitchen of Juan's apartment, which he shares with three other people. One of the occupants, a younger German woman, walked in the kitchen during our lesson and started serving herself a bowl of soup from a pan that was sitting on the stove. I wanted to ask her if she was interested in taking part in our lesson, but in the middle of my sentence, I was deciding if I should use the word *mitmachen* or *teilnehmen*, which both basically mean 'participate.' However, I mixed the words and said, *mitteilen*, which means 'share.' So, in the middle of the lesson, I told this younger woman that she could gladly share her soup with us if she wanted to. Oh, the words we use for 'sharing' the gospel."

Curtis Leston Drake

Which Day for Dessert?

"My companion, Sister Philips, and I were invited to eat supper with the Reynolds [family], a member family. At the end of the supper, Terry, the four-year-old son, said to his mother, 'Can we go and get some ice cream?'

"Sister Reynolds asked, 'Do you want a Sundae?'

"'No,' Terry answered, 'I want to go today!'"

Rebecca Scott

Sacrament Bread and Butter

"While serving in New Zealand, Sister Ahnder and her companion obtained permission from some Tongan investigators to take a few of their younger children to church. During sacrament meeting, the sacramental bread was passed to the congregation. After taking a piece of bread and eating it, one young boy leaned toward Sister Ahnder and seriously said, 'This would be better if it had butter on it.'"

Kathy Liechty

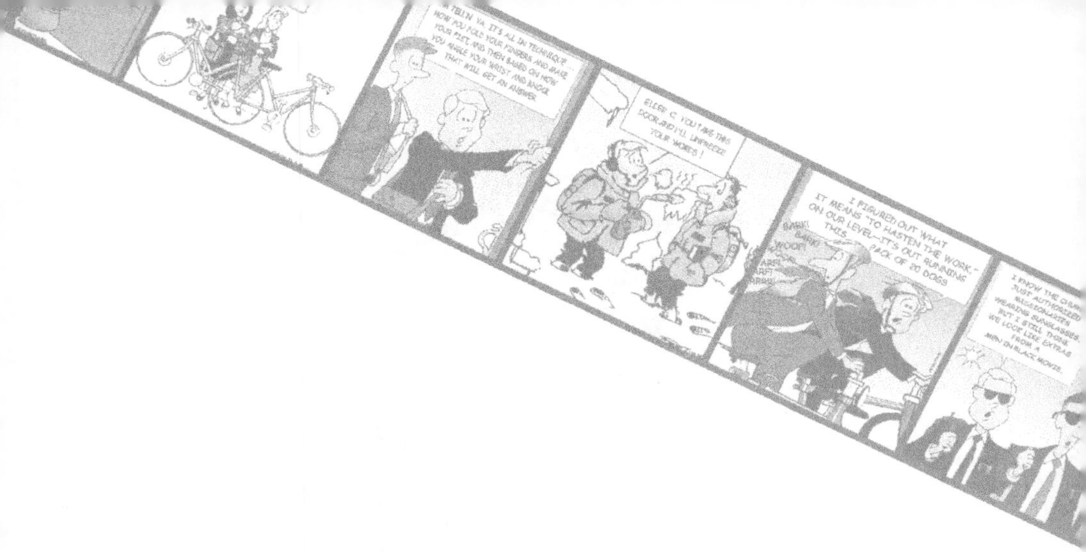
I'M TELLIN YA, IT'S ALL IN TECHNIQUE. HOW YOU FOLD YOUR FINGERS AND MAKE YOUR FIST AND THEN BASED ON HOW YOU ANGLE YOUR WRIST AND KNOCK THAT WILL GET AN ANSWER.
ELDER C. YOU TAKE THIS DOOR AND I'LL UNFREEZE YOUR WORDS!
I FIGURED OUT WHAT IT MEANS "TO HASTEN THE WORK." ON OUR LEVEL—IT'S OUT RUNNING THIS PACK OF 20 DOGS
BARK!
BARK!

A Call for More Stories

To those individuals willing to share their own humorous missionary experiences, please contact either Bruce at bruce@calledtolaugh.com or William at bill@calledtolaugh.com.

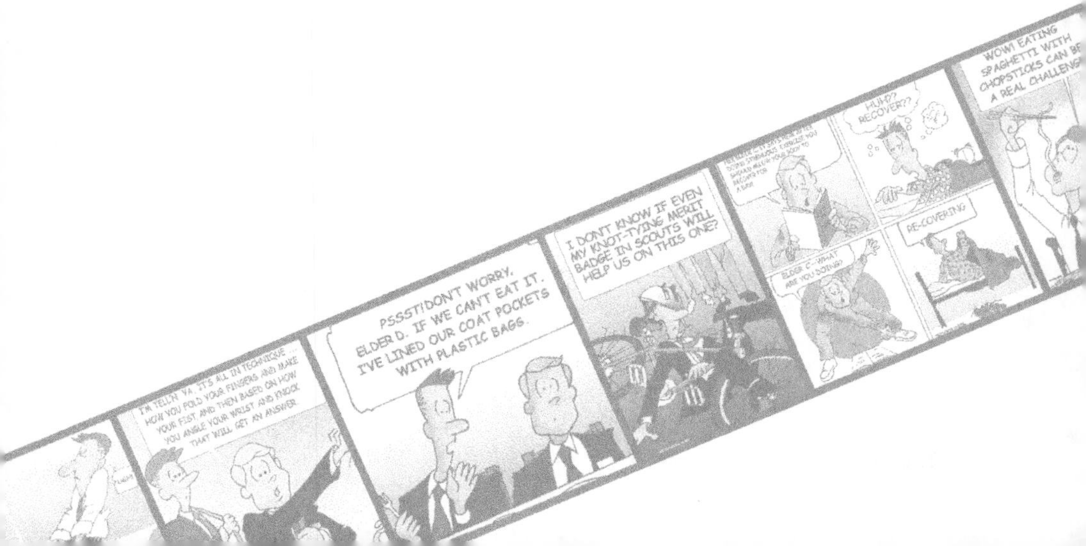
I'M TELLIN YA, IT'S ALL IN TECHNIQUE. HOW YOU FOLD YOUR FINGERS AND MAKE YOUR FIST AND THEN BASED ON HOW YOU ANGLE YOUR WRIST AND KNOCK THAT WILL GET AN ANSWER.
PSSST! DON'T WORRY, ELDER D. IF WE CAN'T EAT IT, I'VE LINED OUR COAT POCKETS WITH PLASTIC BAGS.
I DON'T KNOW IF EVEN MY KNOT-TYING MERIT BADGE IN SCOUTS WILL HELP US ON THIS ONE?
HUH? RECOVER??
RE-COVERING
WOW! EATING SPAGHETTI WITH CHOPSTICKS

About the Author

Bruce E. Dana served an honorable mission for The Church of Jesus Christ of Latter-day Saints in the Northwestern and Pacific Northwest missions. He knows from personal experiences both the spiritual and humorous sides of missionary life. Since that time, various family members have served honorable missions. Brother Dana has served in a variety of Church callings over the years and enjoys teaching the doctrines of the gospel. He also has a keen sense of humor. He is the author of ten other published books, including another humorous volume, *Stories & Jokes of Mormon Folks*.

About the Illustrator

William G. Fortune is a cartoonist, artist, graphic designer. After spending over fifty years in advertising as an Art Director/ Creative Director of Advertising agencies, he retired and moved to St. George, Utah, in March 2014.

He began his advertising career after leaving the Marine Corps and studying at the Academy of Art in San Francisco and Art Center College of Design in Los Angeles and USC film courses in LA. During his career he has worked for national advertising agencies in Los Angeles and Orange County California.

His advertising work has won him national recognition such as an Andy, an IBA Award and a Clio along with a number of local advertising awards. But his first love is cartooning, and he is always looking for opportunities to spend more time doing that.

The cartoon "Elders D & C" was originally created when his son Doug served his mission in Tampa, Florida, and they were drawn and put in the bottom of his letters back to his son. Doug would write home with stories that inspired new concepts and it continued throughout his mission. In 2011 *Meridian Magazine* put out a call for cartoons.

So he decided to take them off the shelf and revise them to fit the computer. Doug passed away eighteen years ago, and the cartoons Elders D and C are done as a tribute to him. Elder D is a characterization of Doug. Elder C was his first companion (who was named Carroll) but he never knew what Carroll looked like, so he is made up for contrast. The title is derived from their initials. Elders D & C has been appearing in *Meridian Magazine* since 2011.

Scan to visit

calledtolaugh.com